FRAMING FAT

COMPETING CONSTRUCTIONS IN CONTEMPORARY CULTURE

SAMANTHA KWAN AND
JENNIFER GRAVES

RUTGERS UNIVERSITY PRESS
New Brunswick, New Jersey, and London

Library of Congress Cataloging-in-Publication Data
Kwan, Samantha.
    Framing fat : competing constructions in contemporary culture / Samantha Kwan,
Jennifer L. Graves.
        pages ; cm
    Includes bibliographical references and index.
    ISBN 978-0-8135-6092-2 (hardcover : alk. paper) — ISBN 978-0-8135-6091-5
(pbk. : alk. paper) — ISBN 978-0-8135-6093-9 (e-book) (print)
    1. Obesity—Social aspects—United States—History. 2. Food habits—United
States—History. 3. Body image—United States. I. Graves, Jennifer L., 1983- II. Title.
RC628.K95 2013
362.196398—dc23   2012033362

A British Cataloging-in-Publication record for this book is available from the British
Library.

Visit our website: http://rutgerspress.rutgers.edu

Manufactured in the United States of America

CONTENTS

FIGURES AND TABLES

ACKNOWLEDGMENTS

Framing Fat would not have been possible without the support of many wonderful individuals. We are indebted to Peter Mickulas for his thoughtful editorship, Jennifer Dropkin for her careful copyediting, and to several anonymous reviewers for their astute comments. As well, we thank Camille Nelson for her meticulous editorial support, manuscript preparation, and indexing work. Our gratitude also extends to Christina Gola, Keiisha Pillai, and Jennifer Wolff for their research assistance, along with Linda Bacon, Esther Rothblum, and Marilyn Wann for their insights on the subject matter, assistance with sources, and help connecting us with others. We are further indebted to members of the Yahoo! Fat Studies discussion group for their advice and assistance with reference materials.

We are grateful to be surrounded by patient partners (Scott V. Savage and Chris Graves), and our sincere appreciation extends to mentors and friends T. Xavia Karner and Louise M. Roth who have, over the years, provided invaluable guidance.

The original dissertation project, which provides the foundation for this book, received financial support from the University of Arizona's Social and Behavioral Sciences Research Institute, along with the National Science Foundation. We are thankful for a University of Houston Women's Studies faculty fellowship, which provided funds for the development of this project.

FRAMING FAT

1 · A CONTESTED FIELD

June 22, 2011: *ABC News* (Carollo and Salahi 2011) reports on research findings out of the Harvard School of Public Health. To understand the relationship between lifestyle and weight, investigators examined three separate studies spanning a twenty-year period that included over 120,000 subjects. They found that weight gain was associated with several foods; at the top of the list of nutritional culprits were potato chips, processed meats, and sugar-sweetened drinks.

August 10, 2010: A *Medical News Today* (George 2010) headline reads, "Research Shows Sugary Drinks Do Not Cause Weight Gain." The article reports on a study published in the journal *Appetite* that monitored the eating, drinking, and exercise habits of fifty-three overweight women. Subjects were placed in one of two groups and blindly given either a sugar-sweetened or an artificially sweetened drink to consume during the study period. Weigh-ins at the end of the four-week study period found no differences in weight gain among the two groups. The study's primary investigator concludes, "Sugar in moderation plays a neutral role in the balanced diet, but an emotionally charged role in the psychology of food choice."

So by some accounts, sugar-sweetened drinks contribute to weight gain. By others, sugar-sweetened drinks do not. Examples of contradictory claims about weight and the fat body abound. Here are two more.

December 1, 2010: The Associated Press (Nano 2010) reports that a study published in the *New England Journal of Medicine* involving approximately 1.5 million people found that adults who were overweight were 13 percent more likely to die during the study period compared to adults in the ideal weight range. The Associated Press quotes a senior author of the study: "Having a little meat on your bones—if that meat happens to be fat—is harmful, not beneficial."

February 2, 2010: The news agency Reuters (Joelving 2010) reports on an Australian study's claim that being overweight can increase longevity. Published in the *Journal of the American Geriatrics Society*, the study followed more than 9,000 adults aged seventy through seventy-five and found that overweight subjects were 13 percent less likely to die during a ten-year period. The conclusion: fat may serve a protective function in old age.

So fat decreases longevity; fat extends longevity.

These are only a few examples of how the mass media regularly bombard us with news about the fat body, including the latest scientific research. Some of this information is consistent at face value, but some of it—like these stories—does not seem to add up.

CONSTRUCTING SOCIAL PROBLEMS

In many ways, we should expect multiple claims about the fat body—what it is, what it signifies, and how we should respond to it. Social scientists have long shown how social issues do not necessarily stem from an objective reality. Instead, multiple claims makers (e.g., social movement actors, institutions, and organizations) vie to define the meaning of social, including medical, phenomena (Best 1989; Blumer 1971; Kitsuse and Spector 1973; Schneider 1985; Spector and Kitsuse 1973). Widespread and popular sentiments about the fat body thus do not represent an unambiguous reality about fat but, rather, the ability of claims makers to shape cultural understandings in the public arena (Hilgartner and Bosk 1988). From this perspective, conflicting information, such as competing research findings about fat, becomes fodder for claims makers—fodder to be used in constructing a version of reality. Often the version of reality constructed by one claims maker is intended to challenge the versions of reality created by rival claims makers.

As social scientists have pointed out, claims makers are diverse and often have competing interests and stakes in a broad variety of social behavior and phenomena. Some claims makers, such as Mothers Against Drunk Driving (Reinarman 1988) or pro-life activists (Luker 1984), act in the capacity of moral entrepreneurs (Becker 1963; Monaghan, Hollands, and Pritchard 2010), crusading vehemently against some form of "deviant" behavior that they claim poses some perceived moral threat. Other claims makers, such as medical professionals and representatives of medical industries—from surgeons to pharmaceutical companies—push a medical response to some condition (Bury 1986; Conrad 1992; Conrad and Schneider 1980).

The role of medical claims makers has been particularly evident over the last several decades owing in part to increased medicalization—the application and expansion of medicine and medical authority over increasing realms of human life (Conrad 1992; Zola 1972). Conditions such as erectile quality (Wienke 2005), dementia in the elderly (Bond 2002), adult attention deficit and hyperactivity (Conrad and Potter 2000), and women's sexual "dysfunction" (Canner 2009; Tiefer 2006) all now fall, in part or in whole, under the umbrella of medical authority. Moreover, since the mid-1980s, technoscientific innovations and accompanying social forms have given rise to a biomedicalization that has, and continues to have, even greater reach than medicalization, both conceptually and clinically (Clarke et al. 2003). With biomedicalization, we witness not only medicine's expansion of control but also its purported ability to transform bodies and lives. This occurs in an environment increasingly characterized by the corporatization and privatization of medicine, the treatment of risk, the technoscientization of biomedicine, the heterogeneous characteristic of health knowledge, and the commodification of health and lifestyles (Clarke et al. 2003). Biomedicalization and these changes in the practice of American medicine have come to shape the types of claims made by those in the medical arena. As we examine in the pages that follow, they also have broad implications for the fat body—a body that signifies much about risk, health, and the self.

In many ways, claims makers' attempts to shape public perception boil down to a matter of framing—an attempt to define "what is it that's going on here?" (Goffman 1974, 25). At the heart of this definitional process are selection and salience (Entman 1993). That is, claims makers often maintain a version of reality that focuses on one aspect of an issue that they argue characterizes its nature, a process Joel Best (1989) refers to as "typification." Framers, whether journalists, institutions, or social movement actors, select and make salient key aspects of a perceived reality in order to promote a particular understanding. For example, while pro-life activists emphasize the moral implications of killing a living being, pro-choice activists focus on the upholding of women's rights. This process of typification can include moral, medical, and political models (Best 1989). These models or frames explicitly or implicitly diagnose causes, make moral judgments, and suggest policy remedies (Best 1989; Gamson 1992; Iyengar 1991; Ryan 1991). At a minimum, claims makers articulate a root cause of an issue, identify a blameworthy culprit, and propose a solution of some kind.

Framing, then, is really about framing competitions—struggles over the production of ideas and meanings (Benford and Snow 2000). According to Stephen Hilgartner and Charles Bosk (1988, 58), "Within each substantive area, different ways of framing [a] situation may compete to be accepted as an authoritative version of reality." Frames attempt to convince individuals (essentially the general public) that a given frame is, in fact, the best interpretation of reality. Frame competitions have winners and losers, although they are rarely zero-sum games. As social movement scholars note, frames are action-oriented sets of beliefs that are designed to mobilize individuals, garner support, and demobilize antagonists (Snow and Benford 1988). In these framing wars, framers turn to multiple tactics and carry with them different weapons.

Thus despite multiple vantage points on a social issue, a framer may success-fully convince large segments of the public that its take is the one and only ver-sion of reality. This view then appears as a concrete truth or as the only natural way to approach a social issue. That is, some frames may become master frames, broad and generic frames that operate as a kind of master algorithm (Benford and Snow 2000; Snow and Benford 1992), thereby increasing their potency or effectiveness. They may even constitute a frequently accessed cultural ideology in one's cultural repertoire or tool kit that informs courses of action (Swidler 1986, 2001). There are implications of such persuasion; to the extent to which one camp can convince the public of a given reality, the more support this camp potentially has to sway public policy on the issue.

CONSTRUCTING FAT

Like other important issues of the day, fat can be interpreted through a construc-tivist optic. Lacking a single inherent truth, fat's meaning has shifted both his-torically and cross-culturally. For example, scholars have documented at length shifting Western beauty ideals (Schwartz 1986; Seid 1989; Stearns 2002). As Jef-fery Sobal (1995) summarizes, in past historical eras, food supplies were uncer-tain and fat was thought to protect against certain infectious disease parasites. During those times, body fat was desirable and signified both health and wealth. However, with the advent of the agricultural and industrial revolutions, food supplies became more stable. By the 1920s, thinness became valued and associ-ated with social mobility, an ideological change facilitated by industrialization and technological innovations of the twentieth century (see Seid 1989). Around the 1950s, views of fat again shifted. Medical professionals began to pathologize obesity and prescribe medical treatments, intensifying the medicalization of obesity. As Sobal maintains, however, this medical labeling is not value neutral, and, around the time of the civil rights movement, size activists began to chal-lenge medical stigmatization. A political model of fat soon emerged.[1] Fat there-fore went from being a form of moral deficiency, to a medical disease, to a source of social oppression, although Sobal argues that all three models continue to be applied to fat individuals, and dynamic competition between models persists.

Anthropologists have also exposed the variability of meanings associated with the overweight body, particularly from a cross-cultural perspective.[2] For example, Don Kulick and Anne Meneley's anthology *Fat: The Anthropology of an Obsession* (2005) illuminates various cultural takes on fat. Westerners may be taken aback by Rebecca Popenoe's (2005) chapter on desert Arabs in Niger who idealize the fat body. Popenoe observed that girls are force-fed to achieve what might be labeled, by Western medical standards, an obese ideal. She also found that, in contrast to the Western practice of wearing as little as possible when stepping on a scale, Nigerien Arab women weighed themselves wearing as many accessories and pieces of clothing as possible. To do otherwise would defeat the goal of weighing more, not less. This remarkably different approach to the fat body, Popenoe surmises, may be attributed to cultural values, environmental realities, and the economic order. In Nigerien Arab society, a former slave population does much of the menial labor, men's economic activities include herding and long-distance trade, and an elite woman's achievement of "weighty immobility signals her ability not to work" (Popenoe 2005, 18). In such a society, the weight a woman gains by consuming foods bought with a man's earnings is a visible symbol of male success.

Yet one does not have to step into a time capsule or travel to another continent to observe how meanings about fat shift. In recent years, scholars have begun to deconstruct Western cultural discourses about body weight. In doing so, they have identified conflicting perspectives on obesity causation, blame, and intervention (Campos 2004; Gaesser 2002; Gard and Wright 2005; Kwan 2009b; Moffat 2010; Rich and Evans 2005; Smith 2009). This growing literature, sometimes referred to as "critical obesity studies" (see Gard 2009) or "fat studies" (see Murray 2008), begins to destabilize so-called truths about body weight and to expose commonly held beliefs about the fat body that, upon closer examination, involve complex assertions by competing claims makers.

There is also a growing number of research studies that critically examine the role of media coverage on the topic of weight. This body of research has led to questions about whether the "obesity epidemic," an oft-articulated phrase, is a public health crisis or a moral panic attributable in part to alarmist reporting (Boero 2007; Campos et al. 2006; Holland et al. 2011; Saguy and Almeling 2008).[3] Researchers analyzing how print media couch issues of blame and responsibility have found that American news media typically frame fat in terms of personal causes and solutions (Kim and Willis 2007; Lawrence 2004; Saguy and Riley 2005). This is in contrast to coverage of eating disorders such as anorexia nervosa, which the media is more likely to ascribe to factors beyond an individual's control (Saguy and Gruys 2010). The emphasis on individualism, and individualistic attributions of responsibility, is particularly prominent in American news reporting compared to reporting in European nations such as France (Saguy, Gruys, and Gong 2010). It also has a long tradition in the United States, where victim blaming and individualistic discourses are apparent for many social issues, including poverty (Ryan 1976). Furthermore, it remains prevalent, despite the increased presence of systematic media frames that acknowledge the role of government, business, and larger social forces in shaping individual choices (Lawrence 2004).

Within today's neoliberal political climate, this media framing is somewhat unsurprising. "Neoliberalism," a term coined in post–World War I Germany

(Steger and Roy 2010), is a contemporary political movement advocating economic liberalization, free trade, and open markets (Boas and Gans-Morse 2009). As a theory of political and economic practice, it proposes that human well-being can best be advanced by liberating individual entrepreneurial freedoms and skills within an institutional framework characterized by strong private property rights, free markets, and free trade (Harvey 2005). Those who embrace neoliberal ideologies often call for the deregulation of the economy, liberalization of trade and industry, and privatization of state-owned enterprises, along with tax cuts, the reduction of social services, and the downsizing of government (Steger and Roy 2010). The ideal of individual freedom is a fundamental component of the doctrine (Harvey 2005), and neoliberalism seeks to govern not through "society" but through the choices of individual citizens (Rose 1996).

As economistic ideology, neoliberalism works with the assumption that these choices are autonomous and rational. The neoliberal subject is presumably rational and acts without undue influence. As such, neoliberalism is closely tied to personal responsibility; if individuals are able to make their own choices and do so in an autonomous and rational manner, then they must deal with the consequences of their choices. This includes any choices they make about their bodies. Subsequently, the body is a domain of personal responsibility, and any risks it might incur are assumed by the individual, not the community. In this view, a public health model that mandates certain health behaviors of its citizens may be viewed as overly authoritarian or even patronizing (Lupton 1995).

Neoliberal approaches to the body, however, have not gone without criticism. For example, Deborah Lupton expresses concern "about the elements of 'victim-blaming' discourse which attracts attention away from the structural, political and economic causes of ill health" (Lupton 1995, 3; see also Crawford 1980). As we later discuss, especially in trying economic times, neoliberal laissez-faire rhetoric plays a key role in heated discussions about the purported rising medical costs associated with the fat body and the food industry's role in creating an environment that encourages unhealthful consumption.

So even though fat may appear to be an unambiguous medical and social problem, it potentially signifies a whole host of meanings for different actors. The contemporary Western understanding of fat can be thought of as a contested field of meanings in a dynamic socioeconomic, political, and cultural landscape constructed by multiple individuals and groups, all of whom have different interests. To be sure, multiple players participate in this game today: bariatric surgeons, diet product manufacturers, pharmaceutical companies, the food industry, fashion designers, fitness trainers, the government, health insurance companies, and fat and thin people alike. Sometimes players work in tandem, sometimes they work against one another. Collectively, their multiple vantage points on the fat body suggest a dynamic and shifting landscape that is subject to negotiation.

Some of these claims makers consciously and coherently generate an understanding of fat; others do so in a less active and less thought-out manner. For example, public health officials warn that overweight and obesity are serious health risks (HHS 2010d). They elaborate on this position at length and draw on the research of public health researchers to support their claims (e.g., Flegal et al. 2010). Similarly, bariatric surgeons, primary-care physicians, and weight-loss drug manufacturers may adopt similar assumptions, even if they are not actively promoting this message on a regular basis. While public health officials deliberately attempt to shape public discourse on overweight and obesity, this latter group supports and reinforces these discourses. In this way, some groups (such as public health officials) can be labeled "cultural producers," while others (such as pharmaceutical companies) are more appropriately labeled "cultural supporters."[4]

The line between these can—and often does—blur; at times, groups may both generate and support a message. In any case, numerous cultural producers (meaning generators) and a host of cultural supporters (meaning adopters) permeate the contested field of fat. As we will see, this is particularly evident in what we refer to as the "aesthetic frame," where there are many players and it is often unclear which are producers and which are supporters. While these distinctions may not be neat, they are nevertheless helpful for analytical purposes.

FAT FRAMES

Framing Fat unpacks our Western contemporary construction of fat. How do key cultural producers define fat and the fat body? How do they approach weight and salient weight-related issues such as aesthetics, health, individual choice, personal responsibility, and social justice? Moreover, what is the relationship among major frames? And what are the implications of these frame constructions for understanding equality? In *Framing Fat*, we map how various cultural producers approach fat, and we examine the discrepant cultural logics in each understanding. Moreover, we show how these constructions are, at times, gendered, raced, and classed, and how they have important consequences for body nonconformists.

Our analysis focuses on several key cultural producers, fully acknowledging that our selection of players is by no means exhaustive or representative of the field of players. We select these cultural producers because they are vocal in their positions on fat and possess strong interests in the way the public understands fat. They also offer publicly accessible cultural artifacts that enable a systematic and replicable analysis. These cultural producers are the Centers for Disease

Control and Prevention (CDC), the Center for Consumer Freedom (CCF), and the National Association to Advance Fat Acceptance (NAAFA).

The Centers for Disease Control and Prevention

The CDC is a federal agency operating under the U.S. Department of Health and Human Services (HHS). It was founded in Atlanta, Georgia, in 1946. Initially descended from the wartime agency Malaria Control in War Areas, in its early years the CDC focused on the fight against malaria (CDC 2010a). Over time, its mission expanded, and the organization began to focus on the treatment and prevention of other diseases such as sexually transmitted diseases (1957) and tuberculosis (1960; see CDC 1996). Today, the CDC is hailed as the nation's premier health promotion, disease prevention, and emergency preparedness agency and as a global leader in public health.

The CDC works to prevent and control infectious and chronic diseases, injuries, workplace hazards, disabilities, and environmental health threats. The agency is also committed to promoting programs that reduce both the health and economic consequences of the leading causes of death and disability to ensure a healthy, productive, and long life for the population. According to the CDC, the agency's main online communication channel (www.cdc.gov) averages over 41 million page views per month. The website's stated goal is to provide users with "credible, reliable health information" on a broad range of topics such as chronic diseases, workplace safety, and healthy living.

One of the diseases the CDC addresses is obesity. The CDC devotes numerous web pages specifically to overweight and obesity issues (2012g). These pages provide extensive information on the two conditions, including how the agency defines overweight and obesity, along with information on their prevalence, causes, and consequences. The agency points out that about one-third of U.S. adults (35.7 percent) are obese and that, while there are no statistically significant differences in prevalence rates by sex, rates of obesity vary by race/ethnicity. For example, non-Hispanic blacks exhibit the highest rates of obesity at 44.1 percent, compared to Mexican Americans (39.3 percent), all Hispanics (37.9 percent), and non-Hispanic whites (32.6 percent; CDC 2012a).

The CDC claims that Americans live in an environment that encourages food intake, where unhealthy foods are abundant and where physical inactivity is rampant. The agency further contends that it actively works to reduce obesity and obesity-related conditions through various avenues. Providing the public with resources on nutrition and physical activity is part of this mission. The agency also expresses special concern about, and devotes specific resources toward combating, childhood overweight and obesity.

Notably, medical interest in these conditions is not recent. Although there is some evidence to indicate that a handful of doctors were concerned about these conditions in the early part of the twentieth century (Stearns 2002), serious medical concern did not emerge until the 1940s when the Metropolitan Life Insurance Company released a series of actuarial tables that supposedly demonstrated that thinner-than-average individuals live longer than individuals who are not (Campos 2004; Oliver 2006). This concern was further exacerbated by the increasing medicalization of the overweight body, and by the mid-1990s the government began to take serious interest in obesity (Oliver 2006).

C. Everett Koop was the first U.S. surgeon general to claim that fat is killing Americans (Campos 2004). In 1994, five years after his tenure under President Ronald Reagan had ended, he launched the Shape Up America! campaign, his self-described "crusade" to place healthy weight and physical activity high on the national agenda (Karra 1994). Koop became the first in a long line of U.S. surgeons general to declare obesity a "public health crisis" that costs the country billions of dollars each year (Campos 2004; Karra 1994; Oliver 2006).

Although the CDC began conducting nutritional research in the 1970s, it first turned its attention to obesity in 1997 when William Dietz became director of the CDC's Division for Nutrition and Physical Activity (Oliver 2006). Dietz was the first leader at the CDC to fully embrace the notion that obesity was a disease and that weight gain was an "epidemic" (Oliver 2006). Dietz's ideas about obesity were widely publicized in a special issue of the *Journal of the American Medical Association* released in 1999 (Oliver 2006). The CDC has fought diligently to end the "obesity epidemic" ever since.

The Center for Consumer Freedom

The CCF is a tax-exempt registered nonprofit 501(c)(3) organization. According to one report by an independent reporter (Shearn 2010), it was born the Guest Choice Network (GCN) in 1999 and renamed the CCF in 2002. It was founded by lobbyist Richard Berman with a $600,000 donation from the Philip Morris tobacco company—a company that continued to contribute another $2.3 million after the CCF's inception. While the CCF initially worked to protect smokers' rights in the face of antismoking activists, its current mission focuses broadly on promoting consumer choices and personal responsibility.

In its goal to help consumers retain control of their decision making and choices, the CCF targets actors who the center claims meddle in the lives of Americans. These include groups that the CCF identifies as activists, self-anointed food police, health campaigners, trial lawyers, personal-finance do-gooders, animal-rights misanthropes, and meddling bureaucrats. According to the CCF, these groups all claim to "know what's best for you" (2012). The CCF sees itself as a defender of the ordinary American, and it pledges to protect Americans' freedom to buy, eat, and drink what they want and to raise their children as they deem fit. The CCF puts forth its message through print, radio, and television advertising campaigns, nationwide op-ed pieces, and websites specifically designed to attack target activist groups. For example, its Animal Scam website (www.animalscam.com) exposes visitors to the "truth about PETA and other animal rights extremists"; its CSPI Scam website (www.cspiscam.com) explains "why the Center for Science in the Public Interest is NOT science in the public interest"; and its Mercury Facts website (www.mercuryfacts.org) asks visitors "Did you know? Mercury levels in the fish we eat are roughly the same as they were 100 years ago." All of these sites claim to debunk myths that erode consumer freedom.

The group's support comes from restaurants, food companies, and individual consumers. Many of its contributors' identities are anonymous. As the CCF states, its contributors "are reasonably apprehensive about privacy and safety in light of the violence and other forms of aggression some activists have adopted as a 'game plan' to impose their views, so we respect their wishes" (2012). According to Shearn's (2010) report, corporate contributors include Monsanto, Tyson Foods, Coca-Cola, and Wendy's International.

In light of the nature of its supporters, the CCF has a special interest in how the public thinks of the body and consumption. Several links on the center's homepage (www.consumerfreedom.com) lead to web pages that outline the group's position on food and drinks (such as meat, seafood, snacks, and soft drinks) and "food radicals" (such as animal-rights groups, celebrity activists, and food police). The CCF's homepage also includes a link to the group's position on the obesity debate. (The CCF's use of the term "debate" is itself revealing, indicating that it finds the issue contentious.) These pages attempt to debunk what the group refers to as "obesity myths" (which it also refers to as "big fat lies") and to attack big government, fat taxes, food police, and trial lawyers. The CCF released the booklet *An Epidemic of Obesity Myths* in 2004 and an updated version in 2005 (CCF 2004a, 2005a). In 2007, it released *Small Choices, Big Bodies: How Countless Daily Decisions Contribute to America's Burgeoning Waistline* (CCF 2007b).

The CCF's close ties to the food and beverage industry have led to accusations that it is nothing more than a food lobby group. For example, because of the CCF's corporate interests and connection to its founder's for-profit lobbying and public relations firm Berman & Company, in 2004 the Citizens for Responsibility and Ethics in Washington (CREW) filed an Internal Revenue Service (IRS) complaint against the CCF (CREW 2004). Internal Revenue Service laws prohibit private individuals from benefiting from nonprofit organizations. Citizens for Responsibility and Ethics in Washington points out that the CCF has no employees and is run out of Berman & Company's offices. It also points out that Richard Berman and his firm have received nearly $2 million from GCN and the CCF.[5]

The National Association to Advance Fat Acceptance

The 1960s was arguably a tumultuous time in U.S. history. It was a period during which, alongside Vietnam war protests, a number of social and civil rights movements set in motion the restructuring of social relations in America. Around this time, citizens also began to fight for the rights of fat Americans. In fact, during the 1960s early fat activists staged a series of public protests, referred to as "fat-ins," modeled on the notorious anti–Vietnam War be-ins. Fat individuals gathered in public places, ate ice cream, and burned diet books and posters of super-model Twiggy (Fletcher 2009). By 1969, the National Association to Aid Fat Americans was founded in New York City by engineer William Fabrey, who was motivated by the discrimination his overweight wife regularly experienced (Fabrey 2001; Fletcher 2009). Initially, the group focused its efforts on letter-writing campaigns and social activities, but toward the 1980s it became more political and was eventually renamed the National Association to Advance Fat Acceptance (NAAFA).

In 1972, several NAAFA members from the West Coast founded the Fat Underground, which maintained that "social pressure and overwhelming medical opinion were perpetuating a campaign of 'genocide' against fat people" (Fletcher 2009). Although the Fat Underground eventually disbanded, NAAFA has remained strong and has provided a powerful voice for fat Americans for over forty years. Today it exists alongside a handful of fat activist organizations such as the International Size Acceptance Association, the Association for Size Diversity and Health, and the Council on Size and Weight Discrimination. Additionally, there is an active blog community, known as the Fatosphere, where bloggers spread the messages of the fat acceptance movement and fight against weight-based stigma (Fletcher 2009; Rabin 2008).

The National Association to Advance Fat Acceptance describes itself as "a non-profit, all volunteer, civil rights organization dedicated to protecting the rights and improving the quality of life for fat people" (2011a). It claims to be the oldest civil rights organization working to end size discrimination in North America. A rolling banner on its online portal (www.naafaonline.com/dev2/index.html) reveals the organization's core position: "Discrimination is wrong. We come in all sizes. Understand it. Support it. Accept it" (NAAFA 2011j). The organization provides fat people with tools for self-empowerment through advocacy, public education, and support. Its vision is a "society in which people of every size are accepted with dignity and equality in all aspects of life" (NAAFA 2011j). The National Association to Advance Fat Acceptance encourages individuals to get involved by donating to the organization, joining the organization, taking action (by, e.g., encouraging lawmakers, the media, and the health-care system to support size equality and a Health At Every Size [HAES] agenda), and sharing experiences that can educate and inspire others.

The National Association to Advance Fat Acceptance's board of directors consists of corporate and community leaders throughout the country. Its board of advisors consists of volunteers who are members of the scientific, medical, and legal communities, some of whom are well-known researchers in their fields. The group has approximately 11,000 members, of which 70 percent are female. Aside from this breakdown by sex, NAAFA does not maintain data on membership demographics.[6] However, others have observed that members are predominantly white, female, and middle class (Gimlin 2002; Saguy and Riley 2005; Sobal 1999).

The group provides extensive resources to its members and to the public about size discrimination, including information about weight discrimination in health care, workplaces, and the education system. In its attempt to eradicate discrimination in the workplace, NAAFA makes available a Size Diversity Toolkit for employers. The association also offers a document for therapists and counselors entitled *Guidelines for Therapists Who Treat Fat Clients* (Bruno and Burgard 2009). Moreover, it has a constitution, bylaws, and official policy documents on a wide range of issues, including adoption, fat admirers, obesity researchers, physical fitness, and weight-loss drugs and surgery. News releases, along with a monthly newsletter, communicate the group's viewpoints. Meanwhile, its annual conference brings together activists, researchers, and health-care practitioners. Other initiatives include scholarships to support student fashion designers who specialize in plus-sized clothing.

The Fashion-Beauty Complex

In sum, these cultural producers represent three distinct fat frames: a health frame (the CDC),[7] a choice and responsibility frame (the CCF), and a social justice frame (NAAFA; see Kwan 2009b). Central to each frame is a core interpretation of the fat body. For the CDC, the fat body is unhealthy; the CCF maintains that the fat body and food consumption are matters of individual choice and personal responsibility; and NAAFA claims that fat is mainly about discrimination and social inequality.

To these three fat frames, we add a fourth: the aesthetic frame. At any given time and place, there are cultural beliefs and assumptions about the aesthetics of body fat. For example, in today's Western world, fat is typically placed at the unattractive end of the beauty continuum. For decades feminist scholarship has exposed the ubiquitous and oppressive presence of cultural beauty ideals that privilege the thin female body (Bordo 2003; Hesse-Biber 1996; Wolf 1991). When it comes to the thin aesthetic, there are many cultural producers and cultural supporters. These include the fashion and cosmetics industries, film and television, weight-loss companies, and cosmetic surgeons, just to name a few. We refer to this conglomerate of fashion, cosmetics, and weight-loss industries, borrowing from Sandra Bartky (1990), as the "fashion-beauty complex." Given that there are numerous producers and supporters, it is next to impossible to pinpoint explicitly a single prominent cultural producer of this rather nebulous frame. Indeed, as Bartky (2010 [1988]) observes, the thin ideal is everywhere and simultaneously nowhere. Yet despite the varied nature and goals of these claims makers, many use popular media and advertisements as tools for selling goods and services, and, moreover, many send the message, directly or indirectly, that fat is ugly.

In sum, we argue that four main fat frames constitute the contested field of fat.[8] As we illustrate, two frames are dominant—the aesthetic frame, promoted by the industries of the fashion-beauty complex, and the CDC's health frame. We define these two frames as dominant because their messages not only ring loud and far, but they also encourage body conformity. That is, they obligate individuals to conform to the body status quo, where compliance is embodied in the nonfat ideal. The other two frames—the CCF's choice and responsibility frame and NAAFA's social justice frame—are reactionary. Unlike the aesthetic and health frames that promote body conformity, these two frames react to and challenge claims made by the dominant frames. In doing so, they send a message, implicitly or explicitly, about difference and diversity, albeit for very different reasons.

FRAME ANALYSIS

Framing Fat is first and foremost about unpacking these key cultural messages about fat. Frame analysis, a form of content analysis, guides our discussion of the aesthetic, health, choice and responsibility, and social justice frames. According to frame analysts, frames are part of a larger unit of public discourse called a "package" (Gamson and Lasch 1983; Gamson and Modigliani 1987). Packages include key frame(s) and "signature elements"—rhetorical devices used to describe representations of a social issue (Gamson and Lasch 1983). Signature elements are either "reasoning" or "framing" devices (Gamson and Lasch 1983). Reasoning devices include causal roots, appeals to principle, and policy consequences. Framing devices include an array of descriptors that facilitate frame articulation and description. These include metaphors, exemplars, catchphrases, depictions, and visual images. Not all signature elements are always present in a given frame, and rival framers often draw on and employ similar elements.

Formal frame analysis involves examining cultural artifacts—such as the documents disseminated by cultural producers—to identify the key signature elements of each frame. Together, these elements constitute what frame analysts refer to as a "framing" or "signature" matrix (Gamson and Lasch 1983). Building on the classic signature matrix, our expanded frame analysis discerns what each frame conveys about fat bodies by identifying the signature elements (both reasoning devices and framing devices) for each frame. Specifically, we identify the following reasoning devices: the central claim or position, the alleged causal roots, the purported consequences, the appeals to principle, and the proposed solutions and policies. We list and define these below. In general, reasoning devices describe a cultural producer's position and focus on the question, What does a frame say? The reasoning devices are

- the *central claim*: the primary assertion that singularly captures the frame's version of reality, often creating a social problem that needs to be addressed;
- *causal roots*: the implied or alleged causal source of the problem;
- the *consequences*: the purported effects or consequences of the problem;
- the *principles*: the underlying values or moral grounds on which the claim rests; and
- the *proposed solutions and policies*: general solutions to the underlying problem and specific policies that will help achieve the proposed solutions and solve the problem, as well as directives given to the public regarding how to act in light of the central claim.

Additionally, we analyze how cultural producers advance their frame's central position through the use of framing devices such as supporting data, metaphors, exemplars, catchphrases, depictions, and visual images. Below, we present these framing devices and their working definitions. While reasoning devices are about *what* a frame says, framing devices address the question of *how* it is being said:

- *supporting data*: evidence used to bolster the claim (or support the proposed solutions and suggested policies);
- *metaphors*: analogies and symbols depicting the frame;
- *exemplars*: events used to illustrate a key point of the frame or illustrative cases that exemplify the frame;
- *catchphrases*: theme statements or slogans that capture the frame's central message;
- *depictions*: characterizations of relevant subjects and opponents ("enemies") of the frame; and
- *visual images*: icons and other illustrative descriptors of the frame.

Both the classic framing matrix (Gamson and Modigliani 1987) and our expanded version potentially create false divisions among the reasoning and framing devices. First, not every frame producer uses all the reasoning and framing devices we have mentioned. Often as much can be discerned by what is mysteriously absent in a given frame as by what is present. As scholars who have conducted similar cultural analyses have put it, "It is vital to consider not simply what is included 'inside' media frames but also the silences in the texts" (Dworkin and Wachs 2004, 622). In other words, what a framer says (or does not say) and how it is said (or not said) are all part of the frame construction process and are central to a full analysis and understanding of a frame.

Second, at times, framers use entirely different devices to convey a message; at other times, they borrow from similar rhetoric. In other words, despite the framing matrix's appearing to suggest that frames advocate a unique vantage point on the fat body, with seemingly unique elements, there remain similarities within and across frames. Identifying and noting these similarities and differences underscores the complexity of the socially constructed meanings of fat in the modern Western world.

Third, in actuality, frames are far too large, complex, and multifaceted to be neatly dissected and broken down into component parts in the way that we are suggesting here. Instead, many of the signature elements overlap and intersect in complex ways. For example, in some cases it may be difficult to distinguish a central claim from its supporting data. In other cases, appeals to principle, which attempt to convince the public why they should care about a given take on a social issue, are linked to consequences. Similarly, the various solutions and policies proposed are sometimes tied in to the supposed causal roots of a given social problem. Or, in a more complicated scenario, the proposed solutions and policies (e.g., eat less and exercise more to lose weight and improve health) imply or provide information about the central claim (e.g., fat is unhealthy), the causal roots (e.g., eating too much and exercising too little), and the consequences (e.g., fat leads to poor health).

In sum, complex cultural discourses cannot be neatly dissected and broken down into component parts. Despite this, we nevertheless rely on the divisions of frame analysis as they enable a thorough and thoughtful analysis, particularly for the sake of comparison. However, recognizing the messy nature of cultural discourses, in *Framing Fat* we do not parcel out with scalpel precision the reasoning and framing devices of the framing matrix. Rather, because we think each framer tells a story about fat, our mission in each case is to uncover that story using the language and tools of the framing matrix as an analytical "guideline," acknowledging whenever relevant any inconsistencies and internal contradictions within a frame, as well as differences and similarities across frames. Despite this acknowledged artificiality of the framing matrix, to provide a visual aid for pedagogical purposes, in chapter 6 we summarize the four frames in a formal framing matrix.

In many ways, then, our frame analysis is a discourse analysis—a close reading of cultural artifacts with the goal of understanding the production and distribution of social knowledge (Blommaert 2005)—in which the signature elements loosely inform our analysis. We analyzed all cultural texts for what

Stuart Hall (1980) refers to as "preferred meaning," the reading or interpretation a cultural producer intends for an audience. Of course, it is possible that audiences do not decode text in the way a cultural producer intends. For example, media content may exhibit an "overspill of meanings" or "polysemic meanings" (Fiske 1986, 1989, 1994), where a plurality of interpretations means audiences can potentially construct their own alternative or even resistant meanings. Yet even though decoding text is a subjective process, given that the primary groups we examine (the CDC, the CCF, and NAAFA) are major stakeholders who consciously attempt to shape public understanding of the fat body, we argue that the preferred meanings of these documents are quite unambiguous, and our frame analysis focuses on these generally unambiguous preferred meanings. In our discussion of frame resonance, we engage how these meanings are then interpreted and used by cultural consumers.

CULTURAL ARTIFACTS

Our frame analysis identifies the signature elements used by the industries of the fashion-beauty complex, the CDC, the CCF, and NAAFA. To do this, we analyze cultural products disseminated by each of these framers. Data selection for the CDC, the CCF, and NAAFA began with a survey of the field of public documents put forth by each group. This meant thoroughly familiarizing ourselves with the materials on each group's website (including direct content, links to other websites, and downloadable publications such as newsletters, fact sheets, and policy documents) and printing off as much of this information as possible to carefully comb through it and preserve it. In our analysis, we take into consideration all of these materials, but we pay special attention to several major documents because they highlight the key messages of the group: for the CDC, *The Surgeon General's Vision for a Healthy and Fit Nation 2010* (HHS 2010d); for the CCF, *An Epidemic of Obesity Myths* (2004a, 2005a) and *Small Choices, Big Bodies* (2007b), both of which are in-depth and lengthy summaries of the CCF's position on obesity; and, for NAAFA, twelve official policy documents (2011k) that clearly articulate the group's perspective. Because some NAAFA board members and key fat acceptance players elaborate on NAAFA's message in outlets beyond these website materials, we also include in our analysis a number of these authors' publications. These individuals are leading actors in the fat acceptance movement, and their texts expand on what appears on the group's website. A list of their published works is featured under "Recommended Reading" on NAAFA's website (2011l).

Because of the amorphous nature of the fashion-beauty complex, we analyze the aesthetic frame using anecdotal evidence from various cultural producers that operate within and/or generate this frame. We focus mainly on advertisements of the fashion, cosmetics, and weight-loss industries. We handle the aesthetic frame differently in our analysis because there is no single cultural producer that promulgates the aesthetic frame. Instead, as others before us have recognized (e.g., Bartky 2010 [1988]), the fashion-beauty complex is nebulous and consists of various groups, many of which use mass media to communicate their messages. Because our goal is to analyze cultural objects that shape the public imagination, we think it is appropriate to focus on the advertisements produced by the industries of this complex. In doing so, we build on a rich history of scholarly analysis that investigates aesthetic and gender ideals through commercial advertising (see Bordo 2003; Cole and Hribar 1995; Goffman 1979; Jhally 1987; Kilbourne 1999, 2012).

Thus for the aesthetic frame we select advertisements from three main areas of the fashion-beauty complex—the cosmetics, fashion, and weight-loss industries—based on their breadth and representativeness, ensuring a range from each industry. While the evidence we present is necessarily anecdotal, the selected advertisements are analytically representative. In other words, while we readily concede that cosmetics, fashion, and weight-loss advertisements are complex, varied, and even contradictory (see Scott 1993), just as popular culture itself is (Fiske 1989), they nevertheless exhibit a general analytical pattern that conveys a powerful message about how the fashion-beauty complex approaches the fat body. Our analysis is also generally consistent with the analyses of others before us (Bordo 2003; Kilbourne 1999, 2012). To ensure the coherence of our analysis, our discussion of the aesthetic frame includes a detailed analysis of one prominent cultural producer, Anti-Gym, that exemplifies this frame.

In sum, we do not randomly select cultural artifacts for our analysis. Rather, after surveying the field of relevant public documents, we select documents that we deem exemplary of each cultural frame. For the CDC, the CCF, and NAAFA, these documents also directly generate the frame; that is, they state the framer's perspective rather than function as frame support. The materials of these three groups also exhibit a high degree of internal coherence; however, in our analysis we are aware that groups may, and do, make contradictory claims, and our analysis explores these internal inconsistencies.

FRAME RESONANCE

Framing is ultimately about framing competitions, that is, attempts by cultural producers to convince cultural consumers of their version of reality. As such, *Framing Fat* also examines frame resonance. Although typically used in reference to social movements, frame resonance can be broadly understood as the extent to which some frames seem to be successful or effective and therefore "resonate" with audiences, while others do not (Snow and Benford 1988). Is a given fat frame influential in the public eye? How do individuals think about the core issues and claims addressed by each frame? To what extent does a frame constitute common ideologies in one's cultural tool kit that are drawn upon to inform strategies of action (Swidler 1986, 2001)? To answer these questions, we draw on insights from a wide range of interdisciplinary scholars who employ various research methodologies to examine how the average American thinks about each frame and its core issues. To ensure a broad snapshot of cultural resonance, we include national poll data and large-scale studies that employ probability samples. As the following chapters illustrate, our look at resonance underscores the raced, classed, and gendered natures of frames.

A NOTE ON LANGUAGE

Language matters. For example, methodologists have shown how the wording of survey questions can elicit very different responses (see Singleton and Straits 2010), and feminists have long pointed out that gender-biased language can evoke feelings of exclusion while gender-neutral language can have an empowering effect (see Kleinman 2002; Richardson 2004 [1987]; Schulz 1975). Similarly, there are many adjectives to describe the size of the nonconforming body—"corpulent," "heavyset," "big boned," just to name a few—and the choice of one term can connote something very different from the choice of another. These words more or less describe the same perceived physical condition, but they potentially signify very different meanings. This is evident with three terms commonly invoked to describe the "body of size"—"fat," "overweight," and "obese." As we discuss in chapter 5, the term "fat" often signifies stigma and deviance (particularly when it is pitted against the term "normal"), but it is a term that fat acceptance activists readily attempt to reclaim (Wann 1998). The terms "overweight" and "obese" are medical labels; while the former typically suggests body nonconformity within limits, the latter indicates an extreme form of body deviance, both aesthetically and medically.

The terms various groups use in their framing endeavors are therefore not coincidental. Knowing this, we do not borrow these terms neutrally. Instead, we employ the terms commonly invoked within a given cultural frame. For example, while citing medical professionals and fat acceptance activists, we, too, use the terms "overweight" or "obese" and "fat," respectively. That is, in general we use the term a given framer references. When we are neither citing other people's work nor alluding to a fat frame, we default to the term "fat." This is because we sympathize with fat acceptance activists who attempt to reclaim the term "fat," and we are in agreement with them when they point out an abundance of credible scholarly evidence that the term has been derogatively constructed in a culture where fat bias, discrimination, and stigma are prevalent (see Puhl and Heuer 2009).

Finally, throughout *Framing Fat*, when referencing assertions made by cultural producers that they allege are fact or truth, we refer to such assertions as "claims" or "allegations." We acknowledge that this may not sit well with those who are wed to a particular frame. We do so to call attention to the social constructionist point of view that threads our analysis: in a contested field of meanings, there are few absolute facts or inherent truths, only assertions made by groups or individuals in an effort to define a situation. Indeed, our goal is to destabilize what dominant paradigms about the fat body have often presented as taken-for-granted "truths."

OVERVIEW

In the pages that follow, we analyze four fat frames, their resonance, and their social significance. We begin with the aesthetic and health frames (chapters 2 and 3)—two dominant and homogenizing cultural discourses that construct fat as a social problem. These frames are likely the ones readers will be familiar with and thus may come across as natural ways of thinking about fat. Fat is typically thought of as physically unattractive and unhealthy, and these messages encourage individuals to lose weight in the name of body image and physical and emotional well-being. Chapters 2 and 3 therefore examine closely the core issues of beauty and health. In chapters 4 and 5, we examine the two reactionary frames, frames that do not construct fat as a social problem. Instead, the food industry's frame emphasizes choice and responsibility, and NAAFA's social justice frame emphasizes body diversity. Furthermore, throughout the frame-specific chapters (chapters 2–5), whenever we engage a given frame we also examine the extent to which its central claim(s), consequences, appeals to principles, and proposed solutions resonate among individuals. As we illustrate in each discussion of resonance, frames are, at times, raced, classed, and/or gendered. In our closing chapter, when we discuss frame competitions and the significance of all four frames, we more closely examine the resonance of causal roots, highlighting how causal claims have implications for social equality.

In sum, the next four chapters each engage an issue that is core to a frame but nevertheless informed to some degree by other frames: aesthetics (chapter 2), health (chapter 3), choice and responsibility (chapter 4), and social justice (chapter 5). We choose to examine the core issues that all four frames generally engage because framing is dialogical (Esacove 2004). That is, frames are directed, however explicitly or implicitly, at one another. A mapping of the cultural landscape of fat begins with a foundational understanding of a cultural producer's frame, but a more thorough understanding of the field includes an analysis of frame competitions—namely how key framers approach similar issues, the conversations between frames, and the relationships among them.

Chapter 2, "Fat as Frightful," examines different approaches to beauty and weight, focusing on the messages about fat bodies presented in the advertisements of the fashion-beauty complex. This aesthetic frame establishes rather unequivocally that the fat body is unattractive. Yet there are other perspectives on fat aesthetics. Thus we turn to the CDC's, the CCF's, and particularly NAAFA's positions on body aesthetics. We examine NAAFA's claims that the fat body can be beautiful, even sexy. We also turn to data illustrating that, despite NAAFA's efforts to reshape public understanding, the thin aesthetic ideal maintains a stranglehold. In sum, chapter 2 explores the aesthetic frame, competing voices on body aesthetics, and the frame's resonance.

Chapter 3, "Fat as Fatal," examines different approaches to health and weight. We focus on the CDC's health frame and its claim that being overweight or obese is unhealthy. We also examine the role of the CDC in constructing the so-called obesity epidemic and the CDC's use of the Body Mass Index (BMI). However, others contest the CDC's messages; both the CCF and NAAFA claim that being obese does not necessarily mean that one is unhealthy. We examine these dissenting voices and also consider how messages about beauty, at times, intertwine with messages about health. Finally, we turn to data illustrating that, despite challenges to the obese-equals-unhealthy rhetoric, public health messages continue to resonate. In sum, chapter 3 explores the health frame, competing voices on body size and health, and the frame's resonance.

Chapter 4, "Fat and Food Politics," examines different approaches to individual choice and personal responsibility, focusing on the food industry's attempt to shape public meanings about the fat body. Unlike representatives of industries that have a stake in helping individuals lose weight, the CCF must encourage caloric consumption. This interest has led to the development of a reactionary fat frame that emphasizes individual choice and personal responsibility. Chapter 4 examines the CCF's choice and responsibility frame as well as how other framers approach issues of individual choice and personal responsibility. Again, we also consider resonance: how do individuals think about weight, individual choice, and personal responsibility? In sum, chapter 4 explores the choice and responsibility frame, competing voices on individual choice, personal responsibility, and body size, and the frame's resonance.

Chapter 5, "Fat and Fair Treatment," examines different approaches to the fat body and social justice. Here we focus on NAAFA's social justice frame. Although we discuss NAAFA's perspectives on body aesthetics, health, and choice and responsibility in chapters 2–4, its central position focuses on inequality. How does NAAFA approach social justice, and how do other cultural producers approach this issue? Chapter 5 examines NAAFA's position on fat bias, discrimination, and inequality. Moreover, it explores the general lack of public support for the social justice frame. In sum, chapter 5 examines the social justice frame, competing voices on social justice, and the frame's resonance.

After looking at these core issues, our final chapter, "Framing Fat Bodies," ties together the four frames and addresses a question central to *Framing Fat*: what are the implications of these different approaches to aesthetics, health, individual choice and personal responsibility, and social justice? Chapter 6 begins with a summary of the four frames and an elaboration of the formal framing matrix that identifies, where appropriate, each frame's signature elements. We then attempt to make sense of the frame resonance we document in chapters 2–5, and in particular why key aspects of the aesthetic, health, and choice and responsibility frames resonate, yet the social justice frame engenders limited support. In our discussion, we examine how the public approaches etiology, as well as the significance of causal attribution. We also revisit biomedicalization and accompanying issues of morality and risk before turning to interframe influences and connections. After a discussion of how public health policy might be better informed by interframe dialogues, we close by revealing the dual meaning of *Framing Fat*. Despite being social constructions, fat frames are used to "frame" body nonconformists—a "framing" based on the distribution of power.

2 · FAT AS FRIGHTFUL

IN NOVEMBER 2008 Susan D'Arcy made a heartfelt plea to the public: "Young girls should not be subjected to images of celebrity women who are so thin. It's unrealistic for girls to have these women as role models" (Stokes 2008). Her request was motivated by tragedy. At the age of thirteen, Ms. D'Arcy's daughter Imogen hanged herself in the bathroom of the family home because she felt "fat and ugly." Her father told the press that his daughter's concerns about her weight were misguided, describing her as of average height and weight, and very popular.

Imogen was not alone; research shows that being overweight and perceiving oneself as overweight increase the risk for suicide in adolescents (Swahn et al. 2009). Many people are literally "dying to be thin" by engaging in unsafe practices in an attempt to control their weight. For instance, in 2009 a 238-pound woman died after crash dieting to lose weight for her wedding (Hagan 2009), and in 2011 a young male army recruit died after developing an acute cardiac dysrhythmia from an electrolyte imbalance brought on by dieting (Associated Press 2011). These cases point to how the thin ideal, an ideal largely proliferated by the mass media, creates a climate in which fat is considered frightful because it is defined as ugly and, as such, is feared, hated, and to be avoided at all costs.

Framing Fat examines four cultural takes on the fat body. In our journey to map this contested field of fat, our first stop is the aesthetic frame of the "fashion-beauty complex" (Bartky 1990). We begin with the aesthetic frame because it is a frame most readers are familiar with and also because it is unique. As we discussed in chapter 1, unlike the other frames, the aesthetic frame has no single cultural producer that we can look to, no clear frame-generating organization, and no specific set of documents, web pages, or policy statements that articulate its position. Instead, the aesthetic frame is all around us—ubiquitous and prolific—and generated primarily by industries via the mass media. As Sandra

Lee Bartky aptly writes in reference to the thin ideal that is so central to the aesthetic frame, it is "everywhere and it is nowhere" (2010 [1988], 88).

THE FASHION-BEAUTY COMPLEX

According to Bartky (1990), the fashion-beauty complex is a multifaceted conglomeration of industries that, in conjunction with consumer culture, conveys a narrow definition and understanding of femininity and womanhood. It includes the fashion, cosmetics, and weight-loss industries, all of which market goods, services, and cultural ideologies that act as a form of patriarchal control. Though Bartky's primary concern is how the fashion-beauty complex oppresses women, the reach of this complex, while remaining gendered, affects both women and men.

The reach and power of these industries are not to be underestimated. According to Shari Dworkin and Faye Linda Wachs (2009), multinational corporations have a large stake in transforming people into the right kinds of objects because this translates into massive profits. This is especially true of the industries of the fashion-beauty complex. For example, market researchers estimate that the U.S. weight-loss industry is worth over $60 billion (Marketdata Enterprises 2011). Industry leaders by market segment include the diet soft-drink industry ($19.8 billion), health clubs ($18.5 billion), bariatric surgeons ($5.12 billion), and commercial weight-loss centers ($3.89 billion; Marketdata Enterprises 2011). The U.S. apparel industry alone generates about $181 billion per year (WeConnectFashion 2011).

Despite the diversity of players that constitute the fashion-beauty complex, common to many of them is the use of mass media and advertising, namely in an effort to sell products. As Mike Featherstone (1982) observes, the foundations of a consumer culture came with the new media of the 1920s (e.g., motion pictures, tabloid press, magazines), and soon after, advertising became the guardian of the new morality. Advertisements enticed individuals to participate in the consumption of commodities and experiences that were once restricted to the privileged classes. Primarily through images, themes such as youth, beauty, and fitness became loosely associated with consumer goals, not only "awakening long-suppressed desires" but also "reminding the individual that he has room for self-improvement in all aspects of his life" (Featherstone 1982, 19). In other words, advertisements market not only goods but also values that tell us who we should aspire to be.

Given the social significance of advertisements in Western consumer culture, in our analysis of the aesthetic frame we focus on the advertisements of the industries of the fashion-beauty complex. Using elements of the framing matrix as a guide, we show how select advertisements from the fashion industry (such as style and clothing companies), the cosmetics industry (such as beauty-product companies), and the weight-loss industry (such as companies in the business of selling diet foods and beverages, weight-loss drugs, and weight-loss services) promote a message about the fat body. The uniqueness of this rather nebulous frame, which lacks a single prominent cultural producer, means that our evidence is perforce anecdotal, and we readily admit that some of the advertisements we profile speak louder than others. Although the advertisements we examine are not necessarily representative of all the advertisements in the fashion-beauty complex, they nevertheless represent a discernible empirical pattern.[1]

In this chapter we illustrate the ways in which the aesthetic frame creates an environment in which fat is defined as a social problem because it is unattractive and it diminishes quality of life. We also profile a chain of workout facilities that illustrates rather remarkably the key points of the aesthetic frame. Because the contested field of fat means that not all cultural producers approach fat as an aesthetic violation, we go on to explore competing messages about the aesthetic desirability of fat. Finally, we turn to resonance. That is, we look at the extent to which the public embraces the aesthetic frame, examining whether it is or is not influential.

THE CENTRAL CLAIM: FAT IS FRIGHTFUL

The central claim of any frame is the primary assertion that singularly captures the frame's version of reality, often creating a social problem that needs to be addressed. The central claim of the aesthetic frame is that the fat body is problematic because it is physically unattractive. Often this central claim is communicated indirectly. For instance, the abundance of thin firm bodies and the marginalization and exclusion of fat bodies in mainstream commercial advertisements conveys the message that fat is undesirable. Some have referred to this absence as "symbolic annihilation," a term previously applied to racial and ethnic minorities in the mainstream media but that has more recently been used to describe the exclusion of fat people from the public eye (Giovanelli and Ostertag 2009).

Many feminist scholars before us have pointed out the prevalence and pervasiveness of a thin (white) feminine Western beauty ideal that has rendered the fat body abject and deviant. They have labeled this ideal a "tyranny of slenderness" (Chernin 1994) and a "beauty myth" (Wolf 1991) that oppresses and objectifies women. These unrealistic body ideals have serious consequences for women's physical, psychological, and social well-being (Bartky 2010 [1988]; Bordo 2003; Collins 2000; Hesse-Biber 1996; Kilbourne 1999, 2012; Milkie 1999; Parker et al. 1995; Spitzack 1990; Thompson 1992; Wolf 1991; Zones 1997). These scholars have also pointed out that the thin aesthetic ideal for women is not only a slim ideal, but one that is taut (Bordo 2003; Dworkin and Wachs 2009; Markula 1995). Masculinities scholars, too, have observed the prevalence of the lean muscular ideal for men as part of a larger cultural understanding of masculinity, the pursuit of which can have negative physical and psychological consequences similar to those experienced by women (Atkinson 2008; Connell 1995; Pope, Phillips, and Olivardia 2000).

Take, for example, the iconic Victoria's Secret advertisements that exemplify the thin feminine ideal. These advertisements typically depict scantily clad voluptuous women. A recent Victoria's Secret print advertisement for the store's "Very Sexy Collection" shows three white women in lingerie dressing and preening in a dressing room. None of the women are fat or even average sized; rather, they are all tall and thin. Large copy dominates the forefront of the advertisement, asking "WHAT IS SEXY?" and making it clear that these women, and the products they are wearing, are the answer. The advertisement conveys three important messages: slender is sexy; fat is consequently frightful;[2] and the products featured in this advertisement can help one appear slender and therefore sexy.

Like this Victoria Secret's advertisement, which openly asks "What is sexy?" and answers the question with a bold cleavage-revealing visual, the fashion-beauty complex conveys its messages by using a combination of words and pictures. In the language of the framing matrix, the copy generates a variety of catchphrases, and the pictures are visual images. These catchphrases and visual images are the primary framing devices used by the fashion-beauty complex, as the abundant and striking images of thin bodies and accompanying copy contained within the vast majority of advertisements make it indisputable that these bodies are "sexy," "hot," "beautiful," "good looking," "pretty," "desirable," and so forth, and consequently that any other body is problematic.

Similar messages come from the advertisements of weight-loss companies. For example, a Jenny Craig advertisement features the American actress Carrie Fisher touting how the program helped her lose thirty pounds. Apparently speaking to the folks at Jenny Craig, she remarks, "Thanks for letting me be pretty one more time." Yet such messages are not restricted to advertisements aimed at a female audience. Weight Watchers, the biggest player in the world of commercial weight-loss services (Schultz 2011), recently launched a $10 million advertising campaign specifically targeting men. These new commercials air mostly during news and sports programming and focus on "manly" weight maintenance issues, such as nutritional knowledge about products like beer and food that can be prepared on the grill (Schultz 2011). Playing to men's sense of competition (particularly with other men), one advertisement features a man boasting that he "looks better" than his friends because he used Weight Watchers online.

While these new advertisements target men, who make up 10 percent of Weight Watchers' customer base (Schultz 2011), they send the same message as the advertisements that target women: fat bodies look bad, thin bodies look good. The difference lies mainly with message packaging. The gendered marketing of weight-loss products and the reframing of weight loss as masculine are in many ways savvy, as hegemonic masculinity (see Connell 1995; Connell and Messerschmidt 2005) relegates weight loss and related activities to women's domain. For example, research shows that "fat talk"—talk about body size and shape that is generally disparaging—is primarily girls' and women's preoccupation (Nichter 2000; Nichter and Vuckovic 1994; Salk and Engeln-Maddox 2011). When men do engage in weight-loss efforts, there is some evidence that they neutralize aesthetic concerns, emphasizing instead the scientific nature of dieting practices (see Mallyon et al. 2010).

The message that thin is beautiful and desirable, and fat is ugly and unacceptable, seems to be ubiquitous in advertisements both within and outside of the fashion-beauty complex. Some advertisements even conflate thinness and beauty to the extent that it is nearly impossible to discuss one without the other. For example, in 2011 PepsiCo released a "new skinny can" in conjunction with New York Fashion Week. PepsiCo's chief marketing officer reportedly said, "Our slim, attractive new can is the perfect complement to today's most stylish looks" (PRNewswire 2011). The initial press release about the "new skinny can" refers to it as "attractive" three times, twice using the phrase "slim, attractive," reinforcing the ongoing conflation of thinness and beauty. So whether the product is Pepsi's sleek-looking soda can, Dell's Vostro V131 laptop computer (marketed under the slogan "Thin and powerful never looked so good"), or Sony Ericsson's Xperia Arc cell phone (described by the company as "amazingly thin"), advertisements frequently normalize the sensibility that thin is beautiful and desirable. By default, fat is ugly and unappealing.

At times this antifat message is overt. For example, one advertisement for the cosmetics company Elizabeth Arden, placed in the high-profile fashion magazine *Vogue*, promotes an antiaging moisturizer called Prevage. The advertisement depicts a slim and shapely mannequin. Copy to the right of the mannequin provides a part-by-part breakdown of the mannequin's problematic body parts. This text is accompanied by arrows pointing directly to each problem area. Descriptors such as "stretch marks," "loss of firmness and elasticity," "weight gain," "loss of tone," "sagging," and "dimpled skin" all stress the need to combat both aging and fat, a battle Prevage purportedly will help wage and win (Elizabeth Arden, Inc. 2012).

One key way advertisers perpetuate the idea that fat is unattractive is by digitally altering the images of already thin women featured in advertisements, ensuring rather unequivocally the symbolic annihilation of the fat body. These altered images are part of the cultural landscape that make up what Naomi Wolf (1991) refers to as the beauty myth, an unrealistic and unattainable cultural ideal of feminine physical beauty, often presumed to be universal. Image-altering practices are so commonplace that a number of celebrities have openly admitted that their images are manipulated (Marikar 2010). The extremes of this editing process were highlighted in 2009 when Ralph Lauren published a dramatically retouched print advertisement in which the model's waist appeared to be smaller than her head. This advertisement created such a stir that Ralph Lauren's representatives eventually issued an apology and withdrew the advertising campaign (Heussner 2009). Because of concerns that retouched images promote unrealistic body expectations for young people, in 2011 the American Medical Association (2011) adopted a new policy to encourage marketers to work with public- and private-sector organizations to develop guidelines that would discourage the altering of photographs.

A poignant illustration of digital alteration involves actress Christina Hendricks, who plays a central character on the American Movie Classics television series *Mad Men*. Hendricks is known for her curvaceous figure and for publicly embracing her size and has even openly stated that she felt beautiful after gaining fifteen pounds (Hunter 2010). However, when the clothing company London Fog featured Hendricks in one of its advertising campaigns, it was apparent that her image had been digitally altered so that her waist would appear smaller, implying that London Fog felt the need to protect the public from Hendricks's body (Wade 2010). By literally reducing and recontouring this curvy female icon, the advertiser made it clear that even women who celebrate their size are more desirable and marketable when trimmed down.

In sum, many of the advertisements of the fashion-beauty complex send the message, whether directly or indirectly, that the fat body, particularly the fat female body, is problematic. The seemingly omnipresent ideal reminds us that our bodies are inadequate—an inadequacy that applies to everyone despite the remote odds of living up to Western cultural body ideals, such as those represented by Mattel's iconic Barbie and Ken dolls. As researchers point out, the probability of attaining Barbie's measurements in real life is under 1 in 100,000, whereas Ken's measurements are attainable for 1 in 50 men (Norton et al. 1996). In this way, as Dworkin and Wachs fittingly observe, media forces generally and advertising specifically conspire with more diffuse notions of power to produce a "culture of lack" (2009, 10). These advertisements imply that we are wanting in some way, and that consumer capitalism will gladly step in to help fill this void. It is through consumerism individuals can improve themselves and construct their ideal selves. Advertisements, like the select few we have profiled, create a world that invites (rather miserable) comparison, leaves us emotionally vulnerable and encourages us to monitor ourselves (Featherstone 1982). In this culture of lack, we are constantly under surveillance, including self-surveillance (see Bartky 2010 [1988]; Foucault 1979, 1980).

CAUSAL ROOTS: PERSONAL FAILURE

In addition to defining reality via a set of central claims, every frame alleges the causal roots of the social problem in question. In the case of the aesthetic frame, these claims come in the form of a set of assumptions. This is because the vast majority of cultural producers that collectively make up the fashion-beauty complex do not directly address the supposed causes of fat. Instead, they propose various solutions to fight fat, and in doing so they imply that the body is malleable and within an individual's control. Consequently, the aesthetic frame works with the assumption, though rarely stated outright, that the source of fatness is personal failure. Whether it is the failure to practice self-restraint or to invest time, energy, or money in oneself, the fat individual is blameworthy. As our chapter 3 discussion of what Robert Crawford (1980) refers to as "healthism" shows, the claim that personal failure is the primary cause of being overweight is also central to the health frame.

Occasionally, however, a company within the fashion-beauty complex will engage the issue of causality more explicitly than others. Because this is the case with the fitness club Anti-Gym, we profile this facility later in this chapter and show how it exemplifies the different elements of the aesthetic frame, including its claims about causality. Anti-Gym serves as a framing exemplar.

Thus both the aesthetic frame we explore here and the health frame we examine in chapter 3 draw upon the framing metaphor that the body is a symbol of accomplishment. This metaphor aligns with the premise, one that others have called attention to, that the body is an identity project that is continuously subject to revision (Giddens 1991; Shilling 2003). While some have emphasized the role of the face in this project (Rivers 1994), others have stressed how body fat reflects the psyche (Bordo 2003). As Susan Bordo writes about unwanted bulges on the body,

> I want to consider them as a metaphor for anxiety about internal processes out of control—uncontained desire, unrestrained hunger, uncontrolled impulse. . . . In advertisements, the construction of the body as an alien attacker, threatening to erupt in an unsightly display of bulging flesh, is a ubiquitous cultural image. . . . The ideal here is of a body that is absolutely tight, contained, "bolted down," firm: in other words, a body that is protected against eruption from within, whose internal processes are under control. Areas that are soft, loose, or "wiggly" are unacceptable, even on extremely thin bodies. (2003, 189–190)

Fashion-beauty complex advertisements remind us that unwieldy, loose, and jiggly fat must be tamed. The taut body, purportedly the result of endless hours at the gym and dietary restrictions (never mind any genetic predispositions one might possess or surgical interventions one might have undertaken), then becomes a reflection of moral fortitude, perseverance, and bodily mastery. As Bordo puts it, it is a symbol of our ability to rein in those "internal processes out of control." Body projects therefore assume a mind-body, subject-object dualism in which individuals rationally and fervently pursue control over the abject (and presumably feminine) body object (Shilling and Mellor 1996).[3] Moreover, that the body is a reflection of the self may account for why individuals perform ongoing impression management (Goffman 1959), including various forms of physical body management such as manipulating clothing and sucking in stomach areas to appear thinner in public settings (Kwan 2010). Fat is to be avoided at all costs because it violates cultural aesthetic codes, and it signifies moral lack.

CONSEQUENCES AND PRINCIPLES: DIMINISHED QUALITY OF LIFE

Frames not only call attention to a social problem and make claims about the source of that problem, but they also outline the consequences of the problem at hand. Moreover, every frame rests on a set of underlying moral values referred to as the appeals to principle. In the case of the aesthetic frame, these two elements of the framing matrix (consequences and appeals) are one in the same. In addition to defining fat as unattractive and implying that the root of fatness lies in personal failure, the cultural producers of the aesthetic frame use advertisements to convince the public that being fat has consequences that will eventually diminish overall quality of life. Specifically, advertisements frequently claim that being fat prevents individuals from looking and feeling good, therefore making them undesirable to others. In other words, the aesthetic frame appeals to our desire for the "good life" and preys on our fears of social isolation and loneliness.

We have already seen this appeal to our desire for the good life play out in the advertisements previously described. These advertisements communicate that being thin will make one more attractive (Prevage) and sexy (Victoria's Secret) and that losing weight will help one look good (Weight Watchers). Being attractive, sexy, and good-looking, will, in turn, lead individuals to a higher quality of life. This message is also transmitted in advertising campaigns for weight-loss drugs when they equate thinness with sexual vitality and happiness. For example, the diet drug Sensa promises to give users a "gym body without going to the gym" so that they can "look and feel sexy again" by revealing their "tight body" (Sensa 2012). Apidexin, another diet drug, relies on testimonials in which clients claim that losing weight by using Apidexin made them feel "awesome" (Apidexin 2011).

One Houston-based bariatric surgeon provides a frank example of this quality-of-life appeal in the form of billboards along Texas highways. The tagline for several of the surgeon's advertisements reads "Lose Weight. Gain Life."

(Bariatric Care Centers 2009). But perhaps the best example comes from the world of fashion. Armani Exchange, a sublabel of the fashion designer Giorgio Armani, produced a print advertisement featuring an extremely slender model crouched at the bottom of the advertisement. A single line of copy at the top reads, "The more you subtract, the more you add." The message conveyed: a small, slender body adds to one's life and a large, fat body somehow subtracts from it.

The Armani Exchange advertisement became somewhat notorious after being highlighted in Jean Kilbourne's *Killing Us Softly* film series, which examines gender representation in advertising. Kilbourne, a feminist author and filmmaker, acknowledges that this advertisement, on the surface, is about minimalist fashion. However, she points out that it is also about cutting women down to size both literally—in terms of the size of their bodies—and figuratively—in terms of their power and voice (Kilbourne 2012). Other writers such as Wolf (1991) have protested such depictions on similar grounds and have added that ideals of thinness that lead to dieting mean that women are in a perpetual state of hunger, a state that makes effective political change difficult.

In sum, the aesthetic frame, through its many visual images and catchphrases, appeals to our desire to live a good life. These advertisements depict thin bodies as physically attractive and sexy, and they pair these bodies with notions of happiness. The not-so-subtle statement is that the fat body leads one down a path of unhappiness. Of note, this pairing parallels a theorized relationship between bodily assets and social outcomes. For example, Chris Shilling writes about how physical capital, capital that "illuminates the value placed upon the size, shape and appearance of the flesh" (2004, 474), can be translated into other forms of capital (see Bourdieu 1978, 1986; Shilling 2003, 2004). When, for example, children of the social elite participate in sporting activities, like polo, that stress manners and deportment, such participation can then translate into both cultural and social capital which in turn can be translated into economic capital.

Similarly, Catherine Hakim (2010), building on these notions of economic, cultural, and social capital developed by Pierre Bourdieu (1986), puts forth a rather controversial fourth form of capital, which she labels "erotic capital." While erotic capital is multifaceted, she indicates that beauty and sexual attractiveness are its core elements, precisely the two central elements found in the advertisements we have examined. Hakim also points out that, whereas beauty involves cultural variations and encompasses body-size ideals, sexual attractiveness is about possessing a sexy body. Just as modern advertisements suggest that these physical assets translate to a good and happy life, according to Hakim, erotic capital is important because it is an asset that translates into many benefits. For example, she maintains that erotic capital enables one to reap rewards in the mating and marriage markets, in the labor market, and in everyday social interactions. In these ways, advertisements that appeal to our sense of the good life tap into a concrete reality; those who look thin and sexy may be happier because they are in fact rewarded in various domains of social life. In chapter 5, we further examine how beauty correlates with positive social outcomes.

PROPOSED SOLUTIONS: FAT IS FIXABLE

As with other frames, the aesthetic frame provides a set of solutions to the social problem it has helped construct. In this case, the aesthetic frame asserts that fat is fixable and that the solution lies in the use of various goods and services. Industries use advertising to manufacture contempt for fat that helps to drive their product sales and boost their bottom lines. A belief in the malleability of the body's appearance is thus a core assumption that closely connects to the frame's assertion that fat is fixable with a combination of willpower and proper product and service usage.

That fat is supposedly fixable and that one ought to do something about this undesirable state is part of our larger transformation culture. Transformation is, as one sociologist puts it, "not only central to consumer culture, it is one of the key tenets of Western modernity" (Featherstone 2010, 200). The so-called American Dream, the rags-to-riches story, and the abundance of self-help literature now available on the $11 billion self-improvement market (Marketdata Enterprises 2008) all purport that we can and should transform ourselves both physically and psychologically in the name of personal improvement. Change will supposedly reveal one's true self and/or align one's outer and inner selves (see Gagné and McGaughey 2002; Throsby 2008). This is in part the rhetoric underscoring the omnipresent cosmetic surgery and makeover culture (Jones 2008; Throsby 2008). In this culture, change becomes an obligation and may even be framed in terms of liberation (Spitzack 1990). As we have demonstrated, advertisements intimate that the attainment of an ideal body through weight-loss transformation will allow individuals to pursue new experiences and attain a quality of life of which they had previously only dreamed. According to Carol Spitzack (1990), this promise of liberation cleverly masks oppressive disciplining bodily practices, particularly for women.

The power and ubiquity of transformation ideologies leaves no body immune. For example, even the pregnant body, which is hailed as maternally successful, is potentially aesthetically problematic and an object of transformation. New mothers are expected to take on a "third shift" of bodily labor (Dworkin and Wachs 2004; 2009). Rather unforgivingly, our transformation culture pressures us all to pursue body work (Gimlin 2000, 2002, 2007; Kwan and Trautner 2009), such as weight-loss efforts, in the name of creating a compliant, conforming, and docile body (Bartky 2000 [1988]; Foucault 1979).

Indeed, many of the advertisements we have examined assert or imply that the body is malleable and that the products and services offered will help consumers obtain the body that they desire. Victoria's Secret promises that its products will make the body appear sexy. Weight Watchers' programs will help alter the body so that it looks better. Prevage's cosmetic cream assures consumers of a transformed body that will hide the signs of aging and fat. The use of diet drugs, like Sensa and Apidexin, will shrink one's body, leading to feelings of sexiness and awesomeness. Bariatric surgery will help gain life.

Examples abound. There are dozens of cosmetic products that allegedly help individuals manipulate their bodies by reducing fat or by masking the stigmatizing bodily evidence that they were once fat. Cellulite reducing creams purport to "shrink thighs, hips and butt" (Cellulite MD 2011) so that people are no longer "forcing [their] body into hiding" (Revitol 2012) and can instead be "normal" and "healthy" (Procellix Cellulite Cream 2012). And for those who have achieved the ideal and firm body, there are products that can conceal previous failings. Use of these products is said to ensure that individuals "don't have to suffer" (Dermology 2011) anymore because of their "embarrassing stretch marks" (Leading Edge Marketing Inc. 2012).

At the end of the day, we are told that fat is fixable and that consumer culture, through its many product offerings, is the key to these fixes. This logic is prevalent even though, as we discuss shortly, weight-loss practices generally fail. Transformation rhetoric too remains ubiquitous despite the fact that even when physical change is successful, the psychological changes that accompany body transformation are dynamic, tenuous, and complicated (see Featherstone 2010; Granberg 2011).

AN ILLUSTRATIVE CASE: ANTI-GYM

In framing language, an exemplar is an event that illustrates key points of a frame. Anti-Gym, while not an event per se, operates in a manner that exemplifies the major elements of the aesthetic frame. Specifically, it features the central, and some of the most controversial, messages of the aesthetic frame.

Anti-Gym is a now-defunct fitness club formerly located in the western United States.[4] Its founder, Michael Karolchyk, proudly promotes fat hatred and has consequently become the target of ridicule and contempt from the fat acceptance community.[5] Anti-Gym's slogan was "No Chubbies Allowed," a "chubby" being defined as "an unmotivated, lazy slob who wants to blame everybody else but themselves for their shortcomings" (Anti-Gym 2011d). This antifat message dominated both Anti-Gym's now-discontinued website and its television and radio advertisements. For instance, its website once openly reinforced a variety of stereotypes about fat people including the beliefs that they refuse to change their behavior, smell bad, are extremely lazy, binge eat and are ashamed of it, and are sexually repulsive (Anti-Gym 2011a). The website's images (which looked more like soft-core pornography than the visuals in typical gym advertise-ments), along with a tagline encouraging Anti-Gym members to "have sex with the lights on," helped cement the message that slender is sexy and fat is frightful. One of Anti-Gym's television commercials even went so far as to suggest that fat women are only attractive to drunk men, while another openly proclaimed, "You are never going to have a hubby if you're a chubby" (Anti-Gym 2011b).

Similar to the other fashion-beauty complex advertisements previously examined, Anti-Gym purported a solution to the "chubby" body. Anti-Gym promised fast and lasting results including a trim tummy, all-night stamina, a look that turns heads (Anti-Gym 2011c), and a great lifestyle (Anti-Gym 2011d). To accomplish these results, Anti-Gym proudly took a tough love approach to fighting fat by promising to "kick your butt" (Anti-Gym 2011c), by assigning "extra cardio for that pizza you just inhaled" (Anti-Gym 2011d), and by ensur-ing that you think of Anti-Gym "the next time you go in for another fudge-pop" (Anti-Gym 2011a).

Through Anti-Gym, core elements of the aesthetic frame surface. Central claim: fat is frightful and thin is attractive and sexy. Consequences and prin-ciples: being fat diminishes overall quality of life largely by making one unde-sirable. And proposed solutions: body size is within an individual's control *if* he or she is willing to use the product being offered. Yet unlike many cultural producers of this frame, Anti-Gym also addresses the purported causes of fat-ness. Namely, its advertisements imply that laziness, slovenliness, redirection of blame, lack of motivation, and lack of restraint are the reasons people become fat. This is acutely evident in Anti-Gym's assertion that "You don't have a 'thy-roid problem'" (Anti-Gym 2011d). According to Anti-Gym, since fat people are to blame for their own predicament, it is acceptable to hate not just fat, but fat people as well.

Anti-Gym also typifies the aesthetic frame because it highlights the enemies of the aesthetic frame. Whereas most fashion-beauty complex advertisements depict the thin ideal (thereby symbolically annihilating the fat nonideal), Anti-Gym reinforces the thin ideal *and* directly engages its fat antithesis. In other words, it directly challenges the enemies of the aesthetic frame, including those who accept fat and the fat body and those who propose that the body is less mal-leable than the aesthetic frame would have the public believe.

COMPETING VOICES: FAT ISN'T ALWAYS FRIGHTFUL

And these "enemies" of the aesthetic frame do exist, as not everyone agrees that fat bodies are aesthetically repulsive. There are a number of individuals and groups who actively refute this claim. In terms of the cultural producers we focus on in *Framing Fat*, neither the Centers for Disease Control and Prevention

(CDC; see chapter 3) nor the Center for Consumer Freedom (CCF; see chapter 4) have much to say about fat aesthetics. In fact, the CDC draws minimal attention to physical appearance, asserting that "the primary concern of overweight and obesity is one of health rather than appearance" (HHS 2001, 23).

In contrast, the National Association to Advance Fat Acceptance (NAAFA) contests the belief that fat bodies are ugly. This contestation is a direct indictment of the fashion-beauty complex, which the association condemns for perpetuating the thin ideal in the name of multimillion dollar profits (see Wann 2009). As we discuss extensively in chapter 5, NAAFA represents the social justice frame.

SOCIAL JUSTICE: FAT AS FOXY

Rejecting the notion that fat is frightful, NAAFA promotes the idea that fat can be physically attractive and even sexy. For example, NAAFA and fat acceptance activists celebrate the fat body and fat-positive images such as the Venus of Willendorf and drawings of fat women in revealing clothing posing provocatively and confidently (Wann 1998). Statements such as "You, too, can be flabulous!" (Wann 1998, 184) also reinforce a fat-positive perspective. In fact, the term "flabulous" is used throughout *Fat!So?*, a book written by former NAAFA board member Marilyn Wann that has become somewhat of a manifesto of the fat acceptance movement. Wann's portrayal of the fat body as a source of beauty and pride is also evident when she invites her readers to contemplate "What do you like about being fat?" (Wann 1998, 24). Notably, NAAFA's promotion of body diversity involves embracing bodies of *all* sizes. For example, the Los Angeles chapter's Myspace website reads, "Whether you are 4-feet tall or 7-feet, 100 or 600 pounds, able-bodied or differently-abled, pear-, barrel-, apple-, or hourglass-shaped . . . NAAFA-LA celebrates people of all shapes and sizes!" (NAAFA-LA 2012).

Another way NAAFA rejects the premise that fat is undesirable is by welcoming fat admiration. Fat admirers are individuals who prefer romantic partners with large bodies. One scholarly study exploring fat admiration found that heterosexual male fat admirers rate fat women positively and react more positively to a much wider range of figures; in other words, they reject sociocultural norms of attractiveness (Swami and Tovee 2009). The National Association to Advance Fat Acceptance's official position on fat admirers asserts that "a preference for a fat partner is as valid as any other preference based on physical characteristics" and that "in a society where at least 65 percent of the population is considered fat, a preference for a fat partner is normal and should be encouraged rather than discouraged" (2011k, "Fat Admirers"). Additionally, NAAFA "condemns the ridiculing and disqualification of fat people as desirable sexual partners as blatant discrimination" (2011k, "Fat Admirers").[6] To this end, the group organizes social outings such as dances, pool parties, and fashion shows to publicly display—and promote the admiration of—fat bodies.

It is noteworthy that closely aligned with NAAFA is the discipline of fat stud-ies, defined by Sondra Solovay and Esther Rothblum, members of NAAFA's board of advisors and editors of the first *Fat Studies Reader*, as "an interdisciplin-ary field of scholarship marked by an aggressive, consistent, rigorous critique of the negative assumptions, stereotypes, and stigma placed on fat and the fat body" (Solovay and Rothblum 2009, 2). These scholars maintain that the core claim of the aesthetic frame, chiefly that fat is frightful, must be examined with a critical eye. To do this, fat studies scholars focus on the social construction of modern attitudes about fat and point out the variability of appearance and body norms across history and between cultures (Fraser 2009; Rothblum 1990). They also underscore that it is within a specific set of economic, cultural, social, and political circumstances that the fat body has come to be understood as physically unattractive.

RESONANCE

But which view of fat bodies dominates the American cultural landscape? How influential is the aesthetic frame's core premise? Is the belief that fat is physically unattractive part of the public imagination? If so, are Americans motivated to fix this supposedly fixable problem?

The answer is a qualified yes. On the one hand, there is quite a bit of evidence indicating that Americans do think of the fat body as frightful and that they believe fat diminishes quality of life. They are also motivated to lose weight in the name of beauty. On the other hand, there is evidence that some subcultures resist the thin aesthetic norm. Weight-loss practices also differ remarkably by social group.

Fat Is Frightful, Slender Is Sexy

First, many people do seem to agree with the central claim of the aesthetic frame that fat is frightful. A number of studies spanning decades have shown that fat people are consistently thought of as shapeless, unappealing (Robinson, Bacon, and O'Reilly 1993), unattractive (Harris, Harris, and Bochner 1982), and aes-thetically displeasing (Wooley and Wooley 1979). Even health-care professionals believe that fat people are unattractive, ugly (Foster et al. 2003), and less sexually appealing than their thinner counterparts (Harvey and Hill 2001).[7]

The results of studies that examine romantic partner preferences provide fur-ther evidence that people think fat is frightful. For example, one study asked col-lege students to rank photographs of hypothetical sexual partners including an obese person, amputees, and individuals with a history of sexually transmitted diseases. Respondents consistently ranked the obese person as the least desirable sexual partner compared to the others (Chen and Brown 2005). Similarly, research on personal advertisements has repeatedly revealed a preference for thin, attractive partners (Andersen et al. 1993; Davis 1990; Greenlees and McGrew 1994; Smith, Waldorf, and Trembath 1990; Wiederman 1993).

Fat is so frightful that individuals are willing to avoid it at nearly any cost. One study found that half of the young women surveyed would rather be hit by a truck than be fat, and over 65 percent reported that they would rather be mean or stupid than be fat (Martin 2007). Among American adults who were asked whether they would choose to be obese, 14 percent reported that they would rather be an alcoholic; 15 percent reported that they would rather be severely depressed; 25 percent reported that they would rather be unable to have children; 30 percent reported that they would rather be divorced; and nearly half (46 percent) indicated that they would rather give up one year of life (Schwartz et al. 2006). Researchers have even reported that 75 percent of obese people would risk death to lose just 20 percent of their body weight (Wee et al. 2006).

Despite what seems like compelling evidence that the aesthetic frame resonates among the general public, scholars have written about counterhegemonic body aesthetics among various racial/ethnic groups. For example, Patricia Hill Collins (2000) maintains that African Americans adopt more flexible conceptions of beauty compared to their white counterparts and reject the slender, fair-skinned ideal that constructs blacks as the Other. In fact, some research confirms that African American girls and women tend to reject the thin ideal and are more accepting of overweight body sizes (Milkie 1999; Parker et al. 1995; Thomas et al. 2008). Collins (2000) maintains that Afrocentric beauty ideals celebrate uniqueness and creativity and thus buffer black girls and women from rigid aesthetic cultural norms. This alternative black aesthetic encourages self-acceptance, particularly within supportive peer and community relationships (see Choate 2005; Collins 2000; Lovejoy 2001). Others have found that African American girls' lack of identification with white media images may serve a protective function to ward off negative body image (Milkie 1999).

There are implications to such alternative aesthetic constructions. For example, researchers point out that higher body satisfaction and self-esteem may come at a cost; comparatively speaking, there is some evidence showing that African Americans tend to underestimate their body shape (Schuler et al. 2008), and an alternative resistant aesthetic ideal that celebrates a larger body may reflect an underlying need to deny health problems (Lovejoy 2001). For this reason, the embodiment of counterhegemonic aesthetic norms by certain minority groups may intensify accusations of individual blame and disproportionately constitute these groups as problematic. If fat aesthetics were the only issue at hand, that some African Americans resist the thin ideal may not, in and of itself, be deemed problematic by, say, public health officials. However, because the fat body also signifies much about health risk (as we discuss in chapter 3), African Americans who embrace a larger body size may be viewed as *especially* problematic for defying both hegemonic aesthetic and health norms—the latter of which, from a public health perspective, has both serious medical and economic implications—a point we revisit in the next chapter.

Fat Is Fixable: Weight-Loss Practices

There is also evidence that the public buys into the aesthetic frame's assertion that people are in control of their body size and have the power to manipulate it. Despite historical changes in beauty ideals, there is a long history of dieting (Schwartz 1986). Today there are even controversial children's storybooks about dieting such as Paul M. Kramer's (2011) *Maggie Goes on a Diet*. Yet perhaps the best evidence of the modern belief that individuals can and want to change their body size comes from the numbers. Annually, Americans spend $19 billion on gym memberships (Cloud 2009) and nearly $60 billion on weight-loss products and services (Marketdata Enterprises 2011).

Additional evidence is seen in the rampant weight-loss and weight-maintenance sentiments and behaviors that are so widespread in the United States. A Gallup poll found that 55 percent of those surveyed want to lose weight (Jones 2009) while another national survey found that 43 percent of respondents indicated that they are trying to lose weight (IFICF 2011). As a whole, the number of people attempting to lose weight is on the rise (Andreyeva et al. 2010). In their efforts to achieve their weight-loss goals, Americans are turning to dieting; estimates indicate that 25 percent of Americans are on a diet at any given time (Pew Research Center 2006). In line with the aesthetic frame, research shows that beauty-related concerns motivate weight-loss efforts (Brink and Ferguson 1998; Crawford et al. 1998; Kwan 2009a). For example, 57 percent of respondents in one national survey said that "improvement in physical appearance" (IFICF 2011, 24) motivated them to lose or maintain weight.

The widespread belief that the body is malleable is also manifest in the high rates of surgical procedures people routinely undergo in an effort to change their body size. For instance, bariatric surgical procedures—80 percent of which are gastric bypass surgeries designed to induce massive and rapid weight loss—are on the rise, increasing by 540 percent in just four years (Santry, Gillen, and Lauderdale 2005). In 2009, 220,000 Americans underwent bariatric surgery (American Society for Metabolic and Bariatric Surgery 2011). Additionally, liposuction, which is purely cosmetic and does not purport to provide any health benefits, remains one of the most common plastic surgery procedures (Gorman 2004), with approximately 283,735 liposuction procedures performed in America in

2009, costing the recipients well over $1 billion (American Society for Aesthetic Plastic Surgery 2009).

Yet, although many Americans want to, and are attempting to, lose weight, not all express equal concern about their weight. Nor do they engage in weight-loss practices at the same rate. (In chapter 3, we show how rates of "overweight" and "obesity" vary by social groups, and, as such, we do not examine them here.) For example, people in their middle adult years worry more than those who are younger (ages eighteen to twenty-nine) or older (ages sixty-five and above; Pew Research Center 2006), and we have already observed how some members of the African American community reject the thin (white) ideal. Some researchers also theorize that as Hispanic and Asian women experience increasingly greater assimilation and enculturation into mainstream American culture, their patterns of body image will eventually resemble those of whites (Altabe and O'Garo 2002; Kawamura 2002).

Alongside these variations, there are discernible patterns by socioeconomic status. For example, adult women and men in higher social classes (defined occupationally) are more likely to perceive themselves as overweight, to monitor their weight, and to try to lose weight compared to their lower socioeconomic status counterparts (Wardle and Griffith 2001). Women in more-privileged classes (defined by income) are also more likely to notice a smaller amount of weight gain compared to those in less-privileged classes (Jeffery and French 1996). A study by Lindsay McLaren and Diana Kuh (2004) reports similar findings. Their sample showed greater weight dissatisfaction among women from the nonmanual social classes (defined by occupation), while downwardly mobile women were more satisfied with their appearance. McLaren and Kuh also stress the importance of education, noting that higher levels of educational attainment were associated with greater weight and appearance dissatisfaction. Again, these findings have important public health implications that we examine in chapter 3. If some individuals with lower socioeconomic status are less likely to identify and/or express dissatisfaction with weight gain, they may be more likely to be labeled by public health authorities as problematic for defying both aesthetic and medical norms.

Of course the ability to transform the body is contingent upon factors directly related to socioeconomic status. First, the body as an identity project involves resources. Whether it is time to go for a run, attend an aerobics class, or sit through a weight-loss support group meeting, weight-loss efforts require a time investment. And leisure time, while increasing generally among Americans since the mid-1960s, varies by a range of demographic factors such as sex, age, and education (Aguiar and Hurst 2007; OECD 2009). Transforming the body also involves a range of financial resources that the privileged classes are more likely to have at their disposal, allowing them to invest in, say, personal trainers, healthful foods, or even cosmetic surgery.

Second, weight-loss efforts require a basic level of know-how. Knowledge of, for instance, the nutritional content of foods and the relationship between food consumption and health varies by sex, race, national origin, income, and education (see Hendrie, Coveney, and Cox 2008; Parmenter, Waller, and Wardle 1999; USDA 2001). Combined, these factors affect the likelihood of "successful" transformation efforts, even though tropes of personal blame and individual failure continue to undergird the myth of meritocracy (see Dworkin and Wachs 2009; Jhally 1987). These time, financial, and knowledge barriers are downplayed given the pervasive cultural ideology that the body is a canvas of the psyche and an indicator of moral fortitude.

There are also important gender differences related to body aesthetics. As we have already pointed out, for decades feminists have criticized the oppressive effects of the thin body norm for women. Female body ideals are seemingly compulsory, such that girls and women are sanctioned and stigmatized more severely when they deviate from them (Rothblum 1992). This is in part because "ideologies of weight closely parallel ideologies of womanhood" (McKinley 1999, 97), where embedded in the construction of womanhood is the thin ideal. In other words, thinness and physical attractiveness are defining characteristics of a woman, above and beyond other characteristics such as intelligence or talent (Bartky 2010 [1988]).

Moreover, some have argued that the mass media, including the fashion-beauty complex advertisements we have just examined, objectify women, making them passive media objects; this objectification includes the work of a "male gaze" that constructs women as objects for viewing by a male heterosexual spectator (Frederickson and Roberts 1997; Mulvey 1975). Objectification can exacerbate the desire to comply with hegemonic body norms, leading to ongoing bodily surveillance (Bartky 2010 [1988]).

For these reasons, among others, women continue to be highly invested in the thin ideal, often more so than men. For example, eating disorders are significantly more prevalent among girls and women (Bordo 2003; National Eating Disorders Association 2011), and there is even evidence that girls as young as three years old have an emotional stake in the thin ideal (Harriger et al. 2010). Research also shows that women express greater concern than men about their weight (see Pew Research Center 2006). For instance, women are more likely than men to perceive themselves as too heavy for their height (Emslie, Hunt, and Macintyre 2001), and adolescent females are more like to worry about gaining weight than are adolescent males (Sweeting and West 2002). A 2008 Gallup poll found that 38 percent of women are "seriously trying to lose weight," compared to men's 22 percent.

At the same time, men do exhibit concern about their physical appearance, although their focus tends to be body shape, muscle mass, and muscle definition

(Pope, Phillips, and Olivardia 2000). For example, Harrison Pope Jr., Katharine Phillips, and Roberto Olivardia (2000) point out that the desire to achieve the Adonis Complex (a lean muscular ideal) has resulted in American men spending billions a year on commercial gym memberships, home exercise equipment, and nutritional supplements that claim to burn fat or build muscle. Analyses of a nationally representative population-based survey of American households also points to a surprisingly high proportion of men with anorexia nervosa and bulimia nervosa, such that men represent about one-fourth of all cases of these disorders (Hudson et al. 2007). These rates are higher than previously estimated, suggesting increasing body dissatisfaction among men across the life course.

Despite these social group differences, Americans continue to spend plenty of time and money on diets, exercise regimes, and medical procedures. They do so in spite of evidence that these efforts may not work and can have serious health risks. For instance, a review of articles in the *Journal of Human Nutrition and Dietetics* spanning five years found that the energy deficit approach to weight management has a high long-term failure rate and that the literature on weight management fails to meet the standards of evidence-based medicine (Aphramor 2010; see also Mann et al. 2007). Others have shown how weight-focused dieting approaches are not as successful as planned in terms of long-term weight loss and do not always lead to positive physiological and psychological outcomes (Bacon et al. 2005). There is even recent research showing that exercise does not necessarily facilitate weight loss; instead, it might actually stimulate hunger and result in weight gain (Church et al. 2009). By some reports, procedures like gastric bypass have failure rates (as defined by a Body Mass Index over 35) of over 20 percent after ten years (Christou, Look, and MacLean 2006).

Additionally, weight cycling—colloquially referred to as "yo-yo dieting"—has been linked to an overall increase in body weight and to an increased risk of cardiovascular disease (Ernsberger and Koletsky 1993; Gaesser 1999; Lissner et al. 1991), and research has shown that dieting can increase the risk of bone damage and disease, decrease fertility, alter brain functioning, produce gallstones, and increase the risk of breast and kidney cancers in women (see Gaesser 2002, 2003). One study even found that dieting increases the risk of premature death (Sørensen et al. 2005)! Yet even with these overwhelming failure rates and the well-documented risks associated with dieting, Americans continue to diet at unprecedented rates.

CONCLUSION

Unlike the frames we discuss in the coming chapters, each of which is associated with a single key cultural producer, the aesthetic frame is promulgated in large part through product advertisements. A hodgepodge of industries that form the fashion-beauty complex sponsor these advertisements. Despite the commercial diversity of these industries, a look at some of their advertisements reveals a cohesive narrative. This narrative defines the fat body as problematic because it is aesthetically unappealing. The inferred source of the problem is personal failure. And it is through the advertised products and services that salvation emerges. By purchasing and using industry offerings, however ineffective or dangerous they might be at times, individuals will supposedly be able to gain control of their body size, elevate their level of attractiveness and desirability, and consequently add to their happiness.

The aesthetic frame generates a self-fulfilling prophecy. By perpetuating the notion that fat results from personal failure and diminishes overall quality of life, the frame creates a climate of fat fear and hatred that in turn leads to disdain for and the mistreatment of fat people that may, in fact, diminish quality of life. The creation of this self-fulfilling prophecy ultimately allows the industries of the fashion-beauty complex to sell their products and services to fat individuals (or to those who fear becoming fat) and remain profitable.

As a whole, we see that the message of the aesthetic frame resonates in the public imagination. This is evidenced in a number of ways, including the amount of money spent on weight-loss endeavors, the widespread and immense fear of becoming or staying fat, and the number of people engaged in weight mainte-nance and body manipulation practices. For this reason we label the aesthetic frame dominant. It is generally how Americans think about fat, and it constitutes a frequently accessed ideology in their cultural tool kits. The logic of this domi-nant aesthetic frame is also hegemonic insofar as it attempts to produce a homo-geneous thin and taut body (for women) or a toned muscular body (for men).

However, not everyone agrees that fat is unattractive. According to NAAFA, fat is not inherently frightful and can even be sexy. It is acceptable, and even nor-mal, to feel attracted to a fat person. While NAAFA's views on fat aesthetics may not have widespread public support, resistant body aesthetics are nevertheless evident among various social groups; dieting practices also vary by social group.

In the contested field of fat—as in all framing contests—for every action there is a reaction, for every believer there is a nonbeliever, and for every advo-cate there is a detractor. The push-and-pull nature of framing contests is central to understanding the way fat is conceptualized and understood in contempo-rary Western culture. We continue to see these pushes and pulls as we examine a second and interrelated cultural take on the fat body in the next chapter: fat as unhealthy.

3 · FAT AS FATAL

By MOST ACCOUNTS, June 17, 1998, was an unremarkable day. Venus Williams celebrated a birthday. Chile tied Austria in a World Cup soccer game. Tori Amos performed in Nürnberg, Germany. And 25 million Americans became overweight without gaining a single pound (Cohen and McDermott 1998).[1] For this feat they could thank the Body Mass Index (BMI), a measurement standard based on a person's height and weight that was adopted by a number of high-ranking health agencies that day. Despite initial controversy and even rejection of the BMI by some experts, adoption of the BMI by health authorities was alleged to be necessary "because of studies linking extra weight to health problems" (Cohen and McDermott 1998).

Over a decade later, the BMI remains a common and accepted measure of whether a person is "underweight," "normal" weight, "overweight," or "obese." Public health officials frequently use the BMI, often as a proxy indicator of health. And if these officials are correct about the BMI serving as a reliable indicator of health, America is facing a health crisis due to its steadily rising BMIs. We are reminded daily that being overweight or obese is not just unhealthy, it is deadly.

These reminders come from a range of medical professionals such as bariatric surgeons who perform weight-loss surgeries and cardiovascular specialists who treat the alleged comorbidities associated with obesity. Professional medical organizations, researchers, disability advocacy groups, politicians, international bodies, and many others also play a role in pushing the message that overweight and obesity are health problems.

THE CENTERS FOR DISEASE CONTROL AND PREVENTION

Chief among these groups is the Centers for Disease Control and Prevention (CDC). The CDC is an agency of the U.S. Department of Health and Human Services (HHS). Recognized as an authoritative voice on overweight and obesity, the CDC provides explicit medical directives about how to address these issues. To fully understand the ways the CDC constructs its health frame and shapes societal understandings of fat, we analyze its public artifacts. We pay special attention to the CDC's online portal to these conditions (www.cdc.gov/obesity) and its publications, such as *The Surgeon General's Vision for a Healthy and Fit Nation* (HHS 2010d). As with every frame we analyze in *Framing Fat*, our aim is to determine both *what* is being said and *how* it is being said.

In this chapter, we investigate different approaches to weight and health. We focus on the CDC's perspective that overweight and obesity are social problems because these conditions pose serious health risks. However, others contest the CDC's message; both the Center for Consumer Freedom (CCF) and National Association to Advance Fat Acceptance (NAAFA) claim that being overweight or obese does not always mean that one is unhealthy. We explore these dissenting voices and also consider how messages about beauty at times intertwine with messages about health. Finally, we examine whether this overweight-equals-unhealthy rhetoric so central to public health messages resonates with the public.

THE CENTRAL CLAIM: BEING OVERWEIGHT OR OBESE CAN BE FATAL

The central claim of any frame is the primary assertion that singularly defines a frame's version of reality, often creating a social problem that needs to be addressed. A systematic analysis of the messages disseminated by the CDC reveals its central claim: overweight and obesity are pressing public health problems.

This claim is pervasive throughout the CDC's public documents and on its website. For instance, the surgeon general's report on these conditions opens with the statement: "Our nation stands at a crossroads. Today's epidemic of overweight and obesity threatens the historic progress we have made in increasing American's quality and years of healthy life" (HHS 2010d, 1). The agency maintains that adult "obesity is common, serious, and costly" (CDC 2010b, 1) and uses the term "crisis" to describe the situation (HHS 2010d, 1).

According to the CDC, the problem is also intensifying. The agency repeatedly stresses that obesity is an "epidemic" (e.g., CDC 2010b; HHS 2010d), a common catchphrase of this frame, alleging that "this epidemic has affected every part of the United States" (CDC 2010b, 1). The CDC backs these assertions by citing a number of statistics, including the claim that two-thirds of U.S. adults are overweight or obese (HHS 2010d) and that, between 1980 and 2008, obesity rates have doubled for adults and increased markedly for all social groups regardless of age, sex, race/ethnicity, socioeconomic status, educational level, or geographic region (CDC 2011f). For effect, the CDC presents data visually in tables, graphs, and other pictorial formats, commonly used framing devices of the health frame.

Among the most powerful of these visual images is an animated slide presentation bearing the caption "Percent of Obese (BMI > 30) in U.S. Adults" that displays longitudinal data on obesity from the CDC's Behavioral Risk Factor Surveillance System (BRFSS) in the form of a series of maps (CDC 2012a). The presentation includes a U.S. map on each slide for every year from 1985 through 2010, and the images depict an increase in obesity as the years (and the slides) progress. This slide show creates a compelling visual illustration of how obesity is sweeping across the nation at alarming rates. As some scholars have argued, this alarmist approach to the obese body is reflected directly in media accounts of obesity, contributing in part to the construction of a moral panic (Boero 2007; Campos et al. 2006; Holland at al. 2011; Saguy and Almeling 2008).

The CDC's warnings of a widespread and worsening health epidemic rely on the Body Mass Index (BMI), a calculation based on an individual's height and weight.[2] Although BMI categories have shifted over time, the CDC currently claims that a BMI of 30.0 or over indicates "obesity" and a BMI between 25.0 and 29.9 indicates "overweight." A "healthy weight" BMI is between 18.5 and 24.9, and a BMI below 18.5 indicates "underweight" (CDC 2012e). The CDC relies on the BMI because, it claims, "for most people, it correlates with their amount of body fat" (CDC 2012e).

The agency acknowledges that the BMI has limitations as a measure but nevertheless contends that it a "useful indicator of overweight and obesity" and that "several studies have found that adults with a high BMI are at increased risk for various diseases" (HHS 2010d, 3). In *The Surgeon General's Vision for a Healthy and Fit Nation*, the CDC also recommends measurement of waist circumference, maintaining that "the BMI does not distinguish between lean tissue and body fat and some growing children or athletic children and adults will have a BMI in the overweight or obese range without having an excess of body fat" (HHS 2010d, 3). Despite these cautions, the widespread use of the BMI on the CDC's website (and even a brief perusal of leading medical journals) suggests that the BMI has become a taken-for-granted measure in the health community.

The CDC's position on obesity as an increasing public health problem can be interpreted as a form of "biopower"—the regulation, surveillance, and control over individuals and populations through knowledge and technologies (see Clarke et al. 2010; Foucault 1984). In Foucauldian terms, biopower exerts control, not through the threat of corporeal extinction, but through the protection of life and the regulation of bodies. This is evident in the CDC's paternalistic yet altruistic health warnings that are hypothetically for the good of the citizenry. Alarmist messages communicate that being above certain body mass thresholds constitutes a public health threat and that something needs to be done to rein in this threat.

Regulation of this threat occurs in part through biomedical knowledge and technologies such as the BMI, a device that purportedly diagnoses and infers health risks. Under the clinical gaze that separates that body from the self (Foucault 1973), the BMI allegedly distinguishes potentially problematic bodies (those at greater risk) in the population from those that are less problematic (those at lower risk). This identification occurs in the name of intervention, whether imposed by authorities such as doctors, parents, or teachers or through individuals themselves in the form of self-surveillance. Diagnostics such as the bathroom scale and the BMI therefore quantify health and health risks for the sake of population management (see Jutel 2001). Indeed biopower operates through appeals to risk. In what Natalie Boero (2007, 2010) labels "postmodern epidemics," not only those bodies that are above the designated BMI thresholds are apparently in danger; all bodies are at risk. That we are all at risk consequently means that we are all potentially to blame.

CAUSAL ROOTS: IT'S *YOUR* FAULT!

Every frame makes claims about the causal roots of a social issue. In its framing efforts, the CDC alleges what it purports to be the roots of excess body weight. It acknowledges a number of potential causes of overweight and obesity, including biological and physical factors, such as genetics and metabolism, and structural elements, such as environmental, cultural, and socioeconomic factors. The CDC even emphasizes the role mothers play; it maintains that excess weight gain, diabetes, and smoking in pregnancy can all put children at risk for obesity early in life, while breastfeeding can help prevent early childhood obesity (HHS 2010d).

One public service message on the CDC's website discusses the complexities of this so-called obesity epidemic (a term not to be lost on a viewer as it is used repeatedly throughout the video). In this podcast, the CDC maintains that obesity is a "complex problem" and that "weight gain is a consequence of complicated changes in the environment, where food is more readily available and opportunities for physical activity are lacking" (CDC 2011g). Reports on the CDC's online portal also acknowledge structural variables such as socioeconomic class and the built environment. For example, it asserts that some Americans do not have access to healthy, affordable foods and that others live in communities that make it difficult or unsafe to be physically active (CDC 2010b). Notably, the CDC addresses structural factors primarily as barriers to behavioral (that is, individual-level) outcomes. In other words, the CDC engages structural factors insofar as they make personal changes in lifestyle difficult to accomplish. The indictment of personal behavior appears to be central. As the surgeon general asserts: "Change starts with the individual choices we as Americans make each day for ourselves and those around us" (HHS 2010d, 5).

The CDC boils down the problem to what it calls the Energy Balance Equation, which it also refers to as the Caloric Balance Equation (see figure 3.1). Specifically, overweight and obesity stem from an imbalance resulting from excessive caloric consumption and/or inadequate physical activity (CDC 2011a). The centrality of this formula in the CDC's overall mission is apparent when the CDC asks, "Why is this epidemic happening?" to which it responds, "Weight gain occurs when people eat too much food and get too little physical activity" (CDC 2010b, 2).

On count 1—that Americans eat too much—the CDC tells us that "high-calorie, good-tasting, and inexpensive foods have become widely available and are heavily advertised. Portion sizes have increased, and we are eating out more frequently" (HHS 2010d, 2, citations removed). Supporting government agencies, such as the U.S. Department of Agriculture, maintain that average American food patterns bear little resemblance to federal dietary guidelines, and data from the CDC's National Health and Nutrition Examination Survey (NHANES) show that "Americans eat too many calories and too much solid fats, added sugars, refined grains, and sodium. Americans also eat too little dietary fiber, vitamin D, calcium, potassium, and unsaturated fatty acids (specifically omega-3s), and other important nutrients that are mostly found in vegetables, fruits, whole grains, low-fat milk and milk products, and seafood" (USDA 2010, B2-1).

On count 2—that Americans get too little physical activity—the CDC chastises Americans for being sedentary, maintaining that many Americans do not

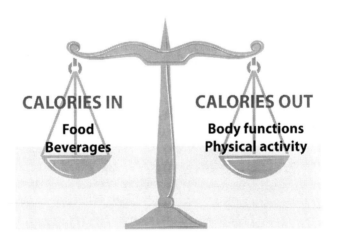

FIGURE 3.1. The Energy Balance Equation
The CDC maintains that overweight and obesity stem from an imbalance in an individual's Energy Balance Equation, resulting from excessive caloric consumption and/or inadequate physical activity. (Credit: The Centers for Disease Control and Prevention.)

follow the *Physical Activity Guidelines for Americans* (HHS 2008). For example, the guidelines recommend that adults participate in at least 150 minutes of moderate intensity or 75 minutes of vigorous intensity physical activity per week (or an equivalent combination). Instead, 25.4 percent of U.S. adults and high school students report no leisure-time physical activity (HHS 2010b).

So, just as we see that the aesthetic frame—the fashion-beauty complex—blames fat individuals for their aesthetic failures, the health frame blames overweight and obese individuals for their health failures. As Robert Crawford (1980, 2006) has brought to our attention, since the 1970s there has been an increasing focus on living a health-conscious lifestyle, particularly among the middle classes. This "healthism," particularly evident in the holistic health and self-care movement, involves a preoccupation with personal health as a primary "focus for the definition and achievement of well-being; a goal which is to be attained primarily through the modification of life styles [*sic*]" (1980, 368). This focus on lifestyle situates health and disease at the individual level. Health is presumably a dynamic, conquerable, and achievable state that is within an individual's control, an achievement we are all exhorted to work toward (see also Edgley and Brisset 1990; Shilling 2003). As Crawford describes—similar to how Talcott Parsons (1951) defined the sick role and exonerated sick individuals from blame so long as they worked with medical professionals to overcome their sicknesses—healthism morally obligates us to be healthy. In other words, with the individualizing of health comes an obligation to be health conscious and to pursue health. Failing to do so means we are blameworthy. Our waistlines expand because we have not, to borrow the CDC's terminology, diligently monitored our Energy Balance Equation. According to Crawford, healthism venerates health and holds it to be an inherent good. However, others assert that healthism can also be viewed as a form of "health fascism" (Edgley and Brisset 1990).

Thus, similar to the beauty frame, the health frame draws on the framing metaphor of the compliant body as a symbol of accomplishment. The rewards accrued for working hard and exercising restraint include the alleged ability to maintain an acceptable weight that purportedly comes with health benefits. Of course, the flip side is that those who do not maintain an acceptable weight compromise their health and become morally suspect; they are assumed to be lazy rather than hardworking, gluttonous rather than restrained, and weak willed rather than determined. These assumptions are to be expected, given that the body is the visible canvas of the psyche (Bordo 2003). The fat body is a sinful body, a body that is out of control, and one that violates Christian asceticism and the Protestant ethic (Edgley and Brisset 1990; Featherstone 2010). Weight management and the healthy body that supposedly comes with it are reputedly signs of personal success and quality of character.

CONSEQUENCES: SOCIAL, HEALTH, AND ECONOMIC

In addition to identifying a number of causal roots, the CDC states what it holds are the consequences of these conditions. With the health frame, the consequences are an integral part of establishing the central claim. Specifically, the central claim is that being overweight or obese is a social problem *because of* its negative health consequences. The CDC focuses on three types of consequences: social effects, health effects, and economic effects.

Social Consequences

Only in passing does the CDC mention the social ramifications of being overweight or obese. Just one sentence in *The Surgeon General's Vision for a Healthy and Fit Nation* highlights social consequences: "Besides suffering from physical illnesses, obese adults and children also may experience social stigmatization and discrimination, as well as psychological problems" (HHS 2010d, 2). Few documents on the CDC's website mention stigma, discrimination, body image issues, or any other social or psychological effects of these conditions. This downplaying of appearance-related stigma goes hand in hand with the CDC's insistence that "the primary concern should be one of health and not appearance" (HHS 2001, 33).[3]

Health Consequences

In contrast, there is no shortage of information about health consequences. The CDC asserts that obesity contributes to "preventable deaths" and that "obese adults are at increased risk for many serious health conditions" (HHS 2010d, 2). Interestingly, while several CDC documents on overweight or obesity once purported that overweight and obesity cause about 400,000 preventable deaths per year, the most recent surgeon general's report on obesity (HHS 2010d) indicates that obesity contributes to an estimated 112,000 preventable deaths a year, a figure with a controversial history that we discuss shortly.

The CDC lists a number of health problems associated with overweight and obesity. These include an increased risk of heart disease, high blood pressure, and stroke; type 2 diabetes; breast, colon, and other forms of cancers; sleep apnea; infertility and abnormal periods in women; gallstones, cirrhosis, and pancreatitis; and arthritis (CDC 2010b; HHS 2010d). The CDC presents this information in tabular format and via a powerful visual that depicts a slightly overweight human body upon which all of these potential health consequences have been diagrammed (see figure 3.2; CDC 2010b).

Economic Consequences

The CDC also focuses on the economic effects of being overweight or obese. The agency contends that health problems associated with these conditions

Medical Complications of Obesity

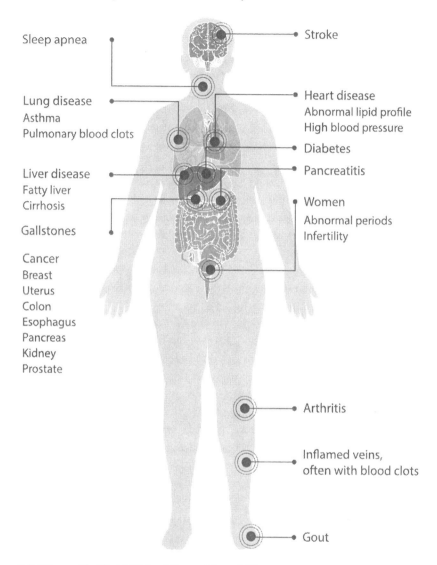

Sleep apnea

Lung disease
Asthma
Pulmonary blood clots

Liver disease
Fatty liver
Cirrhosis

Gallstones

Cancer
Breast
Uterus
Colon
Esophagus
Pancreas
Kidney
Prostate

Stroke

Heart disease
Abnormal lipid profile
High blood pressure

Diabetes

Pancreatitis

Women
Abnormal periods
Infertility

Arthritis

Inflamed veins,
often with blood clots

Gout

FIGURE 3.2. The Health Risks of Overweight and Obesity
According to the CDC, obesity increases an individual's risk of heart disease, liver disease, and certain forms of cancer. (Credit: The Centers for Disease Control and Prevention Vital Signs.)

have a "significant" economic impact on the health-care system (CDC 2012c). The CDC discusses economic consequences in terms of both direct and indirect costs. Direct costs include preventative, diagnostic, and treatment services related to overweight and obesity, while indirect costs pertain to morbidity costs (such as income lost from decreased productivity, restricted activity, and absenteeism) and mortality costs (such as the value of future income lost by premature death; CDC 2012c). The CDC points out that the medical care costs of obesity are "staggering" and that in 2008 dollars, these costs totaled about $147 billion (CDC 2012c). It also alleges that medical expenses for an obese worker are about 42 percent higher compared to those of a worker with a "healthy weight" (CDC 2011b).

Via these economic arguments, the CDC expresses a less than flattering view of not just these conditions but also the individuals that embody them because they allegedly drain the economy and the health-care system by requiring more care than individuals with a "healthy weight." A framing visual helps underscore these economic arguments. On its website, the CDC displays an Obesity Cost Calculator. The icon for the calculator is a bathroom scale with a dollar sign in the window where the weight should be displayed and calculator buttons emblazoned on the platform (CDC 2011e).

Alongside the information provided by the CDC are numerous news articles, including those appearing in *Forbes* (Dykman 2011), the *New York Times* (Darlin 2006), and on MSNBC (Rettner 2011), that have fueled the sense that obesity compounds the current economic crisis and further drains the U.S. health-care system. In recent years, journalists have drawn attention to the economic costs of obesity by citing the CDC on this matter and by turning to the plethora of scholarly studies published on this issue—whether it is a recent report out of George Washington University's School of Public Health and Health Services (Dor et al. 2010) or one of the many studies it builds on (Allison, Zannolli, and Narayan 1999; Arterburn, Maciejewski, and Tsevat 2005; Colditz 1999; Finkel-stein et al. 2009; Wang et al. 2008; Wolf and Colditz 1996).

PRINCIPLES: HEALTH, FISCAL RESPONSIBILITY, EQUALITY, AND OUR CHILDREN'S FUTURE

As we saw in chapter 1, framing analysts point out that framers make claims about the nature, causes, and consequences of a social issue that rest on a set of underlying values or morals. In the language of the framing matrix, these claims are a frame's appeals to principle. These appeals help convince the public that a framer's version of reality is truthful by providing them with reasons to be concerned about the issue at hand. The CDC attempts to convince Americans to care about overweight and obesity by appealing to four specific values, two of which we have already alluded to: health and fiscal responsibility. The CDC further appeals to our sense of social equality and our responsibility to protect our children.

Health

First, the CDC positions overweight and obesity as social problems because they threaten subscribed values such as health, longevity, and productivity. Tacit in the CDC's public health message is the valuing of health. In fact, embedded in Crawford's (1980, 2006) healthism is the critique not only that health is presumed to be an intrinsic good but that it has been venerated as the ultimate good and as a metaphor for all that is valued in life as well. This "super-health," as Crawford puts it, subsumes a panoply of values, including happiness, purpose, self-esteem, creative expression, and a fully productive, self-realized, and expanded life of joy (Crawford 1980, 380).

Fiscal Responsibility

Second, the focus on economic consequences rests on the underlying principle that fiscal responsibility is something Americans value as a nation. To suggest otherwise is to condone government excess and redundancy that smacks of an inefficient socialist regime. Case in point, most Americans agree that health-care costs are a major problem for the country, but they do not support health-care reform, largely because of uncertainty about its cost and effectiveness (Newport 2009a). Particularly in today's economic climate, because of this valued principle, some consider overweight or obese individuals a burden on the public treasury.

Health Disparities

Americans claim to value equality. They take pride in, even if only in spirit, the rhetoric of race, gender, and class equality. Equal opportunity discourses permeate the American cultural landscape and are evident in momentous junctures in the nation's history (such as the implementation of Title VII of the Civil Rights Act of 1964 and *Brown v. Board of Education*[4]). These milestones help begin to transform symbolism into material reality. Today, the notion of equal opportunity includes the opportunity to be healthy.

The CDC underscores how the obesity epidemic threatens equality by highlighting health disparities associated with obesity. For example, the surgeon general maintains that the "burden of obesity is disproportionately borne by some racial and ethnic groups" (HHS 2010d, 2), and the CDC's "Adult Obesity Facts" web page reports that "non-Hispanic blacks have the highest rates of obesity (44.1 percent) compared with Mexican Americans (39.3 percent), all Hispanics (37.9 percent) and non-Hispanic whites (32.6 percent)" (CDC 2012a).

Related to racial/ethnic disparities are socioeconomic disparities, and the CDC points out that there is a relationship between socioeconomic status and these conditions. For example, it maintains that women with higher incomes are less likely to be obese than their lower-income counterparts, although non-Hispanic black and Mexican-American men with higher incomes are more likely to be obese than their lower-income counterparts (CDC 2012a). Interestingly, while the CDC reports no significant relationship between obesity and education among men, women with college degrees are less likely to be obese compared to less-educated women (CDC 2012a).

To explain some of these disparities, the CDC stresses that some Americans have limited access to grocery stores that provide healthy, affordable food, a phenomenon scholars refer to as "food deserts" (Story et al. 2008). This is particularly the case in rural, minority, and lower-income neighborhoods. These communities are overrun with convenience stores and fast food restaurants that abundantly supply high-calorie and high-fat foods (CDC 2010b). The CDC also maintains that poor individuals often live in areas where the absence of parks and recreation centers, lack of public transportation, and concerns about the safety of pedestrian and bicycle routes effectively discourage physical activity (CDC 2010b).

In fact, a plethora of research supports the CDC's claims that there are social disparities associated with obesity. Researchers have shown that both rates of overweight and obesity vary by many social characteristics, including sex, race/ethnicity, and socioeconomic status.[5] For example, racial segregation measured through the black isolation index correlates positively with the risk of being overweight among non-Hispanic blacks (Chang 2006), and high black racial isolation is associated with higher BMIs and higher odds of obesity among women, but not men, a phenomenon researchers say is mediated by the physically disordered nature of these neighborhoods (Chang, Hillier, and Mehta 2009). Others have found that obesity is significantly higher in poor communities and among African Americans, Hispanics, and Native American youths, compared to whites (Thulitha Wickrama, Wickrama, and Bryant 2006; see also Neumark-Sztainer et al. 2002). These disparities begin at early ages, as studies show that young black and Latino children have a greater likelihood of being overweight than white children, regardless of their health insurance status (Haas et al. 2003). Consistent with these findings, researchers have found that fast food restaurants are overrepresented in census tracts with predominantly black residents (Block, Scribner, and DeSalvo 2004).

Researchers have also documented disparities in physical activity across the states (ACSM 2011), noting how "fitter states" are more affluent and more educated (see Florida 2011). They also observe differences in the prevalence of physical activity by race and ethnicity. For example, non-Hispanic blacks and Hispanics are often more inactive during their leisure time compared to non-Hispanic whites (Marshall et al. 2007; see also Crespo et al. 2000).

These select examples of social disparities in overweight and obesity are somewhat expected as health disparities, whether related to tobacco use, physical inactivity, or poor nutrition, are well documented (see Pampel, Krueger, and Denney 2010). In today's neoliberal climate, some predict that these disparities will likely persist. Theorists observe that neoliberalism has resulted in an intensification of capitalism and the expansion of commodification, moves that favor economic elites over the underprivileged (see Harvey 2005). In such contexts, health itself becomes a commodity that, as Crawford (1994) predicts, is often out of the reach of many.

Protecting Our Children

America values, cherishes, and wants to protect its children. This desire stems largely from the belief that, as the late Whitney Houston famously sang, "the children are our future."[6] Child advocates and social commentators have stressed this point when they lay out how U.S. children face all kinds of social ills—from poverty to illiteracy to poor health—all of which compromise the nation's future (Hamburg 1994). In similar fashion, the CDC repeatedly highlights the prevalence of overweight and obesity among children and adolescents in an effort to appeal to our desire to protect our children and, in turn, the future of the United States. Concern for childhood obesity has even crept into U.S. educational policy, as some public schools now distribute weight-related assessment reports to parents (Kantor 2007).

The CDC's discussion of childhood overweight and obesity closely parallels the overall framing of adult overweight and obesity as growing social problems with serious health consequences. For example, the CDC reports on a number of studies, pointing out that obesity affects 17 percent (or 12.5 million) of all children and adolescents aged 2–19 years in the United States, triple the rate from one generation ago (CDC 2012d), and that one in three children are overweight or obese (HHS 2010d). It also reports that the health consequences of overweight and obesity for children and adolescents are similar to those for adults. These include high blood pressure, high cholesterol, impaired glucose tolerance, insulin resistance, and type 2 diabetes (CDC 2012b). Similarly, the CDC underscores economic consequences. In the agency's words, "the financial cost of childhood obesity *tips the scales* at 3 billion dollars annually" (CDC 2010d; emphasis added), also a metaphor of this frame.

PROPOSED SOLUTIONS:
CHANGE STARTS WITH THE INDIVIDUAL

Frames articulate the nature, causes, and effects of a social problem, along with solutions. The CDC's solution to the "obesity epidemic" involves assisting

Americans to balance healthful eating with regular physical activity. The stated goal is a reduction in obesity rates to less than 15 percent of the U.S. population, a goal that no state met in 2010 (CDC 2010c). The agency insists that this mission be carried out via multiple avenues at both the individual and structural level. As the surgeon general states: "Interventions to prevent obesity should focus not only on personal behaviors and biological traits, but also on characteristics of the social and physical environments that offer or limit opportunities for positive health outcomes" (HHS 2010d, 5).

Specifically, the CDC's Division of Nutrition, Physical Activity, and Obesity (DNPAO) works to improve nutrition and physical activity through state programs, technical assistance and training, surveillance and applied research, program implementation and evaluation, translation and dissemination, and partnership development (CDC 2011f). For example, its state-based Nutrition and Physical Activity Program to Prevent Obesity and Other Chronic Diseases funds programs in twenty-five states to work with partners across multiple settings (such as child-care facilities, schools, workplaces, and hospitals) to implement CDC-approved policy, system, and environmental strategies (CDC 2011f).

The agency recommends these structural changes in the hopes that they will make individual-level changes easier for the average American (CDC 2011f). The surgeon general's initial *Call to Action* pointed out over a decade ago that "*Individual behavioral change can occur only in a supportive environment* with accessible and affordable healthy food choices and opportunities for regular physical activity" (HHS 2001, 16; emphasis added). Thus as with the structural *causes* of obesity, the CDC puts forth structural *solutions* mainly as they allow individual solutions to be implemented. In fact, the CDC specifically calls for "policy and environmental approaches that make healthy choices available, affordable, and easy" (CDC 2011f, 2). Specifically, CDC strategies target five areas for increasing healthy choices that in turn, the CDC alleges, will prevent and/or reduce obesity rates. These include increasing the public's consumption of fruits and vegetables; increasing physical activity; increasing breastfeeding initiation, duration, and exclusivity; decreasing the consumption of sugar drinks; and decreasing the consumption of high-calorie, high-energy-dense foods (CDC 2011f).

Given its emphasis on individual behavior, the CDC offers a number of strategies to help individuals lose weight or maintain their current weight. For instance, the "Resources and Publications" menu in the agency's "Overweight and Obesity" pages (CDC 2012i) provides numerous links to tools designed specifically for individuals (including fact sheets and brochures on obesity and weight management). Moreover, its Healthy Weight pages (CDC 2011d) indicate how a new lifestyle (and not dieting) can help individuals lose weight and/or prevent weight gain. Linked through an image of a woman with her arms extended upward in a victorious pose, the CDC also profiles success stories of individuals who have lost weight. The text accompanying these success stories affirms "They did it. So can you!" (CDC 2011d).

At the end of the day, the CDC's solution focuses on individual-level change. As previously mentioned, the surgeon general blatantly claims that "change starts with the individual choices we as Americans make each day for ourselves and those around us" (HHS 2010d, 5). No doubt this is the healthism about which Crawford writes. He observes that while "health problems may originate outside the individual . . . since these problems are also behavioral, solutions are seen to lie within the realm of individual choice" (1980, 368).

And, according to the CDC, those who are able to make these changes will be rewarded for their weight loss, namely by a reduction in the long list of health risks the CDC identifies. But the individuals who lose the weight are not the only ones who reap rewards. For employers, lower body masses not only mean healthier employees but cost-savings as well. For example, the CDC claims that workplace obesity prevention programs can be "an effective way for employers to reduce obesity and lower their health care costs, lower absenteeism and increase employee productivity" (CDC 2011b). And mothers and mothers-to-be who lose weight will pass along benefits in the sense that their children are less likely to be obese (HHS 2010d).

AN ILLUSTRATIVE CASE: LET'S MOVE! CAMPAIGN

In the same way that Anti-Gym illustrates the core tenets of the aesthetic frame, the current First Lady's Let's Move! campaign is illustrative of the health frame. Championing the health frame, Michelle Obama has taken up arms against childhood obesity. Let's Move! is "a comprehensive initiative, launched by the First Lady, dedicated to solving the problem of obesity within a generation" (Let's Move! 2012a). The initiative aims to put children on a path to a healthy future, especially during their earliest months and years. Strategies include providing healthier foods in schools, ensuring that all families have access to healthy and affordable foods, and helping children become more physically active. The campaign directly references the CDC on overweight and obesity as a legitimate source of health information (Let's Move! 2012b).

Within the Let's Move! campaign we see several of the signature elements of the CDC's health frame, including the assertion that being overweight or obese is a problem because it is unhealthy (central claim), the assumption that individuals are to blame for their weight (causes), a focus on the unhealthy outcomes of being overweight or obese (consequences), the promotion of structural-level and individual-level solutions to the twin problems of overweight and obesity (proposed solutions), and an appeal to protect our nation's children (appeals to principle). This high-profile campaign also powerfully illustrates that, while the CDC is a forerunner of the health frame, it is only one of many public and private organizations that promote the message that being overweight or obese is unhealthy.

COMPETING VOICES: FAT ISN'T ALWAYS FATAL

Often a given frame depicts frame opponents—those who disagree with a framer's position and attempt to debunk its version of reality. Interestingly, the CDC makes no explicit mention of opponents or competing views of fat. It does, however, make assumptions about its opponents and about alternative views of the overweight or obese body. The unstated message is that those who contest the health frame are foolish to reject the claims and advice of an authoritative medical agency. After all, who would reject all this "objective" scientific data presented by the government in these graphs and tables? Who would question all these "facts"?

And yet some do! Alongside these powerful messages from the CDC are other approaches to health and body size. Some of these approaches borrow the language of the health frame while others address weight and health matters in a vastly different manner. In this next section, we turn to what our other framers (specifically, the fashion-beauty complex, the food industry, and fat acceptance activists) say about health and body size.

Fashion-Beauty Complex: Beauty Is Health, Health Is Beauty

As we saw in chapter 2, the fashion-beauty complex is similar to the CDC in that it too frames the overweight body as a social problem. Yet unlike the health frame, the central claim of the aesthetic frame is that fat is a social problem because it is physically unattractive. A closer look at the aesthetic frame, however, indicates that those working within the aesthetic frame at times borrow from the language of the health frame to promote their ends.

For example, cultural producers of the aesthetic frame have been known to co-opt and repackage the CDC's message that being overweight is unhealthy and that being unhealthy is not attractive. It does this by conflating health with beauty, and vice versa. One example comes from Diane von Furstenberg, a Belgian American fashion designer and president of the Council of Fashion Designers of America, who publicly proclaimed, "Beauty is health—health, beauty" (Evans 2010). In fact, this conflation of health and beauty has become so pervasive that mainstream publications such as *Self* magazine are often pegged as "health and beauty" focused. There is even an annual Health and Beauty Expo each year in New York City (Gillespie 2010), and some universities have begun hosting annual health and beauty events on their campuses (Lewis 2009).

Advertisers of the fashion-beauty complex, too, blur the line between what is healthy and what is beautiful. For example, Lap-Band, a surgical weight-loss technique, is advertised with the slogan "Healthy is the new beautiful" (Journey-Lite 2007), and Metamucil advertisements indicate that taking this supplement will "beautify your inside" (Proctor & Gamble 2012). Illustrating how individuals confound health and aesthetics, scholars examining feminine beauty ideals in the workplace report that people assume that female coworkers are healthy when they are wearing makeup (Dellinger and Williams 1997).

Research also indicates that individuals believe in the purported connection between health and beauty and that they often confound the two in their everyday lives (Kwan 2009a). For example, interviews with a sample of overweight individuals found that they often think of beauty and health as coming hand in hand and that they do this in three distinct ways (Kwan 2009a). First, interviewees indicate that depictions of the beauty ideal are often depictions of the health ideal. That is, beautiful people are healthy people, and vice versa. Second, interviewees often use beauty indicators as health indicators. For example, they turn to weight loss—gauged either visibly, say, through reduction in rolls of fat or by a number on a scale—as a measure of better health. In other words, interviewees interpreted evidence that they were reaching their aesthetic ideals as a sign they were becoming healthier. Lastly, some interviewees use beauty as a motivator to health goals, articulating that they aspire (first and foremost) to the thin ideal but also acknowledging purported health benefits that might accompany achieving their aesthetic goals.

In similar manner, Carole Spitzack (1990) observes how women are bombarded with cultural imagery in which attractiveness is incorporated into an "aesthetics of health." Women's cultural beauty standards, she maintains, are defined through health, where the beautiful body is defined as a healthy one. This aesthetics of health, however, is not just about being thin; it encompasses all aspects of women's physical appearance, such as skin coloring, muscle conditioning, and facial structures. Spitzack maintains that it even involves correct behavioral and attitudinal outlooks; as she observes, health and beauty are often associated with self-esteem, self-confidence, assertiveness, and sociability. Regardless of its form, the aesthetics of health connects to compliance for women (and men) in powerful ways. By dictating conformity through two intertwining dominant discourses, individuals feel even greater pressure to conform to aesthetic and health norms.

The Food Industry: These Are Health Myths

Other takes on health and body size depart radically from the CDC's version of reality. While the players of the fashion-beauty complex co-opt and repackage certain claims of the health frame, other groups reject outright the CDC's assertions. For instance, the food industry group CCF maintains that being obese does not constitute a social problem. In fact, as we elaborate in chapter 4, the CCF's choice and responsibility frame maintains that the obesity epidemic is really "obesity hype" (CCF 2005a, 1). To protect its interests, the CCF contests many of the CDC's health claims. It rejects the CDC's taken-for-granted measurement (the BMI); it refutes the CDC's supposedly objective data about the negative health consequences of being overweight; and it even says that the CDC is wrong when it comes to the economic burden of obesity.

Rejecting the BMI. The CCF's 2005 publication, *An Epidemic of Obesity Myths,* begins with pictures of several well-known individuals, including actors Brad Pitt and George Clooney (CCF 2005a). A simple question appears beneath their images: "Overweight?" Under pictures of Sylvester Stallone and Mel Gibson, a similar question: "Obese?" A print advertisement disseminated by the CCF that depicts former California governor Arnold Schwarzenegger serves the same purpose. The advertisement reads, "Actor. Governor. Fatso?" (CCF 2011a). These rhetorical questions intimate that the BMI is inaccurate and misleading; we do not typically think of *People* magazine's Sexiest Man Alive (Pitt in 2000 and Clooney in 2006) or the "Terminator" (Schwarzenegger) as overweight or obese and, by association, unhealthy. Through these images and statements, the CCF attempts to expose the "numerical hocus-pocus" (2005a, 6) it claims the BMI really is.

This numerical hocus-pocus, is, according to the CCF, largely the result of a 1998 redefinition of BMI thresholds that made millions of Americans overweight overnight. Until 1998, according to prevailing public health standards, a BMI greater than 27.3 and 27.8 categorized a woman and a man, respectively, as overweight. But in 1998 a National Institutes of Health (NIH) obesity panel lowered the overweight threshold to 25.0 for both sexes, instantly casting more than 35 million Americans into the overweight category.[7] These 35 million Americans essentially woke up one morning to discover that they were no longer of "normal" weight but instead were labeled "overweight."[8]

To further corroborate its position that the BMI is "numerical hocus-pocus" (CCF 2005a, 6), the CCF emphasizes that the NIH redefinition now technically makes 97 percent of players in the National Football League (NFL) overweight and 50 percent of those overweight players obese (CCF 2005a, 6, 8). Drawing support and legitimacy from the NFL, the CCF notes that the NFL too thinks the BMI is "bogus" because it "doesn't consider body muscle versus fat" (2005a, 8).

Yet the CCF does not rely solely on the NFL for support. Its primary strategy is the use of experts, and the group cites numerous experts who warn that the BMI is of limited use in measuring body fat percentages. Of note, the CCF regards body fat percentages as a "generally recognized standard for judging *true* obesity" (2005a, 12; emphasis in original). These expert voices appear in peer-reviewed outlets that the CCF directly quotes, and they range from the *Journal of the American Medical Association* to the *European Journal of Clinical Nutrition.* A quote from the monthly journal of the Association of Physicians in Great Britain exemplifies the CCF's position that, even though the BMI is a poor and unreliable measure that is not valid for all populations, it continues to be widely used: "Although BMI is a generally convenient measure, it lacks a theoretical foundation, and may be compromised by ethnic, cultural, or lifestyle differences. Nonetheless, BMI has been used as a generic risk factor in epidemiological research" (CCF 2005a, 16). According to the CCF, the misleading nature of the BMI is especially true as it pertains to children. In the CCF's words, "many studies have found it is a particularly poor measure of body composition in children" (2005a, 13).[9]

In framing terms, the NIH redefinition is a key exemplar of the CCF's choice and responsibility frame, illustrating precisely the constructed nature of the obesity epidemic. Moreover, this redefinition constitutes a direct blow to the health frame. Sounding rather like social constructionists, the CCF points out that the BMI is a human construct and that public health officials arbitrarily assign cut-off points that determine who is "overweight." In fact, many critical fat scholars have written about the contested nature of the BMI (e.g., Oliver 2006), and even medical professionals have questioned the lowering of the BMI overweight threshold on the basis of mortality (e.g., Strawbridge, Wallhagen, and Shema 2000).

This condemnation of arbitrariness in medical practices is evident in CCF visuals, a key framing device the group uses, including two cartoons that depict *Wheel of Fortune*–like game spinners. One shows a spinner labeled "Today Let's Blame Obesity On": and divided into food-related segments such as pasta, granola, and soda (CCF 2004b). The other, titled "Today's Random Medical News from the New England Journal of Panic-Inducing Gobbledygook" (CCF 2007d),[10] shows three game spinners. The first spinner's segments are labeled with health-related variables such as exercise, smoking, and fatty foods; the second spinner's segments are labeled with medical conditions such as heart disease, depression, and glaucoma; and the third spinner's segments are labeled with affected members of the population such as twins, children, and men ages 25–40. The phrase "can cause" appears between spinners one and two, and "in" appears between spinners two and three. A speech balloon floating beside a television news anchor reads, "According to a report released today . . . ." Depending on the findings of a given day's arbitrary medical study, the message conveyed is that there are potentially many different causal factors that can potentially cause many different conditions in potentially many different populations.

According to the CCF, random (and, as it alludes, groundless) research findings, along with arbitrary BMI cut-off points, do not have empirical biomedical underpinnings but instead represent a set of economic interests. The CCF leaves little doubt who it thinks is behind the current obesity hype: health officials who are funded by the weight-loss industry. In other words, the CCF indicts the health (and aesthetic) frames and their "corrupt" industry alliances.

The group is quick to point out that the decision for reclassification was made by a NIH obesity panel chaired by Xavier Pi-Sunyer—an individual the CCF accuses of receiving support "from virtually every leading weight-loss company" (2005a, 10). The CCF alleges that his involvement in lowering the BMI over-weight threshold created more overweight Americans and, thus, a greater need for weight-loss products.

Challenging the Number of Obesity-Related Deaths. If the NIH's BMI reclas-sification serves as an exemplar that enables the food industry to challenge the health frame, so too does the controversy over the rates of overweight- and obesity-related deaths.[11] According to a CDC study published in March 2004 (Mokdad et al. 2004), 400,000 deaths each year can be attributed to poor diet and physical inactivity. The CCF maintains that after this figure was published, it was extensively adopted by newsmakers, producing rather hyperbolic headlines such as "Obesity on Track as No. 1 Killer" (2005a, 19). Yet the CCF also points out that this number has not gone unchallenged. It cites, for example, an article in *Science* magazine that claims the study's "underlying data are weak" (2005a, 21) and a *Wall Street Journal* cover story, "CDC Study Overstates Obesity as a Cause of Death" (2005a, 25), that clearly questions the study's results. The CCF observes that the article quoted David Allison, who formulated the contentious study's research methods but conceded that "measuring obesity-attributable deaths 'is an evolving science'" (2005a, 24). A citation in the *Harvard Health Policy Review* helped solidify the group's point: "The major problem with this 'obesity kills' statistic is the lack of compelling evidence to substantiate it" (CCF 2005a, 60).[12]

The CCF stresses that the CDC, too, over time, has conceded the problem-atic nature of the 400,000 figure by first lowering it to 365,000 in January 2005, then questioning the study method in an internal memo in February 2005, and then subsequently acknowledging a later study estimating 112,000 obesity-related deaths per year in the United States (Flegal et al. 2005). This newer study by CDC researcher Katherine Flegal and her colleagues (2005) found that the vast majority of weight-related deaths are associated with individuals with a BMI greater than 35 (extreme obesity). This is worth underscoring, as the CCF states up front that it is not trying to "dismiss the genuine health risk of obesity for the heaviest individuals" (2005a, 3).

The CCF's discussion of this 400,000 deaths controversy comes across as a lesson in research methods. The CCF encourages the public to run with Fle-gal's findings instead of Mokdad's or with an earlier study by Allison and his col-leagues (1999) suggesting a figure of about 300,000. It offers a list of reasons for doing so (2005a, 40). These include the assertion that Flegal's study uses more recent and nationally representative data, that she controlled for the influence of age, that she reports deaths due to overweight versus deaths due to obesity, and that she reports on a range of risks. As with its criticisms of Pi-Sunyer, the CCF exposes Allison as a mouthpiece of the weight-loss industry, accusing him of "accepting funding from virtually every major business in the weight-loss industry" (2005a, 52). The group devotes an entire page and half of *An Epidemic of Obesity Myths* (CCF 2005a, 53–54) to listing Allison's supporters, which include a number of major companies ranging from Knoll Pharmaceuticals (the company that manufactures the weight-loss drug Meridia) to Nutrisystem (the popular weight-loss plan).

Illustrating the dynamic nature of frame competitions, the higher estimates (such as 400,000 annual deaths) that once figured prominently on the CDC's "Overweight and Obesity" web pages are now conspicuously absent today. Even the most recent surgeon general's report (HHS 2010d) works with the lower estimate of 112,000 obesity-related deaths, suggesting a victory for the CCF on this matter.

Challenging the CDC's Claims about Life Expectancy. The CCF also takes on the related position that obesity will significantly shorten life expectancy. On its website is a cartoon that depicts two cavemen hinting that scientists really do not know what leads to longer lifespan. One caveman says to the other: "Something's just not right—our air is clean, our water is pure, we all get plenty of exercise, everything we eat is organic and free-range, and yet nobody lives past thirty" (CCF 2007c).[13]

Moreover, related to the CCF's position that being obese does not always reduce lifespan is the assertion that one can be obese and healthy. Again, the group quotes researchers from various sources to support its claim. For example: "'We've studied this from many perspectives in women and men and we get the same answer: It's not the obesity—it's the fitness.'—Steven Blair, P.E.D., Cooper Institute for Aerobics Research, 2004" (CCF 2005a, 77). The argument put forth through this sort of quotation evidence is that whether one is healthy or unhealthy is not dependent on one's weight; rather, health outcomes can be determined by how *fit* one is, something the CCF says is closely connected to physical activity. It is physical inactivity, according to the CCF, that "causes a tremendous burden of disease and death" (CCF 2005a, 82). These claims are overt condemnations of the health frame, which maintains that obesity is a serious health risk that requires lifestyle changes in both activity levels *and* food consumption.

Challenging the Economic Costs of Overweight and Obesity. The CCF also takes issue with the CDC's assertions about the economic costs of obesity (namely, that it costs the U.S. economy nearly $150 billion every year). In fact, the group directly accuses the CDC of generating this myth. In its words, "In December 2001, 'The Surgeon General's Call to Action to Prevent and Decrease Overweight and Obesity,' cited that figure, and the myth was born" (CCF 2005a, 109).

The CCF discredits this figure by turning to a number of framing devices, namely depicting opponents in a negative light and questioning supporting data. First, it argues that one of the studies the CDC cites (Wolf and Colditz 1998) has serious methodological limitations that the authors themselves acknowledge. For example, it maintains that Anne Wolf and Graham Colditz neglected to include height and weight in many of the primary data sources, that they allowed for the double-counting of costs, and that they used a BMI threshold of 29 for obesity instead of the typical 30. Second, it discredits coauthor Colditz by showing that he received funding from Roche, the maker of Xenical, a weight-loss pill. Third, the CCF argues that better studies that control for confounding factors find that there is "no statistically significant relationship between obesity and expenditures" (2005a, 111). In short, the data the CDC presents are not to be trusted.

Social Justice: Health at Every Size

In chapter 5, we examine at length NAAFA's perspective on fat discrimination. However, just as we reviewed NAAFA's views on fat aesthetics in our larger discussion of fat aesthetics, we will review here its views on health. Like the CCF, NAAFA, too, exhibits many points of departure with the CDC.

The National Association to Advance Fat Acceptance, along with other supporters of its social justice frame, alleges that being fat does not always signify lack of health. Much like the CDC and CCF, NAAFA supports its claims about the relationship between fat and health by citing supporting data. For example, it challenges the CDC's assertion that being overweight is unhealthy and potentially deadly by reporting on, through its "Recent News Items" feed on its website, a Mayo Clinic study that found that overweight and obese men with moderate fitness had mortality rates similar to those of the highly fit normal-weight reference group (McAuley et al. 2010). Similarly, NAAFA turns to a study that reports that the most overweight and obese ethnic groups are also some of the most active demographic groups (Belcher et al. 2010).

A new approach to health and weight associated with NAAFA's alternative perspective is Health At Every Size (HAES). On its website, NAAFA states that it supports HAES principles, which it maintains are aligned with its mission of protecting the rights of fat people and improving their quality of life. In 2010, NAAFA hosted its first HAES International Summit, which convened professionals and health advocates from around the world. The keynote speaker was Glenn A. Gaesser, and summit presenters included powerhouse players in both the fat acceptance and HAES movement such as Deb Burgard, Esther Rothblum, and Linda Bacon. On its website, NAAFA also provides interested educators with an Everybody in Schools Curriculum Unit Resource Kit.

According to Bacon, the HAES movement "supports people in adopting health habits for the sake of health and well-being (rather than weight control)" and encourages acceptance of body diversity, flexible eating that values pleasure and honors internal cues, and joy in movement (Bacon 2008, 322). Health At Every Size "acknowledges that good health can best be realized independent from considerations of size" and "supports people—of all sizes—in addressing health directly by adopting healthy behaviors" (Bacon 2008, 257–58). In the *Fat Studies Reader*, Burgard further stresses that "HAES defines health by the process of daily life rather than the outcome of weight" (2009, 44). From this perspective, health is not just a scale measurement but an ongoing and dynamic process that involves "emotional, physical, and spiritual well-being" (Burgard 2009, 42).

Those involved with the HAES movement actively work to refute the alleged facts put forth by the CDC and its allies. For example, turning to research studies, NAAFA and HAES advocates challenge the myths that fat kills people, that losing weight will lead to a longer life, and that anyone can lose weight if they try (Bacon 2008). In contrast, HAES reports that overweight people, on average, live longer than normal weight people, that no study has ever shown that weight loss actually prolongs life, and that biology dictates most people's weight independent of their diet and exercise habits (Bacon 2008). One oft-cited article describes the results of a study that found that significant improvements in overall health can be made, regardless of weight loss, when women learn to recognize and follow internal hunger cues and begin feeling better about their size and shape (Bacon et al. 2005).

The National Association to Advance Fat Acceptance and members of the HAES movement also point out that people's behavior—specifically poor diet and physical inactivity—can lead to health problems regardless of weight and BMI (Bacon 2008). In other words, a thin person who overeats and fails to exercise will likely experience the same health problems as an overweight or obese person who engages in these unhealthy behaviors. The National Association to Advance Fat Acceptance and HAES advocates contend that weight has become an inaccurate proxy by which we gauge health.

In contrast to the CDC's central claim, NAAFA and its HAES allies advance the notion that people can be healthy even if they are considered overweight by BMI standards. For example, the group asserts that "individual fitness can be achieved despite a relatively high ratio of fat-to-lean body mass and affirms that fitness is a desirable and attainable goal for most fat people" (NAAFA 2011k, "Physical Fitness"). This is because, as Gaesser (2002)—whose book *Big Fat Lies: The Truth about Your Weight and Your Health* is recommended reading on NAAFA's website—points out, one can achieve "metabolic fitness." According to Gaesser, metabolic fitness is mainly a matter of "increasing insulin sensitivity and thereby reducing blood insulin levels" (2002, 176). Consequently, maintaining insulin sensitivity and being metabolically fit means "having a metabolism that maximizes vitality and minimizes the risk of disease—particularly those diseases that are influenced by lifestyle, such as heart disease, type 2 diabetes, and cancer. It means living longer *and* living healthier" (Gaesser 2002, 168). So while public health officials at the CDC profess that a high BMI potentially compromises physical health, both the CCF and NAAFA put, so to speak, less weight on these numbers.

While the CDC generally adopts the obese-equals-unhealthy formula, there is, however, some evidence that it has begun to embrace a HAES perspective. Abigail Saguy and Kevin Riley (2005, 909–911) observe that HAES advocates such as Lynn McAfee have had a seat at the table at Food and Drug Administration and NIH meetings and have also influenced important NIH publications. And on January 28, 2010, the surgeon general posted a podcast encouraging Americans to abandon the negative approach to obesity and to adopt a more positive attitude toward being healthy:

> Hello, I'm Dr. Regina Benjamin, United States Surgeon General. Two-thirds of all adults and nearly one in three children are overweight or obese. As a result, our nation has high rates of diabetes and other chronic illnesses. The good news is we can be healthy and fit at any size or any weight. As America's family doctor, I want to change the national conversation from a negative one about obesity and illness, to a positive conversation about being healthy and being fit. So let's start with making healthy choices. Eat nutritious foods, exercise regularly, and have fun doing it. (HHS 2010c)

Further evidence for a potential paradigm shift is seen in the most recent surgeon general's report on obesity (HHS 2010d). Here the surgeon general admits that the nation is at a crossroads and that the "old normal"—one that stresses the importance of recommended numbers for weight and BMI—is now giving way to a "new normal." This new normal focuses on the bigger picture and emphasizes "achieving an optimal level of health and well-being" (HHS 2010d, 12).

Benjamin's podcast and new mindset potentially serves as a framing exemplar because it underscores key assertions made by NAAFA. Her claim that individuals of "any size or any weight" can be healthy and fit resonates with HAES (and thus NAAFA) principles. Yet frame competitions are precisely that—competitions—and Benjamin's announcement has not gone without criticism. In a cultural climate where *The Biggest Loser*, a NBC reality television show about weight loss, has been broadcast for over a decade, Benjamin's podcast has elicited comments such as "This is a joke right?" "Yes, she may have a Ph.D. but she is also fat/borderline obese. And wrong," and "Spoken like a true fatty."[14] As the latter reactions indicate, Benjamin herself has been criticized for being too "overweight" to hold the job of America's family doctor (Donaldson James 2009).

RESONANCE

But how does the average American think about fat bodies and the issue of health? Research suggests that, despite the competing views of the CCF and NAAFA, public health messages resonate in the popular imagination; the CDC's health frame is dominant. In fact, alongside the aesthetic frame, the health frame is the one most individuals connect with and think of as a "natural" taken-for-granted way of understanding the fat body. For this reason, and also because the frame leads to body conformity (e.g., the desire to be thin/ner for women), we label it dominant. The health frame represents a salient component of cultural tool kits that individuals regularly draw on to inform action (Swidler 1986, 2001). The health frame's dominance is evident in a number of studies that indicate that people not only believe the claims of the health frame but that they also regularly engage in behaviors that stem from these claims.

Health Beliefs

Research confirms the cultural legitimacy of the health perspective. For example, one study (Kwan 2009a) involving a nonprobability sample of forty-two in-depth interviews with body nonconformists found that weight-related illnesses concerned nearly all of the participants. The participants were of the opinion that being overweight is unhealthy and that it is tied to disease, disability, and premature death. Moreover, most of the participants had a target weight or weight range and a set number of pounds they hoped to lose, and they believed that reaching this target number would lead to better health. Along with reporting their desires for weight loss, participants overwhelmingly expressed the belief that being healthy meant losing weight, maintaining an active lifestyle, and eating "right."

This study is by no means unique. A national survey commissioned by the Harvard Forums on Health found that most Americans view obesity as a serious health concern (comparable to smoking) and that most believe obesity increases their risk for health problems like high blood pressure, heart disease and diabetes (Lake Snell Perry & Associates 2003). The CDC's framing of childhood obesity has found public support as well. For instance, most respondents in one study considered childhood obesity to be as serious as other major childhood health threats such as tobacco use and violence (Evans et al. 2005).

Research seems to indicate that young people themselves are influenced by the health frame, as adolescents have been shown to perceive obesity as a sickness that can negatively affect health (Serrano et al. 2010). A Gallup Youth Survey poll based on telephone interviews with a national cross section of teenagers found that 76 percent of children think what they eat affects their future health (Robison 2002). Additionally, children and adolescents express a belief in the efficacy of the solutions and the benefits of the expected outcomes laid out in the health frame, reporting that they recognize that being healthy means following a balanced diet and participating in physical activity in order to maintain a satisfactory quality of life (Serrano et al. 2010).

Finally, Americans consider obesity to be one of the top health problems facing the nation today (Saad 2010), suggesting that the CDC's health frame has convinced the public that overweight and obesity are social problems. In one poll, 61 percent of individuals maintained that the CDC is doing an excellent or good job (Saad 2009), indirectly indicating that Americans are broadly satisfied with the CDC's work and messages.

Health Behaviors

In addition to articulating a strong belief in the CDC's core message, the strength and resonance of the health frame is visible through individual health behaviors. The prevalence of weight-loss behaviors suggests that the message that overweight is unhealthy hits home. As we saw in chapter 2, at any given time, numerous Americans are attempting to lose weight. For example, Gallup found that 55 percent of those surveyed in a national poll desired to lose weight (Jones 2009), while another representative survey of U.S. adults found that 43 percent of respondents indicated that they were actually trying to lose weight (IFICF 2011). Adolescents, too, "are concerned about weight and perceptions of weight and are engaging in a variety of weight change activities for weight maintenance and weight change" (Kilpatrick, Ohannessian, and Bartholomew 1999, 148). Gallup Youth Survey reports as many as 12 percent of teenagers admit to currently being on a diet (Robison 2002). Even mentally ill individuals are able to correctly assess whether or not they have a weight problem (Meyer 2002).

Although people cite a number of reasons as to why they want to lose weight—including appearance or vanity, age, competition, and fear (Brink and Ferguson 1998)—multiple studies show that the primary motivation for weight loss is health (Brink and Ferguson 1998; Crawford et al. 1998). That health motivates is somewhat unsurprising; it is seen as a means to various ends. For example, overweight and obese study participants report that they aspire to health to fulfill various social roles such as worker, provider, or spouse, and to live long and meaningful lives (Kwan 2009a).

Yet concern about the alleged health risks of obesity varies among social groups. We discussed earlier in this chapter how overweight and obesity disproportionately affect minorities and underprivileged groups. We also saw in chapter 2 how some social groups, such as African American women, may reject hegemonic cultural ideals of thinness in exchange for ethnic subcultural ideals that celebrate a larger body ideal. Similarly, some studies show variation in how members of some social groups perceive weight and/or express concern for obesity-related health risks.

First, there is some evidence that individuals in general who are overweight or obese do not necessarily recognize that they fall under these medical categories. That is, there seems to be a disconnection between individual perception and the health dictates prescribed by the CDC. For example, one national poll of U.S. adults found that 30 percent of individuals who would be, based on the BMI, labeled medically "overweight," thought of themselves as "normal," while about 70 percent of those in the "obese" category considered themselves "overweight" (Harris Interactive 2010).

Second, there is evidence that some ethnic minorities may be less likely to put themselves in BMI risk categories and, therefore, if the health frame holds, would be placing themselves at greater health risk. For example, researchers have found that African American women do not realistically identify themselves as obese and are more likely than white adults to underestimate their current body weight (Patt et al. 2002; Schuler et al. 2008). Others have found that white adults, women, and high-socioeconomic status individuals are more likely than black adults, men, and low-socioeconomic status individuals to describe themselves as overweight or obese (Schieman, Pudrovska, and Eccles 2007). Preliminary work reported by Matthew Ryan (2011) similarly reports sex and ethnic differences in the perception of weight and health. Specifically, his study of emergency room patients found that about 47 percent of obese and overweight men said they believed their weight was a problem, while about 62 percent of obese or overweight women said their weight was damaging to their health. Ryan also found that 53 percent of overweight and obese black Americans said their weight was bad for their health, compared to 60 percent of overweight and obese whites.

Together, these findings suggest that while Americans are generally concerned about losing weight in the name of health, this concern is not evenly distributed across the population. This has implications for certain minority groups. We have already seen how prevalence rates for obesity are higher among African American and Hispanic populations compared to whites and positively correlate with neighborhood and socioeconomic disadvantage. In chapter 2, we also observed how some racial and ethnic minority groups embrace counterhegemonic aesthetic norms that may buffer members from poor body image. Furthermore, we observed how, for women, concerns about body weight are inversely related to socioeconomic status.

If members of these groups—such as African Americans, Hispanics, or individuals from lower socioeconomic backgrounds—are less likely to define themselves as medically overweight or obese, or at health risk, compared to others, these groups may be labeled by certain claims makers as problematic. Specifically, from a public health standpoint, these groups not only exhibit higher obesity prevalence rates, but they are resisting—however consciously and intentionally or not—both hegemonic beauty expectations and health mandates. Subsequently, these groups may be placed under greater surveillance, both formally (through institutional sanctions) and informally (through public sanctions). Fat frames thus have the ability to asymmetrically affect populations, potentially subjecting vulnerable populations to increased biopower.

Finally, despite this overwhelming support for the health frame, there is some indication that the Health at Every Size perspective has some public support. For example, Lee Monaghan's (2008) interviews with a group of men whom medicine might label "overweight" or "obese" suggest that the HAES perspective may be seeping into the general public. He found that men's talk about weight and physical activity reveals a range of perspectives, including views that might be seen as aligned with HAES. For instance, some of these men prioritized physical fitness over slimness, some discussed natural body diversity, while others openly criticized authoritative public health campaigns.[15] The National Association to Advance Fat Acceptance and HAES support is also evident in the number of individuals who have made the online "HAES Pledge" (HAES 2012). As of May 2012, 4,261 individuals pledged their support for HAES, which is "based on the simple premise that the best way to improve health is to honor your body. It supports people in adopting health habits for the sake of health and well-being (rather than weight control)" (HAES 2012).

CONCLUSION

Medicalization is the process by which human conditions come to be defined and treated as medical problems (Conrad 1992). Through medicalization, social issues and problems once outside medical authority are put directly under its purview. In "The Medicalization and Demedicalization of Obesity" (1995), Jeffery Sobal observes how the medicalization of obesity took off in the 1950s with widespread claims that obesity would be best dealt with through medical interventions. Medicalization has taken several forms, including the naming and popularizing of the term "obesity," the defining of obesity as a disease by medical authorities using diagnostic standards such as the BMI, a range of organizational activities such as the advent of obesity journals and the American Society of Bariatric Physicians (founded in 1949), and the application of a wide range of medical treatments (from surgical techniques to drug therapy). Sobal maintains that while there have been challenges to medicalization (particularly from fat activists such as those at NAAFA), medical models remain prevalent. Indeed, this is evident in the prominent role the CDC continues to play in addressing issues of overweight and obesity.

In fact, today we are observing even more complex, multisited, and multi-directional forms of medicalization (Clarke et al. 2003). According to Adele E. Clarke and colleagues (2003, 2010) medicalization is not just about the expansion of medical control but also about the transformation of bodies and lives, particularly through various interactive processes, including processes that focus on health, risk, and surveillance. This new focus, biomedicalization, is what we see with the CDC's health frame and the healthism that accompanies it. Health becomes a moral obligation, an individual moral responsibility, and we are all subject to the medical gaze that ultimately produces the disciplined conformist body. Biomedicalization comes with elaborate standardized risk-assessment tools such as the BMI to diagnose and judge the many risks that might lead to future illnesses. With biomedicalization, as with Boero's notion of postmodern epidemics, we are all at risk. As such, we are all exhorted to change our personal habits and behaviors to prevent or combat potential disease, disability, or death.

The CDC's health frame, which perpetuates this biomedicalization and accompanying healthism, is presented via a number of avenues (such as web pages, publications, and speeches). These public messages define the obese body as problematic because it is unhealthy and increases the likelihood of death and disease. Like the aesthetic frame, the health frame asserts that the obese body is the result of personal failure and that salvation emerges through behavioral change—messages that generally resonate with the public, as evidenced by the abundance of people who believe that obesity is unhealthy and the large number of people attempting to lose weight in the name of health.

Despite the pervasiveness and resonance of the CDC's health messages, there are other approaches to weight and health. The industries of the fashion-beauty complex imply that fat is more of an aesthetic problem than a health problem. Yet these industries also co-opt the discourse of the health frame, implying that beauty is a sign of health and that health is a sign of beauty. Moreover, the CCF and NAAFA both criticize the health frame. Using the same tools (an arsenal of research), these two groups allege that being obese does not always signify poor health. However, although the CCF and NAAFA align in their challenges of the dominant health frame, as we see in upcoming chapters, the CCF does so in the name of consumer choice, and NAAFA does so in the name of social justice.

4 · FAT AND FOOD POLITICS

IN DECEMBER 2010, Monet Parham, a mother of two from Sacramento, California, filed a class-action lawsuit against McDonald's. Unlike previous suits that accused the restaurant chain of making coffee that was too hot (*Liebeck v. McDonald's*) or serving food that caused two teenage girls to become obese (*Pelman v. McDonald's*), Parham's suit focused on Happy Meal toys. Parham alleged that McDonald's sells toys that bait children and encourage them to develop a preference for Happy Meals. In her words, "we have to say 'no' to our young children so many times, and McDonald's makes that so much harder to do. I object to the fact that McDonald's is getting into my kids' heads without my permission and actually changing what my kids want to eat" (CSPI 2010). Parham's suit has been met with public contempt and criticism. In online forums, participants have called her "stupid," an "idiot," and a "bad parent" (e.g., *New York Daily News* 2010). Her case has been described by one source as a "new low in responsible parenting" (Olson 2010).

In this chapter, we turn to a third approach to body weight that focuses precisely on these types of sentiments that emphasize personal responsibility. In contrast to the industries of the fashion-beauty complex, which focus on the aesthetics of thinness, or the Centers for Disease Control and Prevention (CDC), which focuses on health outcomes, the food industry spotlights individual choice and personal responsibility. This perspective is evident in the messages produced by the food industry group the Center for Consumer Freedom (CCF). Unlike the aesthetic and health frames that construct fat as a problem, the CCF's choice and responsibility frame conveys the message that fat is *not* a social problem.

As we saw in chapter 3, the CCF presents a reactionary frame insofar as its signature elements arise in opposition to the core clams of the CDC's health frame. In this chapter we focus on what the group says about individual choice and personal responsibility. We also examine other takes on these core issues, including the assertions about individual choice and personal responsibility—embedded implicitly or explicitly—in the aesthetic, health, and social justice frames. We conclude by, once again, examining frame resonance, that is, how the public thinks about weight, individual choice, and personal responsibility.

THE CENTER FOR CONSUMER FREEDOM

This chapter examines the CCF's perspective on body weight and how the CCF, on behalf of the food industry, attempts to shape public perceptions of obesity. The CCF is a tax-exempt registered nonprofit 501(c)(3) organization that receives support from restaurants, food companies, and individual consumers. Because of the group's allegedly close ties to large corporate contributors such as Monsanto, Tyson Foods, and Coca-Cola, some of the CCF's critics have accused it of being a lobby group for the food and beverage industry (see chapter 1).

We focus on the CCF despite the existence of other food industry groups that also have a stake in obesity discourses (such as the American Beverage Association, the Food Products Association, and the Grocery Manufacturers of America) because the CCF is a financially powerful group that is *especially* vocal about obesity. As we illustrate in this chapter, the group makes multiple claims about body weight and related issues. Many of these claims rest on three basic premises: obesity is not an epidemic, obesity is not caused by overeating alone, and food consumption (and by extension body size) is a matter of individual choice and personal responsibility. The group articulates its perspective on its website (1997–2012a); in numerous op-ed pieces, cartoons, and advertisements; and in two publications, *An Epidemic of Obesity Myths* (2005a) and *Small Choices, Big Bodies: How Countless Daily Decisions Contribute to America's Burgeoning Waistline* (2007b).[1]

THE CENTRAL CLAIM: OBESITY IS NOT A SOCIAL PROBLEM, BUT "OBESITY MYTHS" ARE

A frame's central claim is the primary assertion that defines the frame's version of reality. In the case of the choice and responsibility frame, these central claims maintain that the tenets of the health frame amount to little more than hype designed to make consumers fearful and worried about weight gain. According to the CCF, the CDC has generated a bunch of "obesity myths," and the group works to expose these myths as "obesity hysteria" (2005a, 1). This is the CCF's central mission, which it aggressively pursues. For example, to get across its message that the obesity epidemic is mere "hype," the CCF invested $600,000 in one advertising campaign alone. This campaign targeted major U.S. newspapers, including newspapers in Atlanta, Georgia, where the CDC is headquartered

(Mayer and Joyce 2005). Through such marketing strategies the group hopes to expose obesity "hype" that it alleges the public has been "force-fed" by "agenda-driven special interests" (CCF 2005a, 3). As we saw in chapter 3, the CCF maintains that CDC "hype" is generated to line the pockets of health officials who are in bed with the weight-loss industry.

As we also saw in chapter 3, the CCF challenges the CDC's "hype" using an arsenal of research quotations, studies, and lessons in research methodology. In its words, it will undermine the CDC's myths by turning to "peer-reviewed publications and esteemed health experts" (2005a, 1).[2] Chapter 3 showed how the CCF contests the CDC's taken-for-granted measurement (the BMI), rejects the CDC's claims about the economic costs of the so-called epidemic, and refutes the CDC's data about the negative health consequences and high mortality rates associated with obesity. The CCF uses the term "junk science" to describe the body of research that propagates these alleged myths.

The CCF turns to graphic displays, cartoons, and drawings in its advertisements to convey its message; they are key visuals of this frame. For example, one CCF print advertisement captures well the CCF's overall message (see figure 4.1). The advertisement's content and its visual presentation all indicate there is no health crisis when it comes to the obese body. The decreasing font sizes and declining levels of hyperbole, along with the use of red ink to strike through apparent errors, all point to the CCF's claim that "the truth is out there." According to the group, Americans are being duped, and with just a little help from the CCF, they will be able to see this. By separating fact from fiction, the CCF hopes it will help savvy consumers make decisions that will protect their self-interests.

CAUSAL ROOTS: WHAT'S TO BLAME AND WHAT'S NOT TO BLAME

Every frame implies a cause to the social issue it grapples with, and the CCF's frame is no different. The CCF acknowledges the health frame's underlying equation that when "energy in" no longer equals "energy out," weight change occurs (2007b, 3). However, it attempts to provide a more nuanced perspective on this equation, arguing that the "Big Two [diet and exercise] . . . do not provide a sufficient model for weight dynamics on their own because many variables affect both sides of the equation" (CCF 2007b, 3). Thus, in addition to debunking the CDC's supposed health myths, the CCF sets out to discredit the CDC's Energy Balance Equation (CDC 2011a), arguing that it is too simplistic to capture the complexities of body weight.

For example, the group points out that while many health reports argue in favor of a single "cause," it is impossible to remove a sole cause from its context. Case in point, it says, is calcium. Calcium is found in cheese, which could be

CDC overstated risks of being overweight
—*Associated Press Headline*

America's Obesity

~~"Epidemic"~~

~~"Plague"~~

~~"Terror"~~

"Hype"?

The truth is out there.

ConsumerFreedom.com

The Center for Consumer Freedom is a nonprofit organization dedicated to protecting consumer choices and promoting common sense.

FIGURE 4.1. Obesity Hype
Through its advertisements, the CCF maintains that the so-called obesity epidemic is obesity "hype." (Credit: The Center for Consumer Freedom.)

part of a sandwich, which might be part of a meal, which is part of an entire diet. The group asks, "How effectively can a study isolate the calcium from every other component in a person's meal or lifestyle?" (CCF 2007b, 4). The group also points out that there is "good science gone bad" (CCF 2007b, 4) and that many studies used by, in its words, "public health activists" do not rely on experimental designs that validly isolate cause and effect. At best, these studies can suggest correlations. Again, the CCF makes its case through lessons in research methodology.[3]

The CCF contends that numerous factors contribute to weight gain. In *Small Choices, Big Bodies* (CCF 2007b, 7–47), the CCF states that physical activity is at an all-time low and that Americans are living sedentary lives. Pharmaceuticals, smoking cessation, increased dieting, and sleep deprivation have also made Americans susceptible to weight gain. Meanwhile, American occupations have changed drastically over time such that many jobs involve less manual labor, more automation, and extensive hours sitting. This is compounded by the prevalence of the automobile as a mode of transportation; fewer Americans are biking or walking to their destinations. The CCF maintains that changes in family life, such as a record number of women in the workforce, the rise in maternal age, and changes in family structure (such as more single parents and fewer siblings), have also led to increases in both adult and childhood obesity.

These causal factors the CCF identifies in *Small Choices, Big Bodies* (2007b) are not only numerous and varied, but some acknowledge the role of historical and social structural changes (such as an increase in sedentary jobs in America, automation, and reliance on automobiles). However, as we see shortly, this nod to social structural factors is cursory and short-lived, and it ultimately bows to personal responsibility.

Just as it does in *An Epidemic of Obesity Myths*, in *Small Choices, Big Bodies* the CCF turns to its usual strategy of relying on research quotes and studies. It presents numerous statistics to back up its claims about changing cultural and social trends and their contribution to America's waistlines. Many of these factors, the group acknowledges, may seem trivial, but according to the CCF, they all matter. Small daily patterns and behaviors eventually contribute, it argues, to big outcomes. Conspicuously, and similar to the CDC's mention of breastfeeding (which we encountered in chapter 3), there is a blaming of women for children's weight—the "mother blame" that others have written about in the context of obesity (see Herndon 2010; Maher, Fraser, and Lindsay 2010; Maher, Fraser, and Wright 2010), and something for which others who make similar scapegoat-like arguments have been criticized (see Boero 2009). For instance, in *An Epidemic of Obesity Myths*, the CCF even references a study that cites infant formula as a cause of overweight status (2005a, 95), implying that shifts in women's schedules and priorities may be to blame for children's weight gain.

Along with the addition of various structural-level contributing factors to the CDC's Energy Balance Equation, the CCF also discredits the Energy Balance Equation by emphasizing the calories-out (rather than calories-in) portion of the CDC's model. This is likely to draw attention to physical inactivity and, consequently, draw attention away from food consumption. The CCF turns to cartoons that poke fun at sedentary Americans, particularly sedentary children. For example, one cartoon depicts a man on a couch with a woman seated next to him. She says: "So how many calories you figure you burned by clicking the remote to change the channel?" (CCF 2009).[4] A second cartoon shows a different couple conversing. The man says to the woman, "I don't know how the kid is getting fat—he plays football for four hours a day!" Meanwhile, that child is in another room playing an NFL football video game (CCF 2005b). A third cartoon portrays three time periods: in 1800 a farm worker trudges along, guiding his plow as a mule pulls it across a field; in 1900 a construction worker uses a pneumatic hammer to drive rivets into a metal column; and in 2000 a white-collar worker sits at his desk, operating a computer via keyboard and mouse (CCF 2007a). These images, and others like them, leave little doubt that the CCF identifies physical inactivity as the primary culprit behind the size of America's waistlines.

The CCF's unabashed use of confrontational op-ed pieces, cartoons, advertisements, and publications suggests that the group does not hesitate to point fingers. Of course, this finger pointing at America's sedentary lifestyles helps to shift blame from the food industry which has been accused of creating an obesogenic environment. In fact, it could be argued that the long list of causal factors in itself is a way of detracting from the "calories-in" part of the CDC's Energy Balance Equation. As we saw in chapter 3, public health officials say that American society has become obesogenic, and they identify increased food intake and unhealthy foods as key characteristics of this environment. In defense, the CCF asserts that overeating is not the primary cause of obesity. Again, it turns to experts to make its case. For example, the group maintains, "'The lack of evidence of a general increase in energy [food] intake among youths despite an increase in the prevalence of overweight suggests that physical inactivity is a major public health challenge in this age group.'—*American Journal of Clinical Nutrition*, 2000" (CCF 2005a, 86).

The CCF also downplays the role of stigmatized foods such as soda and high-fructose corn syrup. It criticizes studies showing a link between soda consumption and childhood obesity, emphasizing that these studies have significant methodological limitations. Instead of relying on this allegedly flawed research, it turns to a different set of research findings showing that, for example, BMI is not influenced by the consumption of regular or diet drinks. Turning to its arsenal of quotes, the CCF defends high-fructose corn syrup against the accusation that it is "especially fattening" (CCF 2005a, 106). It cites New York University nutrition professor Marion Nestle: "'It's basically no different from table sugar. Table sugar is glucose and fructose stuck together. Corn sweeteners are glucose and fructose separated. The body really can't tell them apart'" (CCF 2005a, 106–107).

This defense of high-fructose corn syrup is also evident in a new campaign by the Corn Refiners Association (CRA), whose online portal encourages the public to "take a closer look" and see that "HFCS [high-fructose corn syrup] is simply a form of sugar made from corn" (CRA 2011a). The CRA uses the same strategies as the CCF, citing nutritionists, dieticians, and other experts who provide supporting data maintaining that high fructose corn syrup is "basically the same as sugar," that "there is no scientific evidence that [it] is to blame for obesity and diabetes," and that "the human body absorbs them [high fructose corn syrup and sugar] the same way" (CRA 2011b).

The CRA's campaign reminds us that the CCF is not alone in its framing battles, and there are allied groups that draw on similar strategies to provide reinforcement. In fact, these groups collectively represent what Clare Herrick (2009) refers to as the global food and drink industry (FDI). Herrick observes that the age of obesity has catalyzed the mass vilification of the FDI, and in response, the FDI has shifted blame through two main corporate social responsibility (CSR) strategies. The first is "a repeated adherence to the positive semantics and logic of 'energy balance'" (Herrick 2009, 57), which results in an emphasis on healthier versions of product offerings (such as diet, low-calorie items). The second strategy, directly in line with CCF messages, stresses sedentariness as a "legitimate default causal explanation" (Herrick 2009, 58). This is because, as Herrick points out, "nutritionists and epidemiologists cannot agree conclusively whether it is fat content, energy density, total calories, the type of fat or too much or too little carbohydrate that causes weight gain" (2009, 58). In this way, the food industry's position on physical inactivity is acritical; it takes for granted that sedentary lifestyle is a primary culprit in weight gain—a point the CCF can effectively push in light of ambiguity surrounding the flip side of the CDC's Energy Equation Balance (i.e., caloric intake).

CONSEQUENCES: MISINFORMATION, COMPROMISED CHOICES, LOSS OF FREEDOM

According to the CCF, the current state of affairs is one in which consumers are misinformed about the causes and consequences of obesity. The CDC and other public health officials have allegedly created a cultural milieu in which individuals are not properly informed about the "facts," and, as such, consumers may make misinformed decisions about their food and beverage choices. The CCF argues that the health frame, and the "enemy" health researchers who work in consort with the aesthetic frame in the name of profit, perpetuate the myths that obesity is a health crisis and that the main cause of obesity is food consumption. In response to these myths, consumers may be inclined to reject fast food, avoid demonized foods such as corn syrup, or reduce food intake in general.

The primary consequence of the current state of affairs is a loss of individual choice caused by misinformation. However, as we discuss below, the current state of affairs has also led to a push for food regulations to create a healthier population, a push led by what the CCF refers to on its web pages as "food cops," "health activists," and other "radicals." As we show, the CCF opposes these regulations because, as it argues, they compromise our freedom to decide what to consume. For the CCF, food consumption is a matter of individual choice and personal responsibility; regulations demanded by supposed health zealots compromise our freedom to choose.

PRINCIPLES: OUR BODIES, OUR FREEDOM TO CHOOSE, OUR RESPONSIBILITY

At this point, we can see the language of the framing matrix working in tandem. The CCF maintains that health agencies such as the CDC produce myths about being obese (a central claim); these myths compromise individual choice and freedom (consequences); and the public should care about these myths because choice and freedom, along with the closely connected theme of personal responsibility, are cherished ideals and axiomatic to the American way of life (principles). The principles of individual choice and personal responsibility are so central to this frame, and so uniquely vocalized by the CCF, that it is at times difficult to determine whether they are part of the frame's primary claims or the principles upon which those claims rest. The centrality of these two interconnected issues to the CCF's worldview is also the reason we label the frame the "choice and responsibility frame."

In its public artifacts, the CCF contends that Americans should have the right to make their own decisions, that they should have the freedom to do so without undue interference, and that they should take responsibility for whatever decisions they make. Whether it is the right to smoke, own guns, or eat to one's heart's content, according to the CCF these are god-given freedoms that governments should not take away or interfere with. This rhetoric, in many ways, parallels the rhetoric used by Big Tobacco to maintain sales in the face of evidence that smoking is unhealthy (see Menashe and Siegel 1998).

The underlying metaphor of this frame is thus apprehension of big, evil government. Unfettered state control is a symbol of tyranny and should be feared. One CCF print advertisement illustrates these sentiments. At the center of the advertisement is a large red apple. Copy at the top of the advertisement reads, "Big Apple or Big Brother?" The direct allusion to Big Brother makes the CCF's fear of government surveillance plenty clear. Meanwhile, the subtext of the advertisement, strategically placed like a food label on the apple, reinforces the group's core message that it is not food consumption but, rather, physical inactivity that is to blame: "if [an apple is] consumed without any activity or exercise you will gain weight" (CCF 2011a).

A cartoon on the CCF's website also drives home this fear of controlling big government. It parodies a famous World War I recruiting advertisement that depicts Uncle Sam pointing a finger directly at the viewer and declaring, "I WANT YOU FOR U.S. ARMY." In the parody, Uncle Sam states, "I WANT YOU . . . to stop smoking . . . wear your seatbelt . . . eat your vegetables . . . stay out of the sun . . . lose weight . . . buckle your kids in the back seat . . . talk about race . . . use a condom . . . volunteer . . . eat less red meat" (CCF 2001).[5] The message the CCF conveys through this visual is unmistakable: the government is interfering with our ability to make what should be private personal choices.

Those who challenge the CCF's position, it claims, threaten precious and beloved inalienable rights to act as free citizens. Along with "enemy" researchers and pharmaceutical companies that promote the medicalization of obesity, the CCF attacks what it calls "food cops," "health activists," "government bureaucrats," and "scheming trial lawyers" (like those who take on cases such as Monet Parham's). They, like "junk science" researchers, are enemies of the choice and responsibility frame. By extension, they are enemies of freedom and America. It is not coincidental that, on its web pages and in its public documents, the CCF refers to endorsers of the health frame as "health activists" instead of as advocates or officials. The group intentionally conjures up images of extremists. The use of words such as "radicals," "extremists," and "self-righteous" to depict frame enemies is another strategy used by the CCF.

The CCF takes special aim at the Center for Science in the Public Interest (CSPI), "a consumer advocacy organization whose twin missions are to conduct innovative research and advocacy programs in health and nutrition, and to provide consumers with current, useful information about their health and well-being" (CSPI 2011).[6] The CSPI's positions on food policy—such as its calls for food-labeling reform, a decrease in the marketing of low-nutrition foods to children, and the introduction of nutritional labeling in restaurants—have made it a visible target of CCF advertising campaigns. The CCF's primary tactic for dealing with the CSPI appears to be its cartoons and advertisements. For example, one print advertisement accuses the CSPI of creating phony food scares and junk science. The advertisement displays two boys intimidating a younger boy. The copy reads: "Bullies used to steal your lunch money. Now they scare you out of eating" (CCF 1997–2012b). As seen in this advertisement, hyperbole, humor, and sarcasm are typical of CCF visuals. These strategies help the CCF draw attention to what it believes are the absurd and extreme claims and consequences of the health frame.

PROPOSED SOLUTIONS: LET THE MARKET BE

Because of the CCF's concerns about "big government" and overregulation, it supports a laissez-faire philosophy. While the aesthetic and health frames' policy approaches both dictate action of some sort (namely weight loss), the choice and responsibility frame is mainly about doing nothing. The CCF demands minimal government regulation of the food industry. Again, the CCF contends, individuals should have the freedom to make their own decisions about what to eat and drink. One print advertisement conveys this message (see figure 4.2). Employing its signature sarcasm, the advertisement maintains that we "are too stupid . . . to make good personal decisions about food and beverages." Apparently, food cops and politicians are attacking our food and soda choices. The CCF rhetorically asks, "Have they gone too far?" The group's demand for economic autonomy has meant contesting proposals for regulating the marketing of certain foods, for higher or special food taxes, for food warnings and labels on certain foods and restaurants menus, and for frivolous lawsuits against the food industry.

Similar themes arise in other CCF print advertisements. One attempts to point out the CSPI's antichoice agenda and to criticize the group's demand for food warning labels: "The misnamed Center for Science in the Public Interest has issued hysterical warnings about everything from soup to nuts. Now they're calling for warning labels on soft drinks" (CCF 2011a). Another print advertisement uses the CCF's signature dry humor to accuse the New York Department of Health of being the New York Department of Hype. It sarcastically demands, "What's Next? . . . Let's get a government Department of Menus!" (CCF 2011a). Because of legislation proposed in New York, the CCF is especially vocal about policies in this state.[7]

For the CCF, nutritional content on menus not only interferes with personal choice but is also unlikely to create any meaningful change. In *An Epidemic of Obesity Myths*, the CCF uses its extensive quoting strategy to debunk the myth that mandatory nutritional information on restaurants menus will in fact reduce obesity rates. Nutritional labels are ineffective, it alleges. To back up this claim, the group references a study in a behavioral nutrition journal: "'The pattern of food intake across the different levels of energy density was similar when nutritional information was provided and when it was not.'—*Appetite*, 2002" (CCF 2005a, 99).

If contesting food industry regulation is a CCF priority, then the CCF has cause for concern. As documented by Yale University's Rudd Center for Food Policy and Obesity (Rudd 2011), food-related policies—from food taxes to menu regulations—are being proposed across America. While these so-called health activists, government bureaucrats, and food police continue to press for regulation, the CCF fires back with its neoliberal rhetoric: Let supply and demand regulate the free market. Permit consumers to make their own choices in a capitalist, consumer-driven society. The bottom line is, as several of the CCF's advertisements conclude, "It's your food. It's your drink. It's your freedom" (2011a).

In line with this free-market stance is the CCF's position on litigation. Numerous CCF advertisements convey the group's dissatisfaction with trial

YOU ARE TOO STUPID

...to make good personal decisions
about foods and beverages.

The New York Department of Health Hype
has used your tax dollars to launch an
advertising campaign to demonize soda.

Food cops and politicians are attacking
food and soda choices they don't like.
Have they gone too far?

It's your food. It's your drink. It's your freedom.

Find out more about attacks on your favorite foods and drinks at:

ConsumerFreedom.com

Paid for by The Center for Consumer Freedom

FIGURE 4.2. Individual Choice and Freedom
Acting as stewards of choice and freedom, the CCF maintains that individuals should be able to make their own decisions about what to eat and drink. (Credit: The Center for Consumer Freedom.)

lawyers who represent obese clients who claim they gained weight or suffered adversely from consuming unhealthy foods. This includes the lawyers representing the plaintiff in *Pelman v. McDonald's*,[8] a case made famous by Morgan Spurlock's blockbuster film *Super Size Me* (2004).[9] The CCF digs into its stockpile of advertisements to expose the absurdity of such litigation. It deploys one advertisement that depicts two hippopotamuses conversing: "Fred, Your butt is getting huge. Who can we sue?" Another advertisement reads: "Did you hear the one about the fat guy suing the restaurants? It's no joke" (CCF 2011a). Another cartoon on its website represents particularly well the group's disdain for the trial lawyers who take on these cases. Two lawyers walk by several sunbathers, and one lawyer says to the other: "I made my first million suing fast food for obesity. Now I'm suing bathing suit makers for causing skin cancer" (CCF 2005d).[10]

CCF print materials and web content also target irresponsible parenting while simultaneously taking aim at what it deems frivolous legal cases, such as Monet Parham's recent Happy Meal suit. In one print advertisement, the CCF references parental responsibility, stating that "86% of Americans believe that parents are responsible for their kids' choices." The top of the advertisement reads, "Trial lawyer's next cash cow," and below that text is the image of an enormous potbelly with $100 bills tucked into what appears to be a trial lawyer's waistband (CCF 2011a).

This emphasis on parental and personal responsibility is somewhat striking in light of the CCF's long list of causal factors that includes factors that detract from individual blame. So even though the CCF describes how technological, social, and demographic changes contribute to weight gain (and that it is not food consumption that is the main problem), it ultimately maintains that food consumption and, by extension, the body is a personal responsibility (or, in the case of children, a parent's responsibility). Thus, like the aesthetic and health frames, at the end of the day, the choice and responsibility frame falls back on individualistic logic, blaming and holding individuals accountable for their bodies, along with any decisions regarding them.

AN ILLUSTRATIVE CASE: A SUPER BOWL XLV COMMERCIAL

This chapter focuses on the CCF because, as we stated earlier, the CCF is very vocal about its views on obesity. However, it is important to keep in mind that the group represents a larger discourse in the public arena that other cultural actors and organizations also contribute to and reinforce. The Americans Against Food Taxes' "Give Me a Break" (2011) commercial that aired during Super Bowl XLV serves as a clear example of choice and responsibility framing, highlighting many of the frame's signature elements, including the insinuation that food and beverage intake are not to blame for overweight and obesity, a mention of the potential consequences of food regulation (higher prices and difficulty taking care of a family), and an appeal to our valued ability to make our own choices for ourselves and our families. The American Beverage Association (ABA), which is behind Americans Against Food Taxes, is made up of food industry players such as the Coca-Cola Company, Kraft Foods, and Pepsi Beverages Company (ABA 2012). In the television commercial, a middle-class mother says, as she walks around a grocery store, "Feeding a family is difficult enough in today's economy. Now, some politicians want the government telling me how I should do it. They want to put new taxes on a lot of groceries I buy, like soft drinks, juice drinks, sports drinks, even flavored waters, trying to control what we eat and drink with taxes. Give me a break. I can decide what to buy without government help. The government is just getting too involved in our personal lives" (Americans Against Food Taxes 2011).

The "Give Me a Break" commercial pushes the choice and responsibility frame, as well as exhibits the frame's defensive nature. Its message is unequivocal: politicians and the government are getting too involved; this needs to stop. The male voiceover at the end encapsulates the frame's policy sentiments: "Government needs to trim its budget fat and leave our grocery budgets alone" (Americans Against Food Taxes 2011).

The venue in which this commercial aired suggests that defenders of the choice and responsibility frame are becoming more aggressive in their attempts to shape public perceptions. The Super Bowl is often the most-watched television event of the year. Although Christina Aguilera, who botched the opening singing of the national anthem, might wish to think otherwise, an estimated 111 million viewers watched the Green Bay Packers fend off the Pittsburgh Steelers in Super Bowl XLV (Nielsen 2011). As talk of America's obesogenic environment increases, so, too, may the advertising by supporters of the choice and responsibility frame.

FRAMING WARS AS RESEARCH (QUOTATION) WARS

Framers use a range of framing devices, such as supporting data, metaphors, exemplars, catchphrases, and visual images, to forward their claims. As is clear from the numerous examples we have examined, the CCF's key framing strategy is the use of select experts and quotations from peer-reviewed journals and other publications. In *An Epidemic of Obesity Myths* and *Small Choices, Big Bodies*, these quotations are not always accompanied by the name of an expert (although the expert's name, if not given with the quotation, is always cited in a footnote). Instead, a quotation might be followed by a journal name and year, as the *Harvard Health Policy Review* example (see chapter 3) illustrates. In this way, there seems to be some sense of journal name dropping, given that the CCF does not always appear to evaluate the study. This apparent lack of rigor is also evident in its referencing of semischolarly and mass-market periodicals such as *Science* and the *Wall Street Journal*. Quotations sometimes even come from individuals writing editorials and letters to these journals. For example, after an extensive quotation from an author who questions data linking overweight and death, the CCF provides the following reference information: "Editorial published in the *New England Journal of Medicine*, 1998" (CCF 2005a, 61). Again, the journal, recognized in the health community as rather prestigious, seems to provide the quotation credibility regardless of its author and other details of where and how the quotation appears.

At the same time, the CCF sometimes cites specific authors and their institutional affiliations, seemingly to serve a similar purpose as citing journals. In such cases, it is apparently all about researcher name dropping and institutional name dropping, likely to establish credibility. For example, the CCF cites, "'The health risks of moderate obesity have been greatly overstated.'—Dr. Glenn Gaesser, Professor of Exercise Physiology, University of Virginia, 1997" (2005a, 62).

The impression is that such a claim is valid because it comes from a scholar (of some repute) who is affiliated with a university (of some repute). Yet the quotation itself has little substance, and the text that surrounds it fails to contextualize its controversial claim. In this example and in others, the CCF quotes selectively and affords little or no attention to the context in which the quotation originally appeared. In general, and in contrast to the in-depth coverage of the 400,000 deaths controversy (discussed in chapter 3) and a few select issues it explores in detail, the CCF does not explore the majority of studies it quotes at length. The group's strategy seems to be to extract quotations that vividly illustrate its point, at times with the use of a prestigious journal, author, and/or author's affiliation.

Expert quotations also range in time period of origin. Some go as far back as the 1980s, before the heightened controversies over weight, deaths, and definitions. And they come from a wide range of health and medical sources, from the *Journal of the American Medical Association* to the *Journal of Clinical Epidemiology*. When providing evidence for its claims, the CCF even refers to sources of authority that provide some of the supporting evidence for the health frame that the CCF condemns—sources that the group criticizes as self-interested players that contribute to the obesity hype. These players include the National Institutes of Health (NIH) and journals such as *Obesity*. As we discuss later, *Obesity* is a journal the CCF says is controversial because it was founded by a professional organization that has a stake in medicalizing obesity.

DEPICTION OF ENEMIES: THE "MYTH MAKERS"

In addition to using supporting data as a framing device, the CCF also uses "depictions," defined as characterizations of those who oppose the frame. Despite accusations that it is a food-lobbying group that itself profits generously from its corporate contributors (see chapter 1), the CCF argues that the driving forces behind creating and perpetuating obesity myths are profit-hungry individuals and self-interested groups. The introduction to *An Epidemic of Obesity Myths* states: "This report also details how the $46 billion weight-loss industry is helping to generate obesity hysteria to justify government insurance coverage for obesity drugs and treatments. The pharmaceutical industry in particular is putting its enormous resources behind research that grossly exaggerates the health risks and costs of being overweight, as well as its prevalence" (CCF 2005a, 2).

The weight-loss and pharmaceutical industries are thus the CCF's "enemies"—or what it labels "myth makers." Specifically, the CCF is critical of public health and obesity researchers who have close ties to the weight-loss industry (which endorses the aesthetic frame we examined in chapter 2) and the pharmaceutical industry (which helps reify the assumptions of the health frame we examined in chapter 3). The CCF asserts that the weight-loss industry is a "goldmine" and that the market for obesity drugs is projected to be about "$50 BILLION" (CCF 2005a, 131; emphasis in original). The CCF's insinuation is clear: Who would not want in on this?

Of course, the CCF is not the first to expose the connection between public health researchers and the weight-loss industry and particularly the makers of weight-loss drugs. Writing about the "health industrial complex," J. Eric Oliver observes how this complex is built "upon a symbiotic relationship between health researchers, government bureaucrats, and drug companies" (2006, 31). As he maintains, examples of this symbiotic relationship are plentiful: drug companies sponsor research defining health issues; they fund researchers who sit on NIH boards and have appointments at medical schools; the NIH and CDC rely on research expertise to back requests for congressional funding; and drug companies use CDC-issued health warnings to promote their products.

Whereas in the first edition of *An Epidemic of Obesity Myths* the CCF accused a handful of medical researchers of ethical misdoings (CCF 2004a), in the second edition it boldly describes over a dozen individual researchers and their connections to for-profit industries (CCF 2005a). This is evident in claims such as "public opinion about obesity has been skillfully molded by the pronouncements of financially conflicted researchers and the companies that fund them" (CCF 2005a, 129). In some ways, this is a rather philosophically inconsistent statement coming from a group that represents the food industry, which, based on total food sales, was valued at approximately $1.638 trillion in 2010 (Plunkett Research, Ltd. 2011). Moreover, the CCF, too, is skillfully attempting to mold public discourse on fat and food consumption. And, remarkably, the CCF represents a much larger industry than those its alleged enemies serve; Americans spend close to $500 billion in supermarket and traditional food sales alone

(Plunkett Research, Ltd. 2011), a figure that far exceeds the $60 billion per year they spend on weight-loss products (Marketdata Enterprises 2011). The demonizing of alliances in the name of profit also seems rather duplicitous as there are many instances in which the food industry works with state representatives to influence nutritional policy—policies that eventually affect food sales.[11] This was recently the case when Dairy Management (a creation of the United States Department of Agriculture) teamed up with the pizza chain Domino's to develop a new line of pizza with 40 percent more cheese (Moss 2010). So while one branch of the government espouses weight-loss and caloric-control rhetoric, another branch works with restaurants through such innovations as Dairy Management to expand their menus to include cheese-laden products (Moss 2010).

Three professional nonprofit organizations are also targets of CCF judgment.[12] The CCF accuses these groups of shaping public perceptions about obesity but states that the public "remain[s] unaware of the extremely close ties they maintain with their for-profit sponsors in the weight-loss industry" (CCF 2005a, 133). The three organizations are the American Obesity Association (AOA; now renamed the Obesity Society), the North American Association for the Study of Obesity (NAASO), and the Centers for Obesity Research (CORE).

The CCF charges that the AOA is the lobbying arm of the weight-loss industry. A quotation attributed to the AOA website indicates that the AOA's "fundamental mission is to have obesity regarded as a disease of epidemic proportions" (CCF 2005a, 133). It accomplishes this mission, according to the CCF, through "rhetorical excess," even making the case that obesity costs the United States $238 billion a year—nearly double the figure public health officials acknowledge (CCF 2005a, 137). The CCF maintains that the real purpose of the AOA is to lobby for legislation mandating insurance coverage for weight-loss drugs. One CCF cartoon represents this charge nicely. It depicts a conference speaker at the "Annual Pharmaceutical Industry Conference" whose slide presentation indicates "IF OBESITY = DISEASE THEN DIET DRUGS = INSURANCE$$" (CCF 2005c).

An Epidemic of Obesity Myths also exposes the AOA's close ties to the weight-loss industry. The CCF identifies, for example, a number of AOA donors who are weight-loss industry players, such as GlaxoSmithKline, Pfizer, and Weight Watchers International, and it points out that the AOA's board even includes a chief scientific officer from Weight Watchers (CCF 2005a, 135). The CCF fires similar accusations at NAASO and CORE, contending that they, too, are trying to medicalize obesity and label it a disease in the name of profit. It points out that the parent organization of NAASO, the International Association for the Study of Obesity (IASO), publishes two top journals on the subject—Obesity Research (now renamed Obesity) and the International Journal of Obesity. These journals have on their editorial boards members such as Xavier Pi-Sunyer and

David Allison, whom, as we saw in chapter 3, the CCF accuses of having close ties to the weight-loss industry. The Centers for Obesity Research also has its own journal, entitled *Obesity Management*.

Yet even while alluding to the biased nature of these groups and their journals, the CCF relies on quotations from these very sources. For example, it cites *Obesity Research* to make its case for video games as a cause for childhood obesity (CCF 2005a, 94) and the *International Journal of Obesity* to make its case that sugar-sweetened beverages do not meaningfully affect weight gain (CCF 2005a, 103). The group's inconsistent use of sources is also evident when the CCF quotes nutritionist Marion Nestle. As we saw earlier, the group turns to her to illustrate its point that corn syrup is really no different than table sugar. Yet one CCF website clearly identifies her as an enemy "myth maker," calling her one "of the country's most hysterical anti-food-industry fanatics" (2011b). Again, it appears that by citing authority figures in the field such as Nestle, the CCF concedes their legitimacy and authority—even while it simultaneously accuses them of contributing to obesity "hype."

COMPETING VOICES: TAKING RESPONSIBILITY FOR OUR APPEARANCE, FOR OUR HEALTH

Through the CCF, the food industry takes a stance on individual choice and personal responsibility; however, it is not the only cultural producer that speaks to these issues. The other framers examined in this book do so as well; some engage these issues more so than others.

The industries of the fashion-beauty complex take a position on individual choice and personal responsibility, albeit indirectly. Sociologists have long known that visible physical characteristics such as skin color and gender are diffuse status characteristics (Berger et al. 1977; Correll and Ridgeway 2003). Individuals carry these characteristics from situation to situation and present them to others who may judge their characters, expectations, and abilities based on them. This is also the case with beauty and, by extension, body size. As sociologists Murray Webster Jr. and James Driskell write, "Beauty or ugliness is one of the most accessible features of a person and acts as readily available status information in most encounters" (1983, 162). As we will see in the following chapter, this is particularly evident with body size, which often serves as a cue for judgment.

As we saw in chapter 2, the fashion, cosmetics, and weight-loss industries provide individuals with a plethora of tools to construct and "perfect" their bodies, and individuals—but women, in particular—often feel obliged to take advantage of these tools. These tools range from weight-loss pills to exercise gadgets. The market even provides so-called easy fixes if one can afford them—liposuction, bariatric surgery, and now the possibility of freezing fat cells.[13] In this cultural climate, where the body is a status characteristic, individuals assume that those who choose not to work hard for beauty—whether it is by failing to spend the requisite time, money, and/or energy—should not be rewarded. They deserve to be denied dates, chances for work promotion, higher incomes, and so on. The gendered bias of beauty norms means not only that women must spend more time, money, and energy to conform to these hegemonic beauty ideals but that they are also more highly stigmatized and penalized when they do not live up to cultural expectations (Bartky 2010 [1988]; Bordo 2003; Kwan and Trautner 2009).[14] In short, according to the aesthetic frame, individuals need to work hard at being beautiful; those who do not choose to take responsibility for their bodies and their beauty justifiably suffer the stigma associated with body nonconformity.

With the health frame, as we saw in chapter 3, healthism dictates that we take responsibility for our bodies. However, while the neoliberal rhetoric of the CCF's choice and responsibility frame says we should safeguard our choices so that we can make whatever choices we desire—whether they be healthy or unhealthy—the health frame implores us to make the right choice, that is, the healthy choice. As Samantha Murray (2008) contends, disciplinary medicine's mandate about the fat body is really an illusion. She writes: "Disciplinary medicine relies on the illusion of personal choice for all individuals, whereby each feels they freely choose to take up medical directives relating to healthy lifestyles. In other words, the power of disciplinary medicine functions at a *tacit* level: the virtuous *appeal* of mastering one's body in line with dominant strategies *disguises* the disciplinary effect of medical discourse" (Murray 2008, 12–13; emphasis in original). In the face of health edicts, individuals may feel like they are exercising their own choice to pursue health; however, it is really, as Murray astutely points out, a mythic choice. Individualistic moral discourses, along with self-surveillance, mean that individuals are compelled to pursue health and make the so-called right medical choice.

Failing to make this "right choice" means risking the charge of irresponsibility. This is especially the case for parents, namely mothers, who often carry the primary burden for the health of children and the elderly (Abel 1986; Case and Paxson 2001). Thus, even as increasing biomedicalization means that we place increasing control in the hands of medical authority, our health really is our own responsibility. This is especially the case when diagnostic tools and medical tests are available. For example, others have written about how prenatal diagnostic technologies cannot be neutrally refused, as refusal will be construed as a lack of responsibility (Browner and Press 1996). In the case of prenatal care, willingness to use technological advances means that a pregnant woman is doing "all that can be done" to ensure a healthy pregnancy (Browner and Press 1996, 153).

Similarly, there is an expectation that in light of an array of scientific developments and technologies to predict obesity and related comorbidities—from the BMI to calipers to sophisticated blood tests—individuals should submit to such tests. By doing so, they are behaving responsibly and taking control of their health. Indeed, a whole body of literature is devoted to understanding patient compliance (see Vermeire et al. 2001); there are strong cultural expectations that patients comply with so-called authoritative medical dictates.

Finally, the National Association to Advance Fat Acceptance (NAAFA)'s social justice frame does not readily engage issues of individual choice and personal responsibility. As we see in chapter 5, NAAFA acknowledges that there are multiple causes of fat, from genetic components, to behavioral components, to social structural factors. In this way, the association maintains that individuals do not always have complete choice and control over their bodies and their body size. As such, size-based discrimination is unwarranted and unjust. While NAAFA's perspective on fat respects individual choice and personal responsibility, it primarily calls for social justice and an end to body discrimination.

RESONANCE

Paralleling chapters 2 and 3, after considering a framer's core message, we turn to frame resonance. Do the food industry's views about weight, individual choice, and personal responsibility resonate with the general public? As in previous substantive chapters, in our discussion of resonance, we do not engage resonance regarding the causes of fat; we save this for chapter 6.

The preponderance of evidence indicates that most people agree that individuals are responsible for their own bodies. For example, one survey of a convenience sample of over 400 students at a community college in the southwestern United States found that 93.3 percent of those surveyed agree that overweight individuals are responsible for their own bodies (Kwan 2009c). Qualitative interviews from this population also support the belief in personal responsibility for one's health; one interview respondent's words epitomized these sentiments, stating, "There has to be some amount of responsibility. . . . We have lost our sense of responsibility, in every aspect, including our health" (Kwan 2009c, 490).

Public opinion polls as well suggest that sentiments of personal responsibility (even if broadly conceptualized) remain strong in the public imagination. For example, the majority of Americans believe that economic mobility can be attributed to hard work and personal attributes rather than to external conditions such as bias and institutional discrimination (see Mizell 2011). Even interviews with general physicians show that they conceptualize obesity in terms of personal responsibility and believe that its management rests primarily with the responsibility of the patient (Epstein and Ogden 2005).

This belief in personal responsibility is also evident when surveys ask individuals to voice their opinions about fast food litigation. At about the time of the McDonald's obesity lawsuits, Gallup asked individuals if the fast food industry is responsible for obese people in the country. Sixty-six percent indicated that it was "not too or not at all responsible" (Saad 2003). Gallup also surveyed the public to see if they opposed or favored "holding the fast food industry legally responsible for the diet-related health problems of people who eat fast food on a regular basis." Eighty-nine percent of adults polled indicated that they opposed holding industry responsible, a figure that did not generally change based on the respondent's weight (Saad 2003). The implicit message is that if the food industry is not responsible, then individuals are.

Moreover, research indicates that individuals do not generally care for government regulation of the food industry, whether in the form of food-marketing restrictions or food taxes. A 2008 survey based on a nationally representative sample of over 1,000 respondents found only moderate support for policies that limit unhealthy food and beverage advertising and even less support for soft-drink taxes (Speers et al. 2009). Using a ten-point scale, in which 1 represents no support for a policy and 10 represents strong support, the survey found a mean of 6.23 for policies that limit unhealthy food and beverage advertising and a mean of 4.94 for taxes on soft drinks. (Of note, policies to encourage physical activity and regulate nutrition received high support at a mean of 8.01.) A 2010 survey conducted by National Public Radio with the help of Thomson Reuters also reported that 67 percent of more than 3,000 people surveyed either opposed or expressed no opinion on taxing carbonated, sugary soft drinks (Hensley 2010). Specifically, 51 percent either strongly opposed or opposed these taxes, and 16 percent had no opinion on the matter.

Studies have also found that even when individuals are convinced of the merits of state intervention, they nevertheless maintain that personal responsibility is the bottom line. For example, focus groups with parents show that, first of all, parents are generally not knowledgeable about the pervasiveness of food marketing and its negative impact on children (Rudd 2010). Second, when parents are shown examples of current food-marketing practices, many are convinced of some of the merits of government intervention. However, despite a willingness to support some government interventions, parents nevertheless emphasized that "parental responsibility trumps government involvement" (Rudd 2010, 9). Ultimately, these parents assigned to themselves the responsibility to control their children's exposure to marketing and to teach them about nutrition.

Survey data confirm this self-imposed gold standard of parental responsibility. One study found that while parents admitted that their children have too much access to junk food and are worried that their children will become obese, 78 percent of these parents believe the fault lies with them (Mintel International

Group Ltd. 2011). Additionally, in response to the question "Given our society today, who do you think should have the main responsibility for teaching children how to avoid becoming overweight?" Gallup reported that 89 percent of Americans selected parents, followed by schools (5 percent), the media (2 percent), health-care providers (1 percent), and food providers (1 percent; Lyons 2004).

In fact, many Americans do not really think of obesity as a pressing public *policy* issue. A Pew Research poll (Pew Research Center 2011) that asked Americans to identify what they considered the country's "top priority" found obesity at the very bottom of the list as the country's twenty-second priority, with only 19 percent of individuals polled believing that it should be a top policy priority. It lagged behind the economy, terrorism, health care, illegal immigration, and crime, among other things. This can be interpreted to mean that Americans are not passionate about government intervention on this issue. The message: obesity is not a state responsibility, but a personal one.

We saw in chapter 3 that the public generally rejects the CCF's position on health (opting instead for the CDC's overweight-equals-unhealthy rhetoric). However, the public appears to be on board when it comes to the CCF's views on freedom, individual choice, and personal responsibility. Political science professors J. Eric Oliver and Taeku Lee summarize the approach many Americans take regarding government intervention; in their words, "most Americans are not seriously concerned with obesity, express relatively low support for obesity-targeted policies, and still view obesity as resulting from individual failure" (2005, 923).

Others have theorized related sentiments. For example, Rogan Kersh and James Morone (2002) observe that all the factors needed to successfully move the issue of obesity from the personal to the political realm (in the form of, say, public regulations) are not in place. For instance, despite some parallels between obesity regulation and tobacco regulation, "users are not viewed as endangering society" (2002, 174), but Kersch and Morone admit "that day may come" (2002, 175), particularly as government purse strings tighten and the public increasingly associates obesity with financial drain.

With all four fat frames, we examine how resonance varies by social characteristics. As we saw in previous chapters, there are noteworthy variations in the adoption of the aesthetic and health frames by race/ethnicity, sex, socioeconomic status, and so forth. Similarly, we might expect differential resonance of the choice and responsibility frame. For example, some research suggests that views about personal responsibility (in terms of perspectives toward the welfare state) vary by political affiliation, such that conservatives tend to be more favorable to personal responsibility compared to their less-conservative counterparts (Brown 2009). With this in mind, we can predict that some ethnic subgroups may be less inclined to wholeheartedly endorse personality responsibility when it comes to certain health issues, given that party affiliation varies predictably along racial and ethnic lines. For example, there is some evidence that blacks are more likely to be Democrats than are nonminorities (Newport 2009b).

Moreover, views of personal responsibility might vary based on one's views of, and relation to, the social and physical environment. For example, scholars have documented how rates of obesity and diabetes are low among Mexican Pima Indians, compared to their American counterparts living in southern Arizona (Schulz et al. 2006). These differences have been attributed to lifestyle. As subsistence farmers eating indigenous foods and living physically active lives, Mexican Pimas are less likely to suffer from these conditions compared to their American counterparts, who have greater access to unhealthy foods. It is possible, then, that these two different environments lead to two very different perspectives on personal responsibility. Interviews conducted with members of the Ojibway community in Canada who have been diagnosed with diabetes shed light on this possibility. This research shows a wavering between two endpoints of a continuum (Garro 1995). On the one hand, interviewees see diabetes as a consequence of broader social changes that have led to a diet based on foods full of additives and chemicals. On the other hand, interviewees emphasize personal responsibility, placing blame on individuals for consuming the wrong foods, excessive drinking, or being overweight.

So while national poll and survey data generally point to how Americans overwhelmingly adopt the rhetoric of individual choice and personal responsibility, there may be subgroup variations. Indeed, there is a need for research that examines how perspectives on body size, individual choice, and personal responsibility vary by social group.

CONCLUSION

In our journey to map the contested field of fat, we have come across several players. The industries of the fashion-beauty complex remind us of the fleeting and precarious nature of our bodies and the constant specter of the frightful fat body. Meanwhile, public health officials at the CDC tell us that we can control our food intake and energy expenditure to maintain a "healthy" weight. Together these powerful cultural producers dominate everyday discourses about the fat body. Americans typically think of fat as unattractive and unhealthy—and as a problem that must be overcome.

In contrast, the food industry challenges some of these dominant understandings. The CCF maintains that much of what public health "activists" tell us is hype. The CCF claims that obesity does not do as much damage as we think (either to our health or to our economy), that one can be obese and fit, and that many variables (but particularly physical inactivity) contribute to weight gain.

The CCF contests the health frame with an arsenal of evidence, primarily media headlines and quotes from a range of peer-reviewed journals.

While this frame criticizes health researchers for working in concert with, and being financially motivated by incentives provided by, industries of the fashion-beauty complex, it makes no specific claims about body aesthetics. The CCF is silent about what is an attractive or unattractive body. It seems to tolerate all bodies, so long as they continue to consume. No doubt this is to defend industry interests and to ensure that consumers keep on purchasing foods, healthy or not. Regulation of industry is staunchly contested for this very reason: it is an invasion of our god-given freedoms.

On the whole, we observe public support for the choice and responsibility frame. Individuals believe they are responsible for their own actions, including their bodies and what they put inside them. Government generally should not interfere. There is also some consensus that obesity is not a pressing public policy issue, and there is not widespread and unequivocal support for food industry regulations.

The choice and responsibility frame thus rests on neoliberal discourses of choice, freedom, and responsibility. As Julie Guthman (2009) argues, central to neoliberalism is the rationale of consumer choice. Guthman contends that while both working and consuming hard were prominent features of Fordism in the neoliberal period, today only the consumption side is left to maintain American identity. Consumption becomes sacred, she asserts, and we buy and eat in many regards to become good capitalist subjects. In this neoliberal climate, there is also a "fetish of consumer choice" where "choice represents a sort of right" (Guthman and DePuis 2006). As Guthman and colleague Melanie DePuis (2006) observe, this is exactly the type of "rights discourse" evident in representations of the CCF. Moreover, the neoliberal subject believes that by "exercising our choice to eat we are exercising our freedoms" (Guthman and DePuis 2006, 442). Yet choices and freedoms are closely tied to responsibility. This is because neoliberal governmentality produces "contradictory impulses" (Guthman 2009, 193). We are expected to be enthusiastic consumers, but we are also expected to be self-controlled subjects (Guthman 2009, 193), ones that are, after all, responsible for our actions.

It remains to be seen as, say, Tea Party rhetoric gains momentum in some circles whether we will witness more aggressive defense of the choice and responsibility frame. The CCF's rhetoric was showcased in recent years on the national political stage when, in a 2010 interview with conservative radio host Laura Ingraham, former Republican vice presidential hopeful Sarah Palin remarked on Michelle Obama's antiobesity politics. In reference to Obama's Let's Move! campaign, she urged the First Lady to "get off our back and allow us as individuals to exercise our own God-given rights to make our own decisions" (Henderson

2010). A month later in a broadcast of *Sarah Palin's Alaska*, the former governor is seen preparing s'mores (a fireside staple made of marshmallows, graham crackers, and Hershey's chocolate bars). She takes another jab at the First Lady: these, she says, are "in honor of Michelle Obama, who said the other day we should not have dessert" (Horowitz and Henderson 2010). Yet despite recent partisan politics about repealing a new health-care bill, debates on how to deal with America's economic crisis, and controversies over legislation regarding homosexual service members, several GOP politicians quickly came to Mrs. Obama's defense (Horowitz and Henderson 2010). Outcry over obesity can apparently bring together even the staunchest Republicans and Democrats.

Increased and perhaps increasingly defensive CCF rhetoric may become evident as we witness a surge in counterhegemonic food movements such as veganism, vegetarianism, and organic food consumption, and as noted authors such as Michael Pollan (2009) criticize "food-like substances" and call for a return to a simpler, more natural, and plant-based diet. Jamie Oliver's Emmy Award–winning ABC show, *Food Revolution*, which follows the English chef's attempt to transform the way Americans think about food, may have also added fuel to the fire. And Eric Schlosser's best-selling condemnation of the fast food industry, *Fast Food Nation* (2001), has seen a revival in recent years through a film adaptation. Regardless of how these battles play out, it is certain that they will continue and that the meaning of the fat body will remain contested, as we continue to see in the next chapter on the social justice frame.

5 · FAT AND FAIR TREATMENT

IN 2001, JENNIFER PORTNICK, a 240-pound aerobics instructor who reportedly worked out six times a week and taught back-to-back exercise classes, was denied a franchise by the exercise chain Jazzercise. A company representative maintained, "Jazzercise sells fitness. . . . Consequently, a Jazzercise applicant must have a higher muscle-to-fat ratio and look leaner than the public. People must believe Jazzercise will help them improve, not just maintain their level of fitness. Instructors must set the example and be the role models for Jazzercise enthusiasts" (Fernandez 2002). Ms. Portnick, who happens to live in one of only a handful of U.S. jurisdictions in which height and weight are protected legal categories, turned to the San Francisco Human Rights Commission. She filed a complaint and won.

Ms. Portnick's story is not unique, although her outcome is.[1] There are countless anecdotes of differential treatment allegedly based on body size. In 2009, when Ronald Kratz II reported for his shift on his materials handling job, he was terminated allegedly for being too heavy to perform the work (Sixel 2011). In 2010, film director Kevin Smith was asked to vacate his seat on a Southwest Airlines flight because of his size (Lee 2010). And in 2008, the Japanese government instituted a national policy that measured workers' waistlines.[2] Workers who exceeded the recommended government limit were required to receive "dieting guidance if after three months they do not lose weight" (Onishi 2008).

The common thread of these stories, size discrimination—whether labeled "weightism," "sizism," or "fatism"—is at the heart of the social justice frame we examine in this chapter. As we saw in chapters 2 and 3, this frame is reactionary and contests common beliefs that the fat body is unattractive and unhealthy.

THE NATIONAL ASSOCIATION TO ADVANCE FAT ACCEPTANCE

This chapter focuses on the National Association to Advance Fat Acceptance (NAAFA). While there are many different fat acceptance groups (such as the Fat

Rights Coalition, the Council on Size and Weight Discrimination, and the Association for Size Diversity and Health), we focus on NAAFA because it is vocal and considered "the go-to source" on fat acceptance for the media (NAAFA 2011i). As we mentioned in chapter 1, NAAFA was founded in 1969 as a nonprofit, volunteer-run civil rights organization dedicated to "protecting the rights and improving the quality of life for fat people" (NAAFA 2011a). It currently has about 11,000 members, and its board of advisors includes "scientific, medical and legal leaders from all over the country" (NAAFA 2011b).

The National Association to Advance Fat Acceptance's website provides links to twelve official policies on a range of issues: adoption, activism, dieting, education, employment, fat admirers, feederism, obesity research, physical fitness, size-related legislation, weight-loss drugs, and weight-loss surgery (2011k). Each policy states NAAFA's official position on a given issue, what the group advocates, and what it resolves to do. In addition to posting these official policies, NAAFA also disseminates a monthly newsletter and offers size-diversity tool kits for educators and employers.

In this chapter, through a frame analysis of these public documents as well as supporting documents from influential figures associated with the group, we present the group's social justice frame. As in other frame-specific chapters in *Framing Fat*, we also turn to other framers' positions on social justice and examine the resonance of the social justice frame.

THE CENTRAL CLAIM: FAT IS NOT A SOCIAL PROBLEM, BUT SIZE DISCRIMINATION IS

The central claim of any frame is the primary assertion that singularly captures the frame's version of reality, often creating a social problem that needs to be addressed. However, unlike the aesthetic and health frames, NAAFA claims that the fat body, in and of itself, poses little threat. Instead, the social problem arises in how individuals respond to it. The rolling banner at NAAFA's home page indicates that when it comes to fat, the main issue is discrimination. It reads, "Discrimination is wrong. . . . We come in all sizes. . . . Understand it. Support it. Accept it" (NAAFA 2011j). Claiming that fat prejudice is "one of the last publicly accepted discriminatory practices" (2011a), NAAFA's vision is "a society in which people of every size are accepted with dignity and equality in all aspects of life" (2011a).

And according to NAAFA, size discrimination is prevalent in many arenas of social life. The group points out that in education, for example, teachers hold negative stereotypes of overweight students and perceive them as untidy, emotional, and less likely to succeed. Teachers also have lower expectations for fat students compared to thin students. College administrators, too, exhibit fat bias,

admitting fewer obese applicants than their thinner counterparts, despite comparable academic achievements. As well, the group underscores that overweight
students are teased beginning as early as preschool and continuing through their
college years (2011d).

This size discrimination does not abate when fat individuals enter the workforce. The National Association to Advance Fat Acceptance maintains that "fat
yet equally qualified applicants" (2011m) are perceived negatively by employers,
and fat employees are generally rated more negatively than thin employees. Fat
workers are frequently stereotyped as undisciplined, slovenly, and unambitious.
In NAAFA's words, despite being qualified and highly productive, fat workers
are regularly "underpaid, limited in career advancement, denied benefits and terminated due to their size" (2011m).

The health-care arena is another key site of size discrimination, NAAFA
alleges. Like teachers and employers, doctors also hold negative perceptions of
fat individuals. For example, they tend to respond negatively to obesity, often
ranking it just behind other stigmatized conditions such as drug addiction, alco-
holism, and mental illness (NAAFA 2011g). The group cites a survey of nurses
showing that 31 percent said they would prefer not to care for obese patients and
that 24 percent admitted that obese patients repulsed them (2011g).

CAUSAL ROOTS: BEYOND PERSONAL MORAL FAILURE

All frames include assumptions or statements about the causes of the social issue
at hand. As we saw in chapters 2 and 3, the aesthetic and health frames assume
that the overweight body is the result of personal shortcomings. In contrast,
NAAFA's social justice frame begins with the assumption that fat people are
not blameworthy. According to the group, size discrimination—the real problem at hand—occurs precisely because of assumptions of blameworthiness. In
NAAFA's words, "Our thin-obsessed society firmly believes that fat people are
at fault for their size and it is politically correct to stigmatize and ridicule them"
(2011a). The National Association to Advance Fat Acceptance points out that
cultural messages tend to equate obesity with personal failure (2011h). Specifically, Western culture "places blame on the victim [and] ignores contributing
environmental factors" (NAAFA 2011h).

At the same time, and illustrating how frames can exhibit internal contradictions, former NAAFA board member Marilyn Wann, the author of *Fat!So?
Because You Don't Have to Apologize for Your Size!* (1998), a veritable manifesto of
the size acceptance movement, maintains that weight is predominantly inherited
and only minimally influenced by environmental variables. Wann argues that
individuals can change their activity levels and food consumption patterns yet
continuously return to a set weight range. As she puts it, weight is "influenced

largely by inherited predisposition and only marginally by environmental factors like eating and exercise patterns" (Wann 2009, ix). Wann thus refutes the idea that human body weight is mutable. Instead, she claims that, despite consumption, exercise, and dieting habits, an individual's metabolism tends to adjust such that weight will continuously gravitate toward a set weight range. Other NAAFA-prominent players have referred to this as one's "set point" (see Gaesser 2002). This downplaying of environmental factors illustrates how key players of a frame make divergent claims; in this case, however, these claims all result in the same outcome: the shifting of blame away from fat people.

Some NAAFA allies have cautioned against devoting too much energy to finding a "cause" of fat. This comes at a time when there appears to be an obsession among researchers to locate obesity culprits (with the underlying assumption that if one can identify *the* cause, one can identify *the* solution). These proposed "causes" range from breastfeeding (Hughes 2011) to Caesarian sections (Norton 2011) to a "fat gene" (see LeBesco 2009). However, in her chapter in *The Fat Studies Reader*, edited by NAAFA board members Esther Rothblum and Sondra Solovay, Kathleen LeBesco argues that it remains "unclear what causes people to be fat . . . and debates continue to be waged about whether the quest for a cause is even a desirable endeavor" (2009, 65). While scholars such as LeBesco acknowledge that one should not deny the role of biology, she warns that scientific knowledge does not reveal all there is to know about how body size is socialized and politicized (70). Identifying genetic causes not only implies that fat is a problem of some sort (whether aesthetic, social, or medical), a key point of contest for the social justice frame, but it also raises, as LeBesco spells out, the "specter of consumer eugenics" (65). According to LeBesco, focusing on genetic causes means locating the so-called fat problem within the body itself, thereby opening up the possibility that the solution lies *in* the body through such mechanisms as abortion. She argues that such an approach overlooks the real issue at hand, which is body prejudice (71).

In some ways NAAFA's perspective falls in line with the perspective of the food industry group the Center for Consumer Freedom (CCF). Like NAAFA, the CCF emphasizes many contributing factors to body size, although it downplays the role of food consumption and does not extensively engage genetic predisposition. Recall that, according to the CCF, many factors influence the Centers for Disease Control and Prevention's (CDC's) Energy Balance Equation (CDC 2011a), including modern technologies, employment trends, sleeping patterns, and so on. But there is a major difference between NAAFA and the CCF when it comes to causal roots. Despite acknowledging multiple contributing factors to weight, the CCF ultimately emphasizes personal responsibility. Thus, similar to the aesthetic and health frames, the CCF's choice and responsibility frame indicts individuals for their so-labeled failings. In contrast, NAAFA's approach to causation encourages people attempting to manipulate their body size to refuse to feel guilty or blame themselves when their weight-loss attempts fail (NAAFA 2011k, "Dieting"). We revisit this important issue of causal attribution in chapter 6.

CONSEQUENCES: COMPROMISING PSYCHOLOGICAL, SOCIAL, AND PHYSICAL WELL-BEING

Every frame purports not only a state of affairs and its causes but also implies a set of consequences. In the case of size discrimination, there are many negative consequences for fat people. As NAAFA exclaims, "Size Discrimination Consequences are Real!" (2011h). These consequences include effects on psychological well-being, social mobility, and physical health. For example, with regard to psychological well-being, citing Rebecca Puhl, Tatiana Andreyeva, and Kelly Brownell (2008),[3] NAAFA points out that stigma, negative treatment, and discrimination can create "vulnerability to depression, low self-esteem, poor body image, and suicidal thoughts" and can increase the "likelihood of unhealthy eating patterns and avoidance of physical activity" (2011d).

In terms of social mobility, NAAFA maintains that discrimination potentially affects educational attainment. For example, by the age of sixteen, girls who are obese have fewer years of education than nonobese girls (NAAFA 2011d). In workplaces, NAAFA underscores, overweight people may not even be hired. And when they are, not only do they earn 1–6 percent less than nonoverweight people in comparable positions, but they may also face suspension or dismissal because of their weight despite solid on-the-job performance (NAAFA 2011m). In many social arenas, NAAFA says that fat people are teased, stigmatized, and subjected to derogatory comments by those around them (2011m). All of these negative consequences affect quality of life.

The National Association to Advance Fat Acceptance further alleges that fat discrimination in the health-care system can lead to negative physical health outcomes. The group focuses on three outcomes of size discrimination in health care (NAAFA 2011g). First, because of sizism, fat people avoid proper health care: they are reluctant to seek medical care, they may cancel medical appointments, or they may delay preventive care for fear of stigma (and, it is implied, mistreatment by medical professionals). Second, size discrimination means that doctors spend less time with fat patients and recommend less intervention and fewer preventative health screenings such as cancer screenings. Finally, size discrimination means that appropriate-sized medical equipment (such as magnetic resonance imaging [MRI] machines, blood-pressure cuffs, and stretchers) may not be readily available to fat patients. For fat people, these consequences translate into an unwelcoming environment within a health-care system that was designed to save lives and to promote the well-being of *all* individuals.

In sum, NAAFA contends that size discrimination has serious consequences for psychological, social, and physical well-being. Of note, these claims receive support from a large body of empirical research. For example, research shows that the experience of perceived stigma correlates with negative health consequences such as changes in diastolic blood pressure (Guyll, Matthews, and Bromberger 2001; Schafer and Ferraro 2011). Weight stigmatization has also been found to correlate with poor mental health adjustment, including depression, body image disturbance, and negative self-esteem (Friedman et al. 2005). Moreover, poll data finds that obese people report higher levels of stress, worry, anger, and sadness than "normal weight" individuals (Mendes 2010). Additionally, obese individuals are less likely to report experiencing enjoyment or happiness and are more often diagnosed with depression compared to those with "normal weight" (Mendes 2010). One meta-analysis found a correlation, albeit moderate, between weight and self-esteem (Miller and Downey 1999), and survey-based research broadly has confirmed that physical attractiveness affects psychological well-being (Umberson and Hughes 1987). Researchers in this area, however, are quick to point out that correlation is not tantamount to causation and that causal direction is at times unclear. They maintain that the literature does not show that "obesity" results from poor mental health, and they emphasize that heavyweight people do not suffer unduly from mental disorders (Crandall, Nierman, and Hebl 2009).

Some of these psychosocial outcomes vary by social characteristics. For example, researchers have found that higher Body Mass Indexes (BMIs) predict lower psychological well-being only among women and not men (Bookwala and Boyar 2008) and that depressive symptoms are more evident in obese adolescent females compared to "normal weight females" but not obese adolescent males (Merten, Wickrama, and Williams 2008; see also Vaughan and Halpern 2010). However, some studies report the converse for adolescents—that is, no association between adolescent girls' weight and depressive symptoms—and an association between boys' weights and these symptoms (Frisco, Houle, and Martin 2009). In chapter 2, we have already seen how African American communities may buffer young black girls from negative body image. However, research has not uncovered any significant differences between obese white and African American adolescents in psychosocial outcomes (Merten, Wickrama, and Williams 2008).

PRINCIPLES: APPEALS TO HUMAN RIGHTS

Every frame rests on a set of underlying moral values that facilitates its appeal to the general public. The social justice frame appeals to our desire to protect human rights—an appeal that is integral to NAAFA's collective identity as a "civil rights organization dedicated to protecting [fat people's] rights" (2011a).[4] The group demands fair and equal treatment in all aspects of fat people's lives and promotes the rights of fat people in an effort to improve their quality of life. As it promises on its website, NAAFA's mission will "improve the world—not just for fat people, but for everyone" (2011a). In some respects, the group fulfills a function similar to that of the National Organization for Women (NOW) in the women's rights movement, as well as that of the National Association for the Advancement of Colored People (NAACP) in the African American civil rights movement, serving as a rallying point for movement players.

As part of the larger fat acceptance social movement, NAAFA's tactics and approaches resemble the strategies used by other civil rights groups to achieve equality. For example, similar to liberal feminists who help to broaden the definition of womanhood beyond the roles of stay-at-home wife and mother (see Friedan 1963), through education and the promotion of new media images NAAFA attempts to debunk stereotypes and promote a positive understanding of fat people. Like other social movement crusaders, NAAFA also has a broad repertoire of tactics under its belt; specifically, it "urges fat people and their allies to secure fat people's rights through education and constitutionally protected activities such as letter-writing campaigns, speeches, teach-ins, public rallies, demonstrations, protests, picket lines, and boycotts" (2011k, "Activism").

Some African American groups, along with gay, lesbian, bisexual, transgender, and queer (GLBTQ) communities, have reclaimed terms that once stigmatized their groups (see Chauncey 1994; Kennedy 2002). For example, some homosexuals use "fairy," "queen," and "faggot" to reference members of their own group (Chauncey 1994). As Patricia Hill Collins observes, depending on whether one is referring to "bitch" or "Bitch," the word can represent either subjugation or empowerment, respectively (2004, 123). In similar fashion, NAAFA attempts to reclaim the term "fat" and remove its negative connotation. Marilyn Wann maintains in her popular book that bullies have used the term "fat" to hurt people of size. She writes, "That's why it's time to take this powerful, awe-inspiring word back from the bullies! It's time to put *fat* into the hands of people who will use its power for good, not evil! It's time my fat brothers and sisters, for us to embrace the F-word!!!" (Wann 1998, 18).

Wann urges the avoidance of euphemisms such as "heavy," "large," "voluptuous," "zaftig," and "big-boned," arguing that individuals only need these euphemisms if they find the truth distasteful (1998, 20). For her, fat is not a four-letter word. Indeed, "fat is not a four-letter word" is a catchphrase that is often used by size acceptance activists and fat bloggers. It is also the title of Roy Schroeder's (1992) book, which both NAAFA and the Council on Size and Weight Discrimination, an ally group, tout as recommended reading. The National Association to Advance Fat Acceptance's attempt to reclaim the term "fat" means approaching "fat" just like any other adjective. As Wann writes, "it is just as polite to say *fat* as it is to say *young* or *tall* or *human*" (1998, 20).

Borrowing from the language of other social movements, NAAFA also points out that its mission of fair and equal treatment for people requires the help of "thin allies" who will step up and "publicly object to the mistreatment of fat people" (2011k, "Activism"). The group's appeal to human rights is further apparent in its call for size-related legislation, which doubles up as one of the group's solutions to fat discrimination.

PROPOSED SOLUTIONS: CHANGING THE WAY AMERICA THINKS ABOUT FAT

As we saw in chapters 2 and 3, current cultural discourses stigmatize fat bodies as ugly and unhealthy.[5] Changing these understandings about the unattractiveness and unhealthiness of fat is central to NAAFA's proposed solutions. To combat discrimination, NAAFA proposes that individuals reject dieting and embrace a Health at Every Size (HAES) outlook. As part of this mission, NAAFA works to educate people about salient issues, argues in favor of legislation that would protect height and weight, and calls for regulation of the diet industry.

Stop Dieting and Be Flabulous!

Unlike the health frame and the public health officials that NAAFA hopes to turn into HAES allies, NAAFA sings little praise for the fashion-beauty complex. The aesthetic frame's narrow definition of beauty creates a culture that erases the fat body and stigmatizes it as undesirable. Moreover, it promotes weight loss for fat people, a position that NAAFA contends is oppressive.

The National Association to Advance Fat Acceptance discourages weight-loss practices because "dieting for the sole purpose of losing weight rarely achieves permanent weight loss and can result in negative health consequences" (2011k, "Dieting"). As we saw earlier, NAAFA's social justice frame works with the assumptions of set point theory and maintains that individuals will gravitate toward a set weight range despite behavioral changes. The National Association to Advance Fat Acceptance also warns that "dangerous or ineffective diets" saturate the market (2011k, "Dieting"). Simply stated, diets fail. As Wann, in tongue-in-cheek manner, writes in *Fat!So?* "Percentage of dieters who regain the weight within three years: 90. Percentage of Americans who believe in miracles: 70" (1998, 114).

Similarly, NAAFA discourages the use of drugs for the sole purpose of weight loss (2011k, "Weight-Loss Drugs") and does not endorse weight-loss surgery, warning of inconclusive evidence for the results of these interventions and emphasizing the deaths and severe complications associated with them (2011k,

"Weight-Loss Drugs"). Instead, the group resolves to "promote alternatives to weight-loss diets in a manner which is sensitive to the emotional and financial investment which many fat people have made in repeated weight-loss attempts" (2011k, "Dieting"). This message is consistent with its overall promotion of body and size acceptance.

In framing language, the diet industry is the key enemy of the social justice frame. This is plainly evident in Wann's (1998) book when she includes *Fat!So?* trading cards. These cards depict "heroes" such as Ganesha (a Hindu deity), Lillian Russell (a plus-sized American actress and singer), and Amalie Materna (an Austrian soprano and woman of size), along with "villains" such as William Banting (a nineteenth-century diet guru), Susanna Cocroft (a World War I era diet guru), and C. Everett Koop (a former U.S. surgeon general, previously mentioned in chapter 1).

While NAAFA's use of visual images in promoting the social justice frame is limited (with the exception of a few smiling faces of people of size on its website), Wann's book includes many colorful depictions of fat and fat people. The cover of *Fat!So?* (see figure 5.1) depicts a large scantily clad woman with her skirt whimsically flipped up. The image is similar to the iconic picture taken of Marilyn Monroe as she stood over a New York City subway grate. However, while Monroe flirtatiously attempts to hold her skirt down, the woman on Wann's cover has her arms to the side and open as if to gesture, So what? This and other similar visual depictions of fat people in Wann's book help to recreate a new conception of fat people (and particularly of fat women) as powerful, beautiful, and strong. Fat people should, in Wann's and NAAFA's view, feel comfortable in their own skins and be proud of their bodies. The woman on the cover of Wann's book symbolizes (and, in framing language, is a metaphor for) the social justice frame. Fat is not ugly and shameful: it is bold and beautiful.

This type of body acceptance is evident in another powerful visual in Wann's book. Her Dial-A-Clue is a make-at-home game spinner with twelve segments representing various attitudes toward the body and self (see figure 5.2). This spinner, with a fat arm that serves as a pointer, will help you, the reader, "clue yourself in" (1998, 173). Segments touch on NAAFA's central issue of discrimination (e.g., "You can't cure discrimination with a diet!"), attack the aesthetic frame (e.g., "Get over it! Wear something sleeveless!"), and promote self-acceptance and fat pride (e.g., "You look flabulous!" "Your thighs are not the enemy!" and "Be one of the few, the proud . . . the fat!"). As we saw in chapter 2, "flabulous" is a key catchphrase throughout Wann's book, and it is a direct challenge to conventional beauty ideals that dictate that fat is physically unattractive.

The National Association to Advance Fat Acceptance's take on the weight-loss industry is another point of convergence with the CCF, which also condemns the weight-loss industry and its pharmaceutical allies. For example,

FIGURE 5.1. *Fat!So?*
The cover art of Marilyn Wann's (1998) *Fat!So?* creates a new conception of fat people (and particularly of fat women) as powerful, beautiful, and strong. (Credit: Logo by Ronald Sol.)

NAAFA asserts that its message of size diversity "is often overshadowed by a $49 billion-a-year diet industry that has a vested economic interest in perpetuating discrimination against fat people" (2011a). Similarly, NAAFA indicts "obesity researchers and drug manufacturers who profit from inadequately tested weight-loss drugs" (2011k, "Weight-Loss Drugs"). Thus both NAAFA and the CCF, albeit one more candidly than the other, criticize the weight-loss industry and

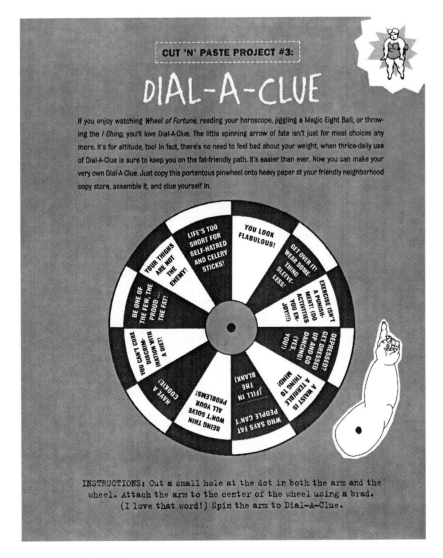

FIGURE 5.2. Dial-A-Clue
This Dial-A-Clue spinner in Marilyn Wann's (1998) *Fat!So?* contests the central claims of
the aesthetic frame and promotes self-acceptance and fat pride. (Credit: Heather Urban.)

the obesity researchers whose ties to the weight-loss industry potentially compromise their ability to conduct sound, ethical research.

Yet the motivations behind each group's condemnation diverge. The National
Association to Advance Fat Acceptance is primarily concerned about the social
and cultural implications of the messages disseminated by the weight-loss industry, while the CCF is primarily concerned about economic viability. The former

condemns the diet industry for creating a culture of fat hatred and normative dieting; the latter condemns the diet industry for creating a culture of normative dieting that may adversely affect food sales, particularly sales of stigmatized foods that the public associates with weight gain. Furthermore, whereas NAAFA criticizes narrow cultural depictions of the beauty ideal and celebrates all body sizes, the CCF is rather silent about which bodies are aesthetically desirable. As a group working primarily on behalf of the food industry, the CCF tolerates all bodies. It accepts fat and thin bodies alike, so long as they eat.

In sum, NAAFA emphasizes size acceptance and self-acceptance. It is not coincidental that these two phrases come hand in hand throughout NAAFA documents. "Size acceptance" and "self-acceptance" are—along with terms such as "weight discrimination," "size discrimination," "fat discrimination," "self-empowerment," "diversity," and "nondieting alternatives"—key catchphrases of the social justice frame.

Embrace HAES

In our discussion of competing views of health, we saw how NAAFA challenges several hegemonic medical understandings associated with the overweight body by promoting a HAES perspective. These HAES principles are fundamental to the fat acceptance movement, and they stress that individuals of all sizes have the potential to be healthy. Health at Every Size principles also include a holistic approach to health, in NAAFA's words, "accepting and respecting the diversity of body shapes and sizes [and] recognizing that health and well-being are multidimensional and that they include physical, social, spiritual, occupational, emotional, and intellectual aspects" (2011f).

An example of a HAES approach is found in Linda Bacon's (2008) book, *Health at Every Size: The Surprising Truth about Your Weight*. Bacon, whose book appears on NAAFA's recommended reading list (2011l), was the keynote speaker at NAAFA's 2009 convention and received their "Outstanding Researcher" award. Consistent with other HAES advocates, Bacon encourages intuitive eating. Intuitive eaters learn to shuck "food rules" about fat and calories and the like, and to follow their bodies' self-nourishing cues. All this is possible only by letting go of weight stigma and the self-judgment that accompanies it. Bacon reiterates the HAES movement's commitment to changing public health policy and the wider culture to support the message of body-acceptance. The program, evaluated through a federally financed, randomized controlled trial, showed that HAES participants fared better on health, physical activity, and self-esteem measures than dieters (Bacon et al. 2005).

The National Association to Advance Fat Acceptance's use of the term "fat" instead of "overweight" or "obese" is in and of itself a reflection of its approach to body diversity; it is a way of reclaiming the term, as well as a denunciation of the health frame's stigmatizing terminology. "Overweight" and "obese" are medical terms that condemn fat people, declaring them deviant and outside a narrow "normal" medical standard. As Rothblum and Solovay write, "'Overweight' is inherently anti-fat. It implies an extreme goal: instead of a bell curve of distribution of human weights, it calls for a lone, towering, unlikely bar group with everyone occupying the same (thin) weights. If a word like 'overweight' is acceptable and even preferable, then weight prejudice becomes accepted and preferred" (2009, xii). In a similar vein, Wann, using her signature sardonic rhetoric, pointedly asks, "Over *whose* weight?" (1998, 19). Through such commentary, NAAFA and its allies question the constructed and arbitrary nature of "normal" weight and its health implications.

In light of its emphasis on health for people of all sizes, NAAFA encourages fat people to participate in physical activities at their own pace and on their own agendas. These activities should be enjoyable, and fat people should be "motivated [to participate in them] by inner goals and interests" (NAAFA 2011k, "Physical Fitness") and not by external coercion from, say, doctors prescribing weight loss. Importantly, fat people should be able to achieve physical fitness and participate in physical activities in an environment free from ridicule and derogatory comments (NAAFA 2011k, "Physical Fitness"). A HAES approach also means all-around wellness, particularly through the promotion of eating in a manner that "balances individual nutritional needs, hunger, satiety, appetite, and pleasure" and "individually appropriate, enjoyable, life-enhancing physical activity" (NAAFA 2011f).

So unlike the health frame's focus on *physical* health, NAAFA's social justice frame implies a broader understanding. Health is about overall well-being and happiness, including physical, psychological, and emotional health. And, according to NAAFA, fat people should achieve this well-being through balance, pleasurable food consumption, and enjoyable physical activity, not through starvation or dieting; they should also be able to participate in this physical activity in a safe environment without fear of stigma and scrutiny. In this way health is an ongoing and dynamic process, not merely a static outcome. As Deb Burgard says in Rothblum and Solovay's *The Fat Studies Reader*, from a HAES perspective, health is a "process of daily life rather than the outcome of weight" (Burgard 2009, 44).

Education

Related to accomplishing these goals is NAAFA's call for education. The National Association to Advance Fat Acceptance's website features education links through which the group aims to educate teachers, health-care providers, media representatives, and others. For example, they have a document for therapists and counselors, a Size Diversity Toolkit for employers, and the Everybody in Schools HAES Toolkit for educators. As we observed earlier, NAAFA educates in large part by debunking myths about fat people that are created by competing framers (see also NAAFA 2011e). The group provides numerous size and weight discrimination resources to fulfill this specific function, including Linda Bacon's (2008) *Health at Every Size: The Surprising Truth about Your Weight*, Paul Campos's (2004) *The Obesity Myth: Why America's Obsession with Weight Is Hazardous to Your Health*, and J. Eric Oliver's (2006) *Fat Politics: The Real Story behind America's Obesity Epidemic*.

As part of its education campaign, and blatantly challenging the fashion-beauty complex's narrow depictions of what is beautiful and sexy, NAAFA advocates that all media channels, from movies to print media, "support the portrayal of fat men and women as romantic interests" (2011k, "Fat Admirers"). The group resolves to teach the public that it is "normal to be attracted to a fat partner" and to "challenge media's negative stereotypes towards fat people" (NAAFA 2011k, "Fat Admirers"). In NAAFA's view, diverse media images of various body types and positive media depictions of fat people will help to combat the stereotypes that create a culture of fat stigma and hatred.

Protecting Height and Weight as Legal Categories

Alongside education efforts, NAAFA hopes to instill cultural change through legislation, in particular, legislation that makes "height and weight protected legal categories" another key catchphrase of the frame. Specifically, the group "demands the inclusion of 'height and weight' as a protected category in existing civil rights statutes and the enactment of additional laws as necessary to ensure protection against size discrimination in employment, education, housing, and public accommodations" (NAAFA 2011k, "Size-Related Legislation"). Its demand applies to local, state, and federal laws and civil rights statutes. For example, in its official policy document "Adoption and Child Custody Discrimination" (2011k, "Adoption"), NAAFA contends that a potential parent's ability to love and care for a child should be the only selection criteria for adoption and that weight should be prohibited as a criterion for removing a child from a home in child-custody cases. As it does in its general request to include height and weight in federal and state legislation, NAAFA asks that these two traits be added to laws on adoption rights, child welfare, and custody laws. The group's request for equal protection for fat people is uncompromising. The word "demand" repeatedly surfaces throughout its documents.

Diet Industry Regulation

The National Association to Advance Fat Acceptance also urges local, state, and federal legislators to enact laws to protect consumers against dangerous or ineffective diets and misleading diet advertising (2011k, "Dieting"). This is in line with its broader plea that regulatory agencies monitor and control the diet industry. Moreover, because of the negative physical and mental health ramifications of dieting and dieting products, NAAFA proposes that commercials for weight-loss diets and diet products be banned from radio and television. The group also recommends that these products be required to display health-warning labels (similar to those found on cigarettes) about their potentially harmful side effects (NAAFA 2011k, "Dieting").

Consistent with its criticisms of the diet industry, NAAFA calls for the regulation of the industry's research and research findings. For example, it proposes that the diet industry study the "'success' rates" of their products and that governmental health agencies such as the CDC track morbidity and mortality caused by dieting (NAAFA 2011k, "Dieting"). The National Association to Advance Fat Acceptance insists that "the primary goal of obesity research should be to improve the health and well being of fat people rather than weight loss" (2011k, "Obesity Research").

Finally, NAAFA advocates transparency regarding the financial ties between, on the one hand, obesity researchers and diet drug advocates and, on the other hand, diet drug manufacturers (2011k, "Weight-Loss Drugs"). As a denunciation of researchers who attempt to find efficient ways to achieve weight loss, NAAFA asserts that research should focus on "non-dieting alternatives to improving the health and well-being of fat people" (2011k, "Obesity Research").

AN ILLUSTRATIVE CASE: A LETTER TO MICHELLE OBAMA

In making its claims, unlike the CDC or the CCF, NAAFA generally does not cite specific references. In fact, to support nearly all of it its allegations of widespread discrimination in three social arenas (education, the workplace, and health care), NAAFA turns to a single citation: an article by Puhl, Andreyeva, and Brownell (2008), faculty members at Yale University's Rudd Center for Food Policy and Obesity. While the group provides only one citation for its claims about discrimination, it does, however, provide lengthy lists of references, including websites, books, and articles under its "Discrimination Resources" and "Reading List" (NAAFA 2011c) links. The "Recent News Items" feed on the group's homepage also provides information about the latest research on body size and health, particularly from a HAES perspective.

It appears that, in contrast to the CDC and CCF, NAAFA is not concerned with linking every claim with specific empirical evidence (at least on its online portal). In this way, NAAFA's message seems diffuse, targeting a broad audience and promoting widespread cultural and *ideological* change. This is by no means to assert that NAAFA is not interested in substantiating its claims with evidence; in fact, it is. But the group tends to rely on its professional allies, such as HAES researchers and fat acceptance scholars, to engage extensively with specific research evidence.

One noteworthy exception is a letter that was addressed to First Lady Michelle Obama and published in the *NAAFA Newsletter* (NAAFA 2010, 1). As we saw in chapter 3, Mrs. Obama is working with the Let's Move! campaign to combat the "childhood obesity epidemic." The National Association to Advance Fat Acceptance's letter to Mrs. Obama is a good example of how the social justice frame directly challenges dominant understandings of fat promoted by advocates of the health frame.[6] In the letter, "NAAFA encourages the First Lady to consider all the research before supporting any program that may do more harm than good" (NAAFA 2010, 1), including evidence that when important figures place importance on weight control, this can contribute to body dissatisfaction, low self-esteem, and weight bias among children and adolescents. The letter cites research to support the claim that a weight-loss approach may be detrimental to physical and mental health, and it urges the First Lady to partner with NAAFA to abandon programs that "create a pervasive bias against fat children" (NAAFA 2010, 1). The numerous citations provided in the letter may be evidence that, when in *direct* conversation with a competing frame, NAAFA recognizes that it must draw from its arsenal the most potent ammunition available in framing wars: specific research evidence.

COMPETING VOICES: BEAUTY ELITES AND HEALTH DISPARITIES

In previous chapters, when we engaged a core issue we also looked at how other key cultural producers approached that issue. Here, we turn to how the industries of the fashion-beauty complex, public health officials, and the food industry approach issues of social justice. As we now discuss, these cultural producers have different takes on social justice, and none explicitly engages the issue of fat discrimination. As such, NAAFA's frame is the primary "injustice frame"—a frame that draws attention to victims and their plight (see Benford and Snow 2000).

Discrimination is actually inherent to the aesthetic frame. This is because hegemonic beauty ideals reward those who have essentially won the genetic lottery. Even Nancy Etcoff, who forwards an evolutionary perspective on beauty, admits that models who exemplify hegemonic beauty ideals are "genetic freaks" (1999, 12). The aesthetic frame is about discerning, discriminating, and separating the beautiful from the ugly. Elitism and exclusion are at the heart of the fashion-beauty complex, although in recent years—and rather paradoxically— some cosmetics companies have marketed their products in a way that exposes this elitism. Examples include Dove's "Campaign for Real Beauty" (Unilever

2012) and the Body Shop's "Love Your Body" advertisement featuring a plus-sized plastic Barbie with the tag line "There are 3 billion women who don't look like supermodels and only 8 who do" (see Elliott 1997). Yet critics maintain that these advertisements still fail in their attempts to challenge the notion that beauty is "an essential part of a woman's identity, personhood, and social success and [legitimize] the notion that every woman should feel beautiful" (Johnston and Taylor 2008, 954). These paradoxical advertisements nevertheless underscore the body discrimination pervasive throughout the fashion-beauty complex.

In chapter 3, we pointed out that the CDC acknowledges the social stigma that comes with being overweight or obese but that this acknowledgment is mainly an afterthought. Instead, the CDC expresses concern with the unequal prevalence rates of these medical conditions. Americans claim to value equality and to take pride in the rhetoric of race, gender, and class equality. Yet the so-called obesity epidemic threatens equality because rates of overweight and obesity are distributed unequally in the population. For example, according to the CDC, non-Hispanic blacks, Mexican Americans, and all Hispanics have higher rates of obesity compared to non-Hispanic whites (2012a). This inequality, however, extends beyond racial and ethnic lines, and the CDC also voices concern that lower-income individuals are more likely to be obese than their higher-income counterparts (CDC 2012a). Highlighting these inequalities is a strategy the CDC uses to create widespread appeal for the health frame.

In contrast, the choice and responsibility frame is silent about social justice. The food industry does not engage this issue. Instead, its main focus is promoting an environment in which individuals have the right to consume whatever they choose. Once again, all bodies are tolerated, so long as they eat and take responsibility for it.

RESONANCE

But how do individuals think about the fat body and social justice, including issues such as size-based stigma and discrimination?

First, research evidence supporting NAAFA's claims of endemic size discrimination is in and of itself indirect evidence of the public's view of size discrimination. Beyond NAAFA's assertions lie a vast body of research empirically verifying the prevalence of fat stigma and discrimination. However, as we explore next, fat stigma and discrimination touch certain segments of the population more so than others. Moreover, sizist or antifat attitudes, while widespread in the population, are correlated with certain social characteristics.

Second, we can gauge how the public views fat and social justice by examining their views on policies related to size discrimination. Such examination reveals limited public openness to combating size-based discrimination through various legal initiatives.[7]

Size Discrimination

The widespread nature of fat stigma and discrimination circuitously suggests that Americans condone the negative treatment of fat individuals. Numerous studies support NAAFA's claims about stigma, illustrating that individuals routinely perceive fat people negatively. Since the 1970s, social psychologists have found that unattractive people (and, by extension, fatter people) are perceived in poorer light compared to their attractive (and, by extension, thinner) counterparts. For example, in 1972, Karen Dion, Ellen Berscheid, and Elaine Walster coined the phrase "what is beautiful is good" to capture the notion that people often perceive attractive persons positively, associating them with success and even talent (Landy and Sigall 1974). This "halo effect" (see Katz 2007) transfers to thin individuals as our Western culture equates thinness with physical attractiveness. And plenty of research evidence shows that individuals associate fat people with a whole list of negative characteristics. Christian S. Crandall, who developed an antifat questionnaire and coined the term "fatism," summarized the research literature well when he wrote, "The majority of research has suggested that being fat is associated with a wide variety of negative characteristics. Fat people are seen as unattractive, aesthetically displeasing, morally and emotionally impaired, alienated from their sexuality, and discontent with themselves. Their physicians describe them as 'weak-willed' and their peers rate them as unlikable" (1994, 883; citations removed). Reviews compiling decades of research confirm such assertions and point to the overwhelming evidence that individuals generally associate fat people with a host of unflattering traits (Brownell et al. 2005; Crandall, Nierman, and Hebl 2009; Puhl and Heuer 2009). National polls further verify the presence of fat bias. For instance, 16 percent of Americans admit that they have less respect for overweight people (Saad 2003), and nearly a third (29 percent) admit that they view those who are "significantly overweight" more negatively (Newport 2008). Recent anthropological work indicates that fat stigma is spreading around the globe (Brewis et al. 2011). Studies even show that individuals may hold an *implicit* antifat bias (a bias that is outside of one's awareness or conscious control) in the absence of an *explicit* antifat bias (Teachman et al. 2003).

And just as NAAFA alleges that it is not just about negative perceptions but a whole host of negative social outcomes, there is an abundance of research showing that fat people experience various forms of discrimination in various arenas of social life (Brownell et al. 2005; Carr and Friedman 2006; Puhl and Heuer 2009). As Tatiana Andreyeva, Rebecca Puhl, and Kelly Brownell (2008) of the Rudd Center for Food Policy and Obesity observe, over the span of a decade, the prevalence of weight/height discrimination has increased 66 percent, from 7 percent in 1995–1996 to 12 percent in 2004–2006, affecting all population groups but the elderly. These statistics were documented by the same team of scholars NAAFA turns to as its key source. This is expected given that these researchers at the Rudd Center for Food Policy and Obesity publish prolifically in this area.

For example, in their systematic review of studies published between 2000 and 2008, Rebecca Puhl and Chelsea A. Heuer (2009) draw attention to the prevalence of employment discrimination based on size. Puhl and Heuer (2009) point out that the experimental research literature finds that obese employees are seen as less conscientious, less agreeable, less emotionally stable, and less extraverted compared to normal-weight counterparts,[8] all of which have implications for workplace interactions, evaluations, and employment outcomes. A meta-analysis of empirical studies examining workplace weight-based bias corroborates these observations (Rudolph et al. 2009). Poll data has even found that 20 percent of Americans (one in five) admit that they would be less likely to hire someone who is overweight (Saad 2003). But discrimination is not just about failing to hire someone based on body size. Research shows that study subjects prefer to pair fat people with low-contact jobs rather than with jobs requiring extensive interpersonal contact (Venturini, Castelli, and Tomelleri 2006). As Mark Roehling's (1999) interdisciplinary review summarizes: there is consistent evidence of weight discrimination at all stages of the employment cycle, including career counseling, placement, pay, promotion, discipline, and discharge.

Studies also indicate that fat stigma and discrimination affect quality of life through interpersonal relationships. For example, analysis of the Midlife Development in the United States survey of more than 3,000 adults found that severely obese individuals report significantly lower levels of support in their family relationship, a finding contingent upon one's adolescent body weight (Carr and Friedman 2006). Robert Crosnoe, Anna Strassmann Mueller, and Kenneth Frank's (2008) analysis of National Longitudinal Study of Adolescent Health (Add Health) data also revealed that increased BMI accompanies decreased likelihood of being identified by others as friends, a finding particularly evident among girls, and a finding that they attribute to stigmatization and homophily.

The gendered (and raced) nature of size discrimination is worth highlighting here. For example, Crosnoe's 2007 analysis of Add Health data found a relationship between obesity and education. Specifically, obese girls are less likely to enter college after high school, especially after attending schools in which obesity was relatively uncommon. In contrast, obese boys' college enrollment did not differ from that of their nonobese peers, regardless of school context. Researchers have also highlighted the importance of schooling on later earnings for stigmatized groups. For example, having less postsecondary schooling than their thinner counterparts has been shown to adversely affect heavy women's later occupational status (Glass, Haas, and Reither 2010). There is also a substantial amount of evidence that women, and particularly white women, suffer an obesity wage penalty that men do not (see Cawley 2004; Conley and Glauber 2007). An analysis by sociologists Dalton Conley and Rebecca Glauber (2007) found that obesity is associated with an 18 percent reduction in women's wages and a 25 percent reduction in women's family income. Moreover, they found that the negative effects of weight are more pronounced for white women than for African American women. In general, research shows that women, but particularly white women, are stigmatized for being obese (Hebl and Heatherton 1998). Meanwhile, African American men are stigmatized less than are large white men (Hebl and Turchin 2005).

Despite the prevalence of antifat attitudes among the public, it is important to qualify that there are differences in who holds antifat attitudes. For example, there is some evidence that men exhibit greater explicit and implicit antifat prejudice toward overweight targets than women (Brochu and Morrison 2007). A widely cited study by Christian Crandall and Monica Biernat (1990) involving a survey of undergraduates also found that those exhibiting antifat attitudes generally adopt an ideologically conservative life outlook. Specifically, dislike of fatness is associated with political conservatism, racism, support for capital punishment, and less support of nontraditional marriages. In the same study, antifat attitudes were *not* related to one's own weight situation, and the relationship between conservative ideology and antifat attitudes was stronger among men than among women.

In other research, Crandall and his colleagues (2001) have also found that holding people responsible for their conditions correlates with antifat prejudice. Interestingly, research involving international subjects finds that attributions of controllability are significantly less important in Mexico for predicting antifat attitudes, compared to the United States, where they are part of a larger social ideology that holds individuals responsible for their life outcomes (Crandall and Martinez 1996). Because of the importance of causal attribution and social justice, we revisit these issues in chapter 6.

Support for Policies Prohibiting Weight Discrimination

Given the prevalence of weight bias, it is unsurprising that there is only moderate public support for including height and weight as protected legal categories in U.S. legislation. In fact, one online survey with a national sample of 1,001 adults found that fewer than half of Americans surveyed agreed that "overweight people should be subject to the same protections and benefits offered to people with physical disabilities" (Puhl and Heuer 2010). Only 27 percent of men and 32 percent of women surveyed agreed with this statement. When asked whether their state should "include weight in their civil rights law in order to protect people from discrimination based on their body weight," men's level of agreement increased to 47 percent and women's to 61 percent, suggesting moderate support for NAAFA's central goal of legally defining height and weight as a protected category. In contrast, a majority of those surveyed (65 percent of men and 81 percent of women) indicated that they would support laws that prohibit employers from refusing to hire, terminating, or denying promotions based on a person's body weight (Puhl and Heuer 2010).

Other studies have found modest public support for laws that prohibit weight discrimination. For example, in their analysis of the American Attitudes Towards Obesity survey, J. Eric Oliver and Taeku Lee (2005) report that nearly a thousand respondents were asked to rate their level of agreement on the following statements: "The government should play a more active role in protecting overweight people from discrimination," and "Overweight people should be subject to the same protections and benefits offered to people with other physical disabilities." They found that both statements elicited similar responses. Specifically, 46 percent of those surveyed agreed or strongly agreed with the statement about the role of government, and 48 percent agreed or strongly agreed with the statement about equal protection. As Oliver and Lee summarize, "Americans are not overwhelmingly in favor of granting special protections for the obese" (2005, 936).

These data are consistent with the current American legal climate. United States law generally does not prohibit size-discrimination by protecting height and weight as legal categories (see Rhode 2010). In fact, just one state (Michigan) and a handful of cities and municipalities (Binghamton, New York; Madison, Wisconsin; San Francisco, California; Santa Cruz, California; Urbana, Illinois; and Washington, DC) protect people of size. In light of the limited number of state and local ordinances that specifically protect against size discrimination, fat individuals who believe they have been the victim of size discrimination must avail themselves of legislation that covers a characteristic that is in fact protected by law such as sex, race/ethnicity, age, and disability status. This typically means calling on Title VII of the Civil Rights Act of 1964, the Rehabilitation Act (RA) of 1973, or the Americans with Disability Act (ADA) of 1990. However, not only are these formal avenues scant, their success rates are rather dismal (see Rhode 2010; Solovay 2000; Trautner and Kwan 2010).

CONCLUSION

In Western societies where two influential fat frames create a culture in which the fat body is considered problematic because it is considered unattractive and unhealthy, NAAFA boldly voices the unthinkable: The overweight body—or in NAAFA's terminology, the *fat* body—is not a social problem. Other groups and actors have merely constructed it as such. The real problem is fat discrimination.

According to NAAFA, we live in a fat-phobic culture where fat hatred abounds, a reality perpetuated by media fear mongering, and where news reporting seems to associate fat with the demise of everything—from the health-care system, to America's ability to fight terrorism, to global warming (Landau 2009; Martin 2009; Park 2010). The National Association to Advance Fat Acceptance seems to have a credible point here. Examples of fat stigma and discrimination are easy to come by. These include the blatant fat loathing of the now defunct Anti-Gym we examined in chapter 2, the presence of fat hatred groups on Facebook (Carmon 2010), and the ever-increasing bullying that fat children endure (Weinstock and Krehbiel 2009). Through education and institutional changes such as formal legal protection, improved regulation of the diet industry, and positive media depictions, NAAFA hopes to create a society in which all individuals, regardless of size, feel welcome.

Our examination of the resonance of NAAFA's social justice frame suggests that there is ample empirical evidence to support NAAFA's claim that size discrimination is rife and that individuals do perceive and treat fat people negatively. The group's claim is backed by meta-analyses, literature reviews, and countless studies. Moreover, as we saw in chapters 2 and 3, there is widespread belief that the fat body is both unattractive and unhealthy. On a daily basis, Americans wage a war against fat as evidenced through weight-loss practices in the name of aesthetic desirability and physical well-being. In this way, NAAFA principles fail to penetrate public sentiments on the fat body. Fat acceptance and body acceptance continue to present daily struggles for many Americans. Moreover, the call to include height and weight as protected legal categories appears to have moderate support at best.

Given the formidable task NAAFA has ahead of it, only time will tell if size equality will eventually become part of the everyday social and moral fabric of American society. In the meantime, fat individuals and fat acceptance activists will continue to voice their discontent at being removed from airplanes for being overweight; file lawsuits when companies presume that fat is tantamount to unfit and therefore deny equal opportunity based on this inaccurate presumption; and react to oppressive state policies by mailing fat origami cranes to the Japanese government to send a message that such policies, based on the misbegotten belief that a waistline can accurately predict health,[9] will not be tolerated.

6 · FRAMING FAT BODIES

SINCE THE SECOND-WAVE feminist movement, gender scholars have written about the deleterious effects of cultural beauty ideals (Bartky 1990; Bordo 2003; Hesse-Biber 1996; Wolf 1991). They have documented the harmful effects of these ideals on both the psyche and the material body and shown how preoccupation with the thin ideal has stymied women's social advancement (Wolf 1991; Zones 1997). These findings have also elicited an ongoing debate about the relationship between cultural structure and women's agency (Davis 1991). While this scholarship has uncovered important knowledge of cultural body norms and their effects, it has failed to provide a comprehensive understanding of the relationship between body ideals and social actors. Feminist cultural analyses of body ideals typically focus on a single discourse; in this case, what we refer to as the aesthetic frame. This singular focus limits a full understanding of cultural body ideals and the relationship between individuals and culture. For this reason, *Framing Fat* lays out multiple competing cultural logics on the fat body.

Framing Fat maps the contested field of fat, showing how the fat body is not just about an aesthetic ideal but also about a health ideal and how issues of choice and responsibility and discrimination are central to these constructions. Despite the existence of numerous players in this field, we have examined four sets of cultural producers. We selected these cultural producers because of their visibility, prominence, and accessibility. All of these producers' cultural artifacts are publicly available, thereby enabling a systematic and replicable analysis. We make no claims about the substantive representativeness of each producer, although we maintain that each receives both direct and indirect reinforcement from cultural supporters. The fashion-beauty complex promulgates the aesthetic frame through the industries of the cosmetics, fashion, and weight-loss industries; the Centers for Disease Control and Prevention (CDC) promotes the health frame with endorsements by public health officials, weight-loss surgeons, and health practitioners; the Center for Consumer Freedom (CCF) pushes the choice and responsibility frame with the help of other food and beverage groups; and the National Association to Advance Fat Acceptance (NAAFA) gives voice to the social justice frame with the backing of fat studies scholars and other fat acceptance groups in the United States and abroad. None of these frames, as we have seen, is always consistent; they all, at times, exhibit internal contradictions. Nevertheless, each tells a rather coherent story.

Like others before us (Guthman and DePuis 2006), we acknowledge that public meanings about fat are complex. We understand that these four frames by no means tell an exhaustive story. Our goal in *Framing Fat* is to uncover these four stories with as much breadth, depth, and nuance as space affords and, through them, illuminate the constructed nature of the fat body. While historians and anthropologists shed light on this construction by looking historically and cross-culturally at dynamic meanings about the body, we focus primarily on how four cultural discourses play out today in the public sphere.

Our analysis is certainly not the first to deconstruct competing meanings about the fat body. We build on the seminal work of others who have examined various perspectives on obesity causation, blame, and intervention (Campos 2004; Gaesser 2002; Gard and Wright 2005; Moffat 2010; Rich and Evans 2005; Smith 2009). We stand on the shoulders of scholars who have investigated the media's framing of the "obesity epidemic" (Boero 2007; Campos et al. 2006; Holland 2011; Saguy and Almeling 2008). We are further indebted to the growing field of critical obesity studies that has laid out a foundation for destabilizing so-called truths about the fat body (Gard 2009; Monaghan 2008; Murray 2008). Our goal in *Framing Fat* is to continue this destabilization by exposing how, under closer scrutiny, commonly held beliefs about the fat body constitute a complex landscape of claims put forth by a diverse range of claims makers.

In this concluding chapter, we bring together the four frames and address a lingering question: What are the implications of these various approaches? We begin with a summary of all four frames, and as promised, we provide for illustrative and pedagogical purposes the framing matrix in tabular form (see table 6.1). After recapping the resonance that we have documented in previous pages, we attempt to make sense of the observed resonance of frames, in particular why key aspects of the aesthetic, health, and choice and responsibility frames resonate, yet the social justice frame engenders limited support. This discussion includes an exploration of the salience of causal claims, the relationship between causal attribution and social justice, and frame credibility. We also revisit biomedicalization and the accompanying issues of morality and risk. We then discuss intraframe connections before turning to public policy implications. We close by examining the issues of body diversity and social justice.

TABLE 6.1 Framing Matrix of Fat Frames

	Aesthetic frame	Health frame	Choice and responsibility frame	Social justice frame
Cultural producer	Fashion-beauty complex	Centers for Disease Control and Prevention (CDC)	Center for Consumer Freedom (CCF)	National Association to Advance Fat Acceptance (NAAFA)
Supporting producer(s)	Mass media	Other public health organizations, providers, and practitioners	Other food and beverage groups	Other fat acceptance groups
Motivation	Profit	Public health	Profit	Social justice
Frame type	Dominant	Dominant	Reactionary	Reactionary
Social problem	Fat is a social problem because fat bodies are unattractive.	Overweight and obesity are social problems because they are unhealthy.	Obesity is not a social problem, but governmental and other forms of interference with personal freedom and individual choice are social problems.	Fat is not a social problem, but size-based discrimination that affects the lived experiences of fat people is a social problem.
			Reasoning devices		
Central claim	Fat is frightful.	Being overweight or obese can be fatal.	Food consumption, lifestyle, and (by extension) body size are individual choices and a matter of personal responsibility.	Fat bias, stigma, and discrimination are prevalent and problematic.
Causal roots	Individual causes: failure to discipline the body; failure to use the proper products and services	Individual causes: failure to discipline the body; failure to achieve caloric balance by adjusting food consumption and physical activity patterns	Individual causes: lack of physical activity, not food consumption patterns	Individual causes of fat: multiple, including inherited genetic predisposition
		Structural (influencing individual) causes: differential access to healthy foods and physical activity as a barrier to achieving caloric balance	Structural (influencing individual) causes: changes in the workplace, technologies, family life, transportation, etc.	Structural causes of fat: multiple environmental factors
				Structural causes of size discrimination: fat-hating society (including individuals, cultural ideologies, and institutions), largely created and reinforced by the aesthetic and health frames

TABLE 6.1 (Continued)

	Aesthetic frame	Health frame	Choice and responsibility frame	Social justice frame
Consequences	Looking and feeling bad; being unattractive and undesirable; experiencing a diminished quality of life	Major: morbidity; mortality; economic costs Minor: social stigma	Misinformation and thus misinformed choices about consumption; loss of freedom and the ability to choose; promotion of an anticapitalist society	Compromised psychological, physical, and social well-being of fat people
Principles (appeals to)	Desire for a high quality of life	Desire to achieve health, promote fiscal responsibility, uphold equality, and protect future generations	Personal responsibility and the right to make individual choices (about lifestyle)	Desire to protect human rights
Proposed solutions and policies	Weight loss through self-discipline and by using the proper products and services	Individual: weight loss through self-discipline and lifestyle adjustment Societal: state programs, surveillance and applied research, program implementation and evaluation, and partnership development	Do nothing; let the market be; reject proposed laws that would tax or regulate consumer food choices.	Eliminate size discrimination through education, media reform, and legal changes; encourage individuals to embrace size acceptance and a Health at Every Size perspective; regulate diet and weight-loss industries.

(continued)

TABLE 6.1 (Continued)

	Aesthetic frame	Health frame	Choice and responsibility frame	Social justice frame
Framing devices				
Supporting data	This frame does not rest on explicit data; its message is implicit.	Research and statistics from scholarly studies, including studies conducted by CDC and other public health researchers	Quotes and data from scholarly studies and health experts	Research and statistics from scholarly studies on size discrimination and Health at Every Size
Metaphors	The beautiful body as a symbol of accomplishment	The healthy body as a symbol of accomplishment	The evils of big government	The fat (and particularly fat female) body as a symbol of beauty and empowerment
Exemplars	Anti-Gym	Let's Move! campaign	"Give Me a Break" Super Bowl XLV commercial; 1998 National Institutes of Health redefinition of BMI; CDC release of new death figure of 112,000 (from the previous 400,000)	Letter to Mrs. Obama; Surgeon General's podcast (HHS 2010c) and report (HHS 2010d)
Catchphrases (and words)	"Pretty"; "feel your best"; "better looking"; "sexy"; "desirable"	Overweight and obesity are "major public health problems"; obesity is an "epidemic"; "the primary concern of overweight and obesity is one of health and not appearance"; "choose a healthy weight for life."	"An epidemic of obesity myths"; "the truth is out there"; "good science gone bad"; "personal responsibility"; "common sense"; obesity "hysteria," "hype," and "junk science"	"Discrimination is wrong . . ."; "Health At Every Size"; "over whose weight?"; "Fat is not a four-letter word"; "Fat! So?"; "diets don't work"

TABLE 6.1 (*Continued*)

	Aesthetic frame	Health frame	Choice and responsibility frame	Social justice frame
Depictions (of enemies)	Implied: Those who do not conform to the thin aesthetic ideal are lacking in discipline.	Implied: Those who contest the "objective" scientific data and "facts" provided by the CDC, a legitimate and authoritative medical agency, are ignorant.	"Radicals," "extremists," and "self-righteous" "food cops"; "health activists," "government bureaucrats," "anti-food-industry fanatics"; the Center for Science in the Public Interest, and scheming trial lawyers who threaten individual's right to choose what to eat and the food industry's right to sell what it wants are unjustly imposing their will on others and threatening personal freedom; "myth makers" such as specific medical researchers (and obesity organizations) who are connected to the weight-loss industry and conduct biased research in the name of profit misleading the public and interfering with its ability to make informed choices	Industries of the fashion-beauty complex that produce and promote ineffective and dangerous products and services in the name of profit are creating a dangerous beauty ideal that compromises the physical, emotional, and social well-being of fat people; obesity researchers who focus on curing obesity in the name of profit, instead of focusing on nondieting alternatives to improve the well-being of fat people, are endorsing a climate of fat hatred.
Visual images	Advertisements and other mass media artifacts	Maps, tables, diagrams, charts, videos, etc., that illustrate the prevalence, urgency, and rise of overweight and obesity	Cartoons and advertisements that often employ ridicule and sarcasm to emphasize individual choice and personal responsibility to debunk "obesity myths"	Few visual images, although Wann (1998) uses drawings and photographs of fat bodies in *Fat!So?* in an effort to celebrate and destigmatize the fat body

SOURCE: Compiled by the authors.

NOTE: This is an expanded version of a table initially published in *Sociological Inquiry* (Kwan 2009b).

FOUR STORIES

Framing Fat lays out the messages put forth by four cultural producers as well as each cultural producer's take on four interrelated themes—body aesthetics, health, individual choice and personal responsibility, and social justice. We summarize the framing elements of the four frames in table 6.1.

Our journey began with the aesthetic frame of the fashion-beauty complex (Bartky 1990). We noted earlier that this is a unique frame insofar as no sole cultural producer gives voice to this complex. Because of the amorphous nature of the fashion-beauty complex, we selected advertisements from each of the industries that constitutes it (the cosmetics, fashion, and weight-loss industries). Our intent was not, by any means, to anthropomorphize this complex or to represent it as a homogeneous entity that consciously produces a coherent message. The evidence we present is perforce anecdotal, and we readily concede that advertisements are complex, varied, and at times contradictory. Nevertheless, we argue that these advertisements exhibit a general analytical pattern that conveys a powerful message about the fat body.

Column 2 in table 6.1 presents the core message of the aesthetic frame: the fat body is problematic because it is aesthetically unappealing. Thin is sexy, and fat is a frightful state that purportedly diminishes quality of life. The solution to this problematic condition lies with individual change and self-discipline, particularly through the use of products and services. The aesthetic frame portrays the aesthetically pleasing body as a symbol of accomplishment; it signifies moral fortitude, perseverance, and commitment to change. According to the advertisements of the fashion-beauty complex, individuals who are willing to invest the time, money, and energy to achieve and maintain a muscular (male) body or a taut and slim (female) body will be rewarded with sexual vitality, social magnetism, and the good life.

Yet, as we saw, there are other approaches to fat aesthetics. The National Association to Advance Fat Acceptance maintains that fat can be physically attractive, even sexy. Through fat-positive images and by welcoming fat admiration, NAAFA attempts to rework the fat-equals-unattractive formula endemic to the advertisements of the fashion-beauty complex.

Alongside the aesthetic frame is a second frame that constructs the fat body as problematic. Column 3 of table 6.1 presents the signature elements of the CDC's health frame. The CDC, in the name of public health, communicates that overweight and obesity constitute a health epidemic that requires immediate action. Overweight and obesity can be fatal, and they can lead to a host of health risks, including heart disease, diabetes, and several forms of cancer. But it is not just the health consequences that concern the CDC; these conditions have economic ramifications, and they also compromise the nation's commitment to equality as prevalence rates of these conditions are particularly high among disadvantaged populations. Moreover, childhood obesity potentially compromises the well-being of future generations. According to the CDC, blame falls on an individual's failure to achieve caloric balance by adjusting food consumption and physical activity patterns. Although the CDC acknowledges the structural barriers that individuals encounter in their attempts to achieve this balance, it portrays, as does the aesthetic frame, the healthy body as a symbol of accomplishment.

Despite the pervasiveness of the CDC's health message, there are alternative approaches to body weight and health. The CCF refutes the CDC's data about the negative health consequences of being overweight, challenges the CDC's emphasis on the food consumption side of the Energy Balance Equation, and even says that the CDC is wrong when it comes to the economic burden of obesity. The National Association to Advance Fat Acceptance, too, contests the CDC's health rhetoric, attesting that individuals can be healthy at every size.

A third frame emphasizes individual choice and personal responsibility. Unlike the aesthetic and health frames, the CCF's choice and responsibility frame maintains that the obese body is not a social problem (see column 4, table 6.1). Instead, it points to government and other forms of interference with personal freedom. Downplaying food consumption, the CCF attributes the overweight body to changes in modern society that affect the CDC's Energy Balance Equation, particularly those that affect physical activity levels. Given its refusal to consider the obese body problematic (either aesthetically or medically), the CCF lays out no solution for it. Rather, the CCF advocates laissez-faire economics by criticizing proposed laws that would tax or regulate consumer food choices. This approach is in line with its overall goal of protecting consumers' interests as well as consumers' ability to make food and beverage consumption choices that they personally (and responsibly) deem fit.

Assumptions about choice and responsibility are manifest in other frames as well. For example, the aesthetic frame encourages individuals to take responsibility for their physical appearance, implying that those who do not take such responsibility justifiably suffer the shame and stigma associated with body nonconformity. Meanwhile, the health frame's mandates compel individuals to make the so-called right choice and to conform responsibly to its health edicts. These mandates are bolstered by a profusion of scientific evidence put forth by the CDC that supposedly only a fool would reject.

Finally, in the last column of table 6.1 are the signature elements of NAAFA's social justice frame. The National Association to Advance Fat Acceptance emphasizes multiple causes of fat, including genetic predisposition and environmental factors, and maintains that fat is not always, as the two dominant frames allege, fixable. It also contends that we live in a sizist society where fat stigma, bias, and discrimination are rampant. These social injustices compromise the psychological, physical, and social well-being of fat people. Appealing to human rights, NAAFA attempts to eliminate size-based discrimination through the promotion of body acceptance and a Health at Every Size (HAES) paradigm, legal reforms, and educational outreach programs.

Although NAAFA's is the only frame that has injustice as its central focus, other frames carry messages about social inequality. On the one hand, discrimination and inequality are endemic to the aesthetic frame since beauty ideals fundamentally reward the select few who have won the genetic lottery. On the other hand, the CDC's health frame expresses indirect concern for social equality by drawing attention to the high prevalence of overweight and obesity in minority and disadvantaged populations.

FRAME RESONANCE OF CORE TENETS

In the long run, frames are about frame competitions and persuading an audience of a certain version of reality. The notion of resonance, loosely adopted from the social movements literature, accounts for why some frames seem to be effective while others do not (Benford and Snow 2000; Snow and Benford 1988). As Rhys H. Williams summarizes, "Whatever frames actors use must 'resonate' if audiences are to respond. Some frames 'work' better than others because they resonate with audiences who are prepared to hear the claim, or have experiences commensurate with the claims being made. In this sense resonance is the 'fit' between frames and audiences' previous beliefs, worldviews, and life experiences" (2004, 105). Frames that resonate among audiences may be adopted as part of their everyday cultural tool kits and repertoires, subsequently informing personal decisions and courses of action (Swidler 1986, 2001). Understanding who wins and who loses these framing wars is particularly important in an environment where consumers are bombarded with numerous, oftentimes mixed, messages about food, exercise, and health (Dixon and Winter 2007).

Framing Fat examines the resonance of four cultural frames. Each frame attempts to manipulate cultural ideologies and meanings associated with the fat body to convince cultural consumers that their story is a compelling one that they should adopt. Ideological persuasion, however, varies by intentionality, coherence, and organization. For example, the fashion-beauty complex's efforts to shape cultural beliefs are less intentional, coherent, and organized than the more sustained and cohesive tactics of NAAFA, an organization best described as a social movement because it represents ordinary people attempting to make collective claims on others (see Tilly 2004).

Resonance is not a zero-sum game. Like a Foucauldian conceptualization of power that is always accompanied by resistance (Foucault 1979), our observations show how cultural frames can be adapted by some segments of the population while simultaneously resisted by others. For example, as we saw with the aesthetic frame, survey and poll data indicate that individuals generally agree that fat is physically unappealing and to be avoided. This is supported by the pervasiveness of dieting practices and surgical weight-loss procedures. Yet not all Americans are equally concerned about waistline aesthetics. Variations exist along racial/ethnic, gender, and socioeconomic lines—the last of which directly affects one's ability to conform successfully to aesthetic norms. Still, body trans-formation practices persist despite well-documented failure rates and serious health risks.

Survey data also confirm the cultural resonance of the health frame's core tenets. Americans view obesity as a serious health threat and are motivated to lose weight in the name of health. At the same time, there is evidence to suggest that certain subgroups (such as men, some racial/ethnic minorities, and indi-viduals in lower socioeconomic status groups) are less likely to consider them-selves medically overweight or obese. Health at Every Size (HAES) principles, too, evince some public support, as research suggests that HAES language has seeped into some laypersons' understandings of their bodies.

There is compelling evidence that Americans also subscribe to the core tenets of the choice and responsibility frame. Surveys point to limited support for insti-tutional interventions, such as holding the food industry legally responsible for diet-related health problems, limiting unhealthy food and beverage advertising, and taxing soft drinks. Overall, public sentiment appears to be that lifestyle is an individual choice and that obesity is not a state responsibility but a personal one.

Finally, data confirm that NAAFA is correct when it maintains that fat bias, stigma, and discrimination are widespread. Individual studies, literature reviews, and meta-analyses all attest that we live in a sizist society. Size discrimination affects quality of life and is particularly harmful to women who suffer more severely the burden of weight-based stigma. Despite the prevalence of weight discrimination, research indicates that antifat attitudes are more common among some social groups, such as men, individuals with an ideologically con-servative worldview, and those who hold individuals responsible for their health conditions. We also learned that American law generally does not prohibit size discrimination and that public support for protecting height and weight as legal categories is moderate at best.

BODY COMPLIANCE VERSUS BODY DIVERSITY

We label the aesthetic and health frames dominant. These frames resonate. Their core tenets—that fat is physically unattractive and unhealthy—are part of the popular imagination. People tend to think of the fat body this way, and these views motivate weight-loss behaviors. Their cultural persuasiveness can also be seen in the terms typically used to describe the fat body. Despite attempts by fat acceptance activists and scholars to reclaim it, the term "fat" remains highly stigmatized. Medical terms such as "overweight" and "obese," along with euphemisms such as "big boned," "heavyset," and "corpulent," remain commonplace in everyday talk, media outlets, and mainstream scholarship.

Moreover, the aesthetic and health frames compel individuals to conform to the body status quo: the former in the name of cultural beauty norms, the latter in the name of physical well-being. With these frames, anything but the thin or "normal"-sized body is seen as abject; it is aesthetically and/or medically "deviant." These frames are thus hegemonic; they work within narrowly defined cultural norms and mandate compliance. The end result is nothing less than a disciplined docile body. The aesthetic and health frames are thus dominant because they influence public sentiments about the fat body and result in individual actions that lead to body uniformity and conformity.

Yet the *central* claim of the choice and responsibility frame also resonates. So even though the CCF rejects the CDC's health messages, and even though the public generally rejects the CCF's oppositional stance on health (running instead with the CDC's sentiment that overweight or obese does in fact signify unhealthy), the CCF's core message—that the body, food consumption, and lifestyle are individual choices involving personal responsibility—actually sits well with the public. Why then do we not label the choice and responsibility frame dominant?

In contrast to the aesthetic and health frames, the choice and responsibility frame makes no explicit statements about what individuals *ought* to do with their bodies. This frame protects consumers' choices and places the burden of responsibility on the individual, with no proclamations about compliance. The CCF does not tell the public to lose weight, to go on a diet, or to hit the gym. Acting as stewards of choice and freedom, the CCF endeavors to protect freedom of choice, and it encourages individuals to make whatever decisions they desire. In a rather roundabout way, the choice and responsibility frame advocates body difference and diversity. It does not encourage deference to hegemonic aesthetic or health norms; instead, it champions autonomous and responsible decision making. Individual decisions may result in a culturally compliant and disciplined body, or they may not.

We have similar reasons for declining to label the social justice frame dominant. It, too, rejects body compliance; however, unlike the choice and responsibility frame, it does so overtly. The social justice frame proudly promotes body difference and diversity. The National Association to Advance Fat Acceptance celebrates all body sizes aesthetically, and it questions narrow health tenets that assert that only a "normal"-sized body can be healthy. It rejects oppressive and risky weight-loss regimens that might compromise physical and mental well-being in the name of the thin body. Association advocates and allies refuse to bow to cultural imperatives that result in docile bodies. They proudly resist and redefine hegemonic norms. By doing so, NAAFA members and advocates promote a form of "embodied resistance" (Bobel and Kwan 2011).

In sum, we have two dominant frames that promote a standardized "normal" body and two that promote body diversity and difference. We label these latter frames reactionary because they promote this diversity and difference but also because they contest the claims of one or both dominant frames. However, these two reactionary frames are driven by very different motivations (see table 6.1).

The CCF puts forth its message for the purpose of protecting consumer interests, and, when all is said and done, food industry profits. Those profits are threatened by the CDC, which labels obesity a health crisis and alleges that the solution lies in the hands of individuals through a change in the Energy Balance Equation. (Recall that half of the Energy Balance Equation is caloric consumption.) The CCF must encourage caloric intake in light of these accusations.

In contrast, while membership and revenue are important for organizational survival, NAAFA is motivated not primarily by profit but, rather, by ideological change. It champions new ways of thinking about the fat body and crusades for body acceptance in hopes of creating a better society where *all* bodies feel welcome. In NAAFA's view, what is central is neither body compliance nor profit. Rather, it is social justice. For this reason, NAAFA's frame is not only reactionary; it is subversive. As the only subversive frame of the four, it attempts to rework extant hegemonic cultural and social structures. This unique attribute of NAAFA becomes even more demarcated when we turn to causal attribution.

CAUSAL CLAIMS AND THE RESONANCE OF CAUSAL CLAIMS

Up to this point, we have limited our examination of resonance to the substantive issues central to each frame, omitting a close look at public sentiments about causal claims. Yet each set of cultural producers makes assumptions about what causes individuals to gain weight. These assumptions have important implications for understanding why some frames seem to sway public opinion more so than others.

As we saw in chapter 2, the vast majority of cultural producers that collectively make up the fashion-beauty complex do not overtly address the cause or causes of fat bodies. Proposing various solutions to fight fat, however, implies that the body is malleable and within an individual's control. Though rarely stated outright, the aesthetic frame assumes that fat people have personally failed. This is conspicuously evident in our profile of Anti-Gym, which depicts fat people as lazy, slovenly, and unmotivated individuals who want to place blame on anything other than themselves.

Captured in its visual of a woman with her arms extended above her head with the accompanying copy "They did it. So can you!" are the CDC's causal assumptions. As we have seen, the CDC explains the problem of weight gain using its Energy Balance Equation, which underscores lifestyle choices. Although the health frame acknowledges a number of potential causes (such as genetics, metabolism, and environmental factors), the CDC asserts that the main causes of overweight and obesity are the choices individuals make regarding food intake and physical activity. Once more, individuals are to blame.

The CCF cautions against this simplistic view of weight gain, maintaining that it is difficult to isolate a single cause (read: a single food); instead, it suggests multiple factors. The CCF documents how historical shifts, such as changes in occupations, technologies, and transportation, have affected weight gain and physical activity levels. It also notes that physical activity is at an all-time low and that the public is misled when it associates vilified foods such as high-fructose corn syrup with obesity. At the same time the group draws attention to multiple— including structural—forces, it nevertheless defaults to individual blame, thus corroborating its overall approach to choice and responsibility. We have observed through its many public documents that the CCF protects the choice to consume so long as individuals take *personal responsibility* for these choices. The upshot once again: individuals are blameworthy.

In contrast to these three frames, NAAFA's social justice frame begins with a different premise. Fat people are *not* blameworthy. Blaming individuals for their bodies, the group argues, is the basis for stigma and ridicule, precisely the sentiments and behaviors it is trying to fight. Individual blame not only fails to acknowledge contributing environmental factors and genetic predisposition, but erroneously assumes that body weight is readily mutable.

Thus of the four frames, three indict individual choices and assign blame either directly or indirectly to the individual. But how does the average American think about causal claims? What do people believe causes fat? What or who do they blame?

To start, a Gallup poll (McMurray 2004) asked a sample of Americans if "obesity is a disease" or if it is "more a problem of bad eating and bad lifestyle habits." Seventy-five percent of respondents indicated eating and lifestyle habits, compared to 21 percent who indicated disease. Women (at 25 percent) were slightly more likely than men (at 17 percent) to agree that obesity is a disease, and younger adults eighteen to twenty-nine years of age (at 34 percent) were more likely to agree than elderly Americans sixty-five years of age or older (at 10 percent). This Gallup poll found minimal variation in response by weight status.

This nationwide poll data showing that a majority of Americans attribute obesity to lifestyle factors finds support from several academic studies. Analysis of over 3,000 respondents of the 2007 Health Information National Trends

Survey (HINTS) revealed that 72 percent of those surveyed endorsed the belief that lifestyle behaviors have "a lot" to do with causing obesity (Wang and Coups 2010). These researchers also found a positive relationship between, on the one hand, respondents' level of physical activity and, on the other hand, the belief in lifestyle causes. Moreover, individuals with college degrees (compared to those with high school educations) and Hispanics (compared to non-Hispanic whites) were more likely to maintain that obesity is caused by overeating and not exercising. Survey respondents' sex, age, and body mass index had no impact on this causal belief.

It is not only laypersons who associate lifestyle factors with obesity. Jane Ogden and Zakk Flanagan (2008) asked 73 general practitioners (GPs) and 311 laypersons if they thought obesity's causes were biological (such as genetics or hormones), psychological (such as low self-esteem or depressive tendencies), behavioral (such as eating too much or exercising too little), social (such as unemployment or low income), or structural (such as today's fast food culture or the high price of good, healthy food). The vast majority—97.3 percent of GPs and 79.2 percent of laypersons—indicated that behavioral factors cause obesity. While both GPs and laypersons acknowledged the role of biological, psychological, social, and structural factors, albeit with varying levels of endorsement, these results suggest that a majority of individuals blame behavioral choices for weight gain.

J. Eric Oliver and Taeku Lee's (2005) analysis of the American Attitudes Towards Obesity survey out of the Survey Research Center at Princeton University similarly revealed that the most popular explanation for obesity, favored by 65 percent of 909 adult respondents, was "lack of willpower to diet or exercise." And like Ogden and Flanagan, these researchers found that respondents recognize multiple and even contradictory causes of obesity. They blamed environmental factors such as unhealthy food in restaurants (62 percent), ineffective diets (57 percent), and genetically inherited traits (40 percent). Colleen Barry and her colleagues (2009) observed a comparable willingness to acknowledge multiple causes in their study involving a nationally representative web sample of over one thousand subjects. Surveying respondents about seven obesity metaphors (specifically, sinful behavior, addiction, time crunch, eating disorder, disability, industry manipulation, and toxic environment), they report that nearly half of the sample (46.5 percent) acknowledged three to four causal narratives.

At least one qualitative study involving interviews with health professionals, policy makers, and overweight laypersons corroborates these findings (Greener, Douglas, and van Teijlingen 2010). Health professionals and overweight laypersons viewed the problem of obesity as arising from personal shortcomings but also recognized social and environmental factors. Interestingly, only the policy makers interviewed "scarcely discussed individual choice or lifestyle. . . . [Instead,] they tended to take a fully environmental view in relation to the causation of obesity" (Greener, Douglas, and van Teijlingen 2010, 1046). At the same time they adopted this fully environmental view, these policy makers conceded the unlikelihood of implementing any social policy changes that stemmed from it (such as town planning and food industry regulation) without political will or popular support.

Thus, whether we turn to nationwide poll data, findings from nationally representative survey data, or the results of studies based on nonprobability sampling designs, a common theme emerges. Individuals acknowledge multiple causes of weight gain, yet the rhetoric of individual blame, particularly through the indictment of lifestyle factors, is pervasive. While likely shaped in part by the three cultural fat frames that emphasize individual behavior, these sentiments also go hand in hand with media characterizations of obesity. As aforementioned, researchers analyzing print media find that the American news media typically couches obesity in terms of personal causes and solutions (Kim and Willis 2007; Lawrence 2004; Saguy, Gruys, and Gong 2010; Saguy and Riley 2005).

CAUSAL ATTRIBUTION, SOCIAL JUSTICE, AND FRAME SALIENCE

How individuals think about causation matters. Attribution theory suggests that when fat people are seen as responsible for their condition, they are more likely to be evaluated negatively. For example, a classic study by William DeJong (1980) found that the stigma of obesity is more severe when individuals perceive this condition to be controllable. In turn, the introduction of a discounting factor that places causality outside the individual lessens stigma. Specifically, subjects evaluate more negatively (i.e., they see as less likeable, more lazy, and more self-indulgent) fat individuals who they are told do *not* have a discounting condition such as a thyroid condition (compared to those afflicted with such conditions). DeJong's research suggests that it is not necessarily physical appearance per se that leads to stigma and to the negative perception and treatment of fat people; rather, it is the assumption of causal responsibility.[1] Given the tendency of the public to focus on individual-level causes, the widespread presence of size-based bias, stigma, and discrimination really should come as no surprise.

Stanford law professor Deborah L. Rhode's (2010) analysis of physical characteristics and discrimination provides insight here. According to Rhode, physical characteristics can be conceptualized along a continuum. On the one end are characteristics that individuals typically view as immutable, traits such as age, sex, and race. Because the public generally agrees that these characteristics are unchangeable, discrimination based on them has come to be regarded as unwarranted, unjustified, and illegal. At the other end of the continuum are characteristics such as hairstyles, clothing, and body art. Individuals tend to think these latter characteristics stem from personal choices, and as a result are open to derision.

As we have seen, the public frequently places body size on this latter end of the continuum. Body size discrimination is therefore deemed justifiable because fat is presumably the result of lifestyle choices. Or, as Abigail C. Saguy, Kjerstin Gruys, and Shanna Gong summarize in their analysis of media frames, "One important reason that the group-based discrimination frame has little traction in the case of body size is that the latter is typically viewed as a *behavior,* like smoking, rather than as an *ascribed characteristic,* akin to race or sex" (2010, 601). By this logic, formal protection of body size under state or federal law is unwarranted. Indeed, a major challenge faced by the social justice frame is transforming how Americans perceive the *causes* of weight gain.

That public opinion points to individual lifestyle as a key cause of weight gain explains in part the strong resonance of the aesthetic, health, and choice and responsibility frames. However, we acknowledge the difficulty of parsing causal claims; we will never know for certain whether frames create public opinion or whether they find a home only when public opinion matches them. Regardless, all three of these frames rest on causal roots that seem sensible in the public eye and mesh with the public's understanding of blame.

To borrow from the language of social movement scholars, they exhibit salience. According to Robert Benford and David Snow (2000), two sets of interacting factors account for variation in frame resonance: salience and credibility. While the former refers to the extent to which a frame's message fits with the audience's worldviews, the latter involves issues such as claim consistency, empirical evidence, and claims-maker credibility. Frames that culturally resonate with an audience's cultural narratives, assumptions, and ideologies offer greater salience and therefore greater prospects of mobilization (Benford and Snow 2000). In other words, the aesthetic, health, and choice and responsibility frames resonate in large part because they rest on an ideology that is *salient* in the public imagination: fat individuals, because of the choices they make, are to be blamed for the condition of their bodies.

FRAME RESONANCE AND FRAME CREDIBILITY

Credibility matters, too, and is a function of empirical credibility, which involves the extent to which claims can be empirically verified, consistency, which involves the uniformity of claims and beliefs, and the credibility of frame articulators, which involves the status and/or perceived expertise of the claims maker (Benford and Snow 2000).

With the exception of the unique aesthetic frame, which relies on mass media to implicitly make its claims, the frames we have examined make their cases with the support of scholarly research.[2] As we discussed in chapter 4, framing wars are essentially research and data wars. Framers turn to scholarly quotations, paraphrasings, and citations to convey their key points. For the CCF, this often means quoting from prestigious academic journals and turning to well-known researchers. Similarly, the CDC relies on its arsenal of facts and figures, citing its own public health researchers, who publish in outlets such as the *Journal of the American Medical Association*, and NAAFA relies on the credibility of research out of Yale University's Rudd Center for Food Policy and Obesity when making arguments about size-based discrimination. To a certain degree, one could argue that empirical credibility is relatively equal across these three frames; they are all able to back their statements with relatively believable empirical evidence.

But what about the consistency of these claims? We have seen how frames exhibit some degree of internal inconsistency that potentially jeopardizes their credibility. For example, some NAAFA documents play up environmental causal factors, while others dismiss it. The CCF also falls prey to inconsistent messages, citing as authorities researchers it concurrently slams for creating "obesity" myths and resorting to scholarly journals that it contends are suspect because of the organizations that manage them.

These inconsistencies, however, are relatively minor and, one could argue, possibly lost on the public for at least two reasons. First, they require rather close scrutiny of a framer's entire body of public artifacts. It is likely that the average individual does not have the time, energy, or interest to undertake such a task, which upon only untenured academics would embark. Second, these relatively imperceptible inconsistencies may be overshadowed by the larger narratives of all four frames, which are, by and large, cohesive.

Palpable and visible public discontent with corporate greed, as evident in the 2011 Occupy Wall Street movement, suggests that, at least in terms of framer credibility, the aesthetic and choice and responsibility frames are at a disadvantage since both the fashion-beauty complex and the food industry are profit-driven and represent capitalist interests. Whereas the aesthetic frame attains its financial goals implicitly through frame rhetoric, the choice and responsibility frame does so explicitly through the endorsement of neoliberal rhetoric and economics. Yet, as we have seen, despite these corporate underpinnings, these two frames exhibit strong resonance, with the aesthetic frame even informing strategies of action such as dieting and other weight-loss behaviors. Multiple reasons likely account for the mainstream popularity of these frames despite their framers' dubious credibility. For one, it is possible that either the frames' core claims or the powerful individualistic rhetoric behind them supersede framer credibility. It is also possible that individuals fail to acknowledge (or they intentionally endorse or overlook) the capitalist motivations behind these groups.

Framer credibility plays a crucial role for the CDC and NAAFA, both of which disseminate medical messages about the fat body in the public sphere. It is here that the CDC has a marked advantage. As Paul Starr (1982) documents, well into the twentieth century, an assortment of medical providers such as surgeons, homeopaths, and midwives littered the American health-care landscape. It was not until the culmination of a series of forces that American medicine transformed into an authoritative (and credible) profession. These forces included internal developments such as greater cohesiveness and dependency within the profession because of the growth of hospitals and specializations; changes in social and economic life, such as advances in science and technology; and institutional changes such as the standardization of education and licensing of physicians. These transformations eventually located cultural authority in the hands of doctors who now held the power to define a body as either sick or well (Starr 1982). Today, medical authorities carry much credibility, which transfers broadly to those who advocate the health frame—from public health authorities to individual medical practitioners.

In contrast, NAAFA, whose members have already been cast as suspect because of popular beliefs about morality, lifestyle, and responsibility, engenders far less claims-maker credibility. The same negative stereotypes and epithets that fat individuals have been labeled are often used to question the credibility of those who advocate the social justice frame. For example, after NAAFA spokeswoman Peggy Howell commented on Academy Award nominee Gabourey Sidibe's weight, maintaining, "You cannot tell by looking at a person if they are healthy. Fat does not equal disease and thin does not equal healthy" (TMZ 2010), the public chimed in with a slew of sizist attacks to discount Howell's claims, including the retort that "NAAFA is a bunch of sick fatties trying to justify their obese existence" (TMZ 2010).

Similarly, researchers studying NAAFA have observed that a large majority of its members are white women who fall into upper weight categories (Gimlin 2002; Saguy and Riley 2005; Sobal 1999). The gendered nature of NAAFA's group membership is not surprising and likely reflects the well-established claim that men have greater cultural leeway when they do not conform to cultural beauty expectations (e.g., Deutsch et al. 1986). However, this narrow demographic (namely, white women) potentially alienates thin allies, racial and ethnic minorities, and men, all of whom could help NAAFA establish greater credibility and wider appeal.

FAT BODIES, BIOMEDICALIZATION, AND SURVEILLANCE

The individualistic rhetoric so salient in the public imagination is axiomatic to the health frame and its notion of biopower, which deserves special attention here. As we saw earlier, biopower exerts control by means of the regulation, surveillance, and control of individuals and populations, particularly through knowledge and technologies (see Clarke et al. 2010; Foucault 1984). The protection of life and regulation of bodies central to biopower surfaces powerfully in public health agencies, such as the CDC, that purportedly pursue their mission in the name of public welfare. For example, through the use of the Body Mass Index (BMI), a diagnostic tool that allegedly predicts health risks, health officials are able to distinguish those at greater risk from those at less risk. Yet, as scholars have pointed out, it is not only those above the designated BMI thresholds who are at risk; all bodies are at risk (Boero 2007). Thus, unlike sufferers of diseases in which etiology is limited by prescribed genetic conditions, everyone is susceptible to becoming "overweight" or "obese." This is particularly the case in a modern environment which public health officials have labeled "obesogenic." At the end of the day, identification of risk (greater or less) occurs for the sake of later intervention. This intervention more often than not involves behavioral changes and surveillance, the latter of which takes the form of both self-surveillance and surveillance by others—from generalized others we do not know (Mead 1934) to the doctors, parents, employers, teachers, and friends we do know.

Of course, medicine is happy to step in to "protect" us and ensure we live long and healthy lives. This is the crux of biomedicalization. Unlike medicalization, which involves medicine exerting clinical and social control over particular conditions, biomedicalization transforms bodies and lives by creating a culture that emphasizes health, risk, and surveillance (Clarke et al. 2003). As Adele E. Clarke and her colleagues write, "In the biomedicalization era, the focus is no longer on illness, disability, and disease as matters of fate, but on health as a matter [of] ongoing moral self-transformation" (2003, 172). Those identified to be at risk— essentially all of us—are expected to participate in ongoing self-surveillance and management of lifestyle choices that affect the CDC's Energy Balance Equation. Or, as Natalie Boero describes, "processes of biomedicalization do not simply replace medicalization and discourses of morality via-à-vis health; rather, biomedicalization draws on and breaks with these discourses in employing the complex language of personal responsibility for health, risk, and the success or failure of biomedicine" (2003, 307). The dynamics of biomedicalization mean that, even though public health messages are normative, prescriptive, and ubiquitous, bodily "success" lies solely in the hands of individuals through ongoing management and transformation.

This moral obligation toward one's health is what Robert Crawford (1980, 2006) described several decades ago when he coined the term "healthism." Over the years we have witnessed an increasing preoccupation with obtaining health through lifestyle modification. Health is presumably an achievable state attainable by all. Drawing parallels with Talcott Parsons's (1951) sick role, Crawford maintains that, just as sick individuals should work with medical professionals to overcome their sickness, healthism obligates us all to pursue health. So if we are *all* susceptible to obesity and developing the health risks that, by the CDC's accounts, accompany this condition (such as heart disease, type 2 diabetes, and certain forms of cancers), we should all actively pursue health through the ongoing scrutiny of lifestyle. This mandate is nonnegotiable in tough economic times where public health agencies (and news media), with the backing of academic research, draw attention to the allegedly soaring economic costs of obesity. Defiance signifies a drain on public coffers and a public burden to the state; failing or refusing to do all one can to pursue health becomes even more morally suspect.

This is especially true of mothers, who carry the special burden of the well-being and weight of their children (Herndon 2010; Maher, Fraser, and Lindsay 2010; Maher, Fraser, and Wright 2010). And it is true of some racial/ethnic minorities and individuals from lower socioeconomic backgrounds, who, as we saw in previous chapters, not only exhibit higher obesity prevalence rates but may embrace counterhegemonic aesthetic norms as well. These groups may also be less likely to define themselves as medically overweight or obese or to express concern about their weight, compared to, say, whites and more socioeconomically privileged counterparts. Regardless of whether members of these groups are actively defying aesthetic and medical norms, they may be constituted as problematic by public health officials. They are moral suspects and potential burdens on the health-care system and public coffers. Subsequently, they may be placed under greater surveillance. Indeed, as others have observed, the moral panic over the fat body originates in part from public anxieties about minorities and disadvantaged groups (Herndon 2005; Oliver 2006; Saguy and Riley 2005).

The sheer availability of choices can exacerbate moral suspicion. For example, as we discussed, when diagnostic tools and technologies become available, patients cannot neutrally refuse them as refusal can be construed as failing to do "all that can be done" to ensure one's health (Browner and Press 1996). Refusal becomes an act of defiance that smacks of moral irresponsibility. In light of an array of scientific developments and technologies to predict obesity and related co-morbidities (e.g., BMI calculations, calipers, and blood tests), there is an expectation that individuals, as good citizens and patients, submit to these diagnostic tools. Choice, morality, and obligation are inescapably enmeshed (see Hughes 2002).

Some have argued that the moral undertones of public health messages, and of disciplinary medicine in general, mean that in actuality individuals do not possess *real* choices. Disciplinary medicine relies on an illusion of personal choice in which individuals think they can freely choose to adopt medical directives related to lifestyle, yet this is a mythic choice (Murray 2008). Healthism compels us to make only one choice, the one that complies with public health prescriptives. This is in line with what others have said about medical knowledge, broadly. Described as "authoritative knowledge," medical knowledge exhibits legitimacy and persuasion because it seems "natural, reasonable, and *consensually constructed*" (Jordan 1997, 57; our emphasis). Yet it can be far from consensual, and thus the health frame and its public health approach to the fat body can be interpreted as a form of "health fascism" (Edgley and Brissett 1990). It is neither about altruism nor public good; rather, it is about disciplinary control and management of the populace.

INTERFRAME CONNECTIONS

In chapter 1, we acknowledged that complex cultural discourses cannot be neatly dissected into component parts and that we employ a framing matrix as an analytical guideline to facilitate our analysis. The framing matrix in table 6.1 can be somewhat deceptive, giving the illusion that frames are stand alone, unconnected, and distinct. Yet frames are dialogical (Esacove 2004) and ought not to be analyzed in isolation. We have already recapped how competing sets of actors approach similar issues and how the two reactionary frames pit themselves against the hegemonic claims of the two dominant frames. We have not addressed, however, the ways in which frames may also work together to bolster one another and even implicitly undermine other frames. Here, we underscore a few examples of interframe influences and connections.

For example, recall how the reactionary frames have accused the dominant frames of working together. Both the CCF and NAAFA allege that financial incentives provided by diet drug manufacturers contaminate ethical research and result in a symbiotic relationship that others say is part of a larger health industrial complex (Oliver 2006). Furthermore, as we saw in chapter 2, the fashion-beauty complex often co-opts the language of the health frame. Such "beauty is health and health is beauty" talk pushes body compliance from two different yet equally powerful directions. In a culture that defines thinness as beautiful, this motto can be read as "thin *is* healthy and health *is* thinness." The danger of such logic, discussed elsewhere (see Kwan 2009a), is primarily that aesthetic gauges of health can be misleading, particularly compared to bio-physiological measures. (Or, in NAAFA's terminology, aesthetic markers of physical fitness do not accurately gauge metabolic fitness.) Nevertheless, the end result remains: the two dominant discourses, each of which mandates a compliant and docile body in its own right, effectively work in tandem to produce the same outcome.

There are also instances in which dominant and reactionary frames come together. For example, Marion Nestle (1993, 2002) has written extensively about the influence of food and agriculture lobbies on the content of the United States

Department of Agriculture (USDA) Food Pyramid and other nutritional guide-lines. As we saw in chapter 4, the USDA's Dairy Management program has col-laborated with the Domino's pizza chain to develop a new line of cheesier pizzas. So while one branch of the government espouses weight loss and caloric con-trol, another branch works with restaurants to expand their menus to include calorie-laden products. The food industry has also been known to employ differ-ent strategies to co-opt the health frame. Jeffrey P. Koplan and Kelly D. Brownell (2010) have rather skeptically pointed out that these strategies include directly associating themselves with a health organization; reformulating products by adding vitamins, minerals, and fibers to foods of poor nutritional quality and then marketing them as healthy options; and even endorsing Michelle Obama's Let's Move! campaign.

We have also seen connections between NAAFA's subversive social justice frame and the two dominant frames. Researchers have documented that HAES advocate Lynn McAfee has had a seat at the table at FDA and NIH meetings and has also influenced important NIH publications (Saguy and Riley 2005, 909–911). That NAAFA offers scholarships to student fashion designers to specialize in plus-size fashions indicates that the organization has begun to directly shape the product offerings of the fashion-beauty complex. The asso-ciation's expert commentary on entertainment news shows and websites such as *TMZ* (2010) and *Entertainment Tonight* (see Chang 2006)—programs that typically obsess about beauty and superficial matters—further suggests that the group is, at the very least, dialoguing with the fashion-beauty complex and related media industries.

Interestingly, there seems to be minimal connection between the two reac-tionary frames. This is somewhat striking in light of their commonalities. Both frames attack the core assertions of the health frame; both frames rework the overweight-equals-unhealthy formula, maintaining that large bodies can still be fit; both frames rely on, at times, the same authoritative figure, Glenn Gaesser; both frames condemn obesity researchers who fail to conduct unbiased research as a result of their financial ties to various industries; and both frames protect food consumption, whether as a right to be practiced free from governmental interference (CCF 2005a) or as a pleasure to be enjoyed without stigmatization or judgment for one's dietary preferences (NAAFA 2011k, "Dieting").

This lack of dialogue and absence of an alliance between the social justice frame and the choice and responsibility frame may be due to the motivations mentioned earlier. The CCF is profit driven, while NAAFA's organizational mis-sion is to attain social justice through cultural and structural change. The lack of an alliance may also be attributable to how these two groups approach causal claims: as we have seen, unlike the CCF, which falls back on arguments of indi-vidual blame, NAAFA attempts to shift blame away from the individual.

POLICY IMPLICATIONS, FRAME DIALOGUES, AND
LESSONS FOR PUBLIC HEALTH OFFICIALS

All frames offer solutions to the problem they define as fundamental. While three of the frames we have examined contain explicit policy directives, one frame does not. The fashion-beauty complex is not a conscious actor attempting to directly manipulate public policy, and as such the aesthetic frame does not offer explicit policy objectives. The three remaining frames do. The health frame advocates policy objectives aimed at protecting public health, the choice and responsibility frame promotes policies that comport with its goals of protecting consumer choice and the free market, and the social justice frame pursues policies geared toward modifying the way the fat body is viewed and treated in an effort to combat size discrimination. Although these frames have decidedly different policy slants, a closer look reveals that they may not be entirely incompatible. We have already seen how frames exhibit overlap and connections, and it seems that public health authorities may be able to learn from other frames where public policy is concerned.[3]

The health frame's underlying policy objectives aim to, when all is said and done, cultivate a healthy population, in part through reducing overweight and obesity rates. The title of one report by the nonprofit nonpartisan organization Trust for America's Health (2006) captures how well these policies are faring: *F as in Fat: How Obesity Policies Are Failing in America.* According to this report, despite interventions targeting three levels—children, adults, and community design—the so-called obesity epidemic is not abating. In May 2012, public health researchers, including those working at the CDC, published the report "Obesity and Severe Obesity Forecasts through 2030" (Finkelstein et al. 2012). If current trends continue, these researchers predict an obesity prevalence rate of 42 percent by 2030. Moreover, as we saw in chapter 3, in 2010 no state reached the goal of 15 percent adult obesity prevalence. Today, visitors to the CDC's Adult Obesity web pages are greeted with the message: "During the past 20 years, there has been a dramatic increase in obesity in the United States and rates remain high" (CDC 2012f). In short, from a public health standpoint, the problem has not subsided.

Anjali Jain's comprehensive review of obesity programs sheds light on the source of this failure. As she states, "It is time to be realistic with individuals about the limited effectiveness of lifestyle interventions and obesity drugs, and to focus on public health interventions rather than individual treatments to halt the obesity epidemic" (2005, 1390). A statement in the Trust for America's Health report acknowledges this very point, indicating that most adult obesity-related efforts in the United States have focused on weight-loss efforts (2005, 40).

It is plausible then that the failure of current public policy strategies to combat the so-called obesity epidemic can be attributed in part to an overemphasis on weight-related behavioral changes and a de-emphasis of broader community interventions, along with long-term weight-management strategies. Despite policy makers' and experts' call for multitiered interventions (and even laypersons' recognition of multiple causal factors), public policy gravitates toward individualized policies.

Such individualized approaches are not surprising given public views on obesity causation and the link between perceived etiology and policy recommendations. Scholars have shown that the strongest predictors of obesity policy are beliefs about its etiology (Oliver and Lee 2005) and that the metaphors people use to understand obesity (e.g., obesity is a sin, a disability, an addiction) are reliable predictors of public policy support (Barry et al. 2009). As Joe Greener, Flora Douglas, and Edwin van Teijlingen (2010) observe, unlike health professionals and overweight laypersons, policy makers as a group acknowledge socioecological causes of obesity and, subsequently, are the ones pushing for environmental interventions. However, these researchers contend that policy makers do so rather warily; policy makers acknowledge that large-scale environmental policy changes are unlikely in the absence of public support and in a climate that typically favors behavioral-level changes.

In recent years, however, there have been a number of innovative federal policy initiatives that address structural changes and the built environment in order to facilitate effective and long-term lifestyle changes. For example, Michelle Obama's Let's Move! campaign was instrumental in the passage of the Healthy, Hunger-Free Kids Act of 2010, which "authorizes funding for federal school meal and child nutrition programs and increases access to healthy food for low-income children" by extending existing programs and providing an additional $4.5 billion in new funding over a ten-year period (Let's Move! 2010). One of the most important changes brought about by this act was a revision of the National School Lunch Program; it raised nutrition standards by mandating the inclusion of more fruits, vegetables, and whole grains; decreasing portion sizes; and limiting access to full-fat milk (USDA 2012).

Moreover, the American Recovery and Reinvestment Act of 2009 provided $650 million to the CDC for a program titled Communities Putting Prevention to Work (CPPW), which "emphasizes policy and environmental change at both the state and local levels, focused on increasing levels of physical activity; improving nutrition; [and] decreasing obesity prevalence" (CDC 2011c, 21–22). Specifically, $230 million was awarded to the CDC's Division of Nutrition, Physical Activity, and Obesity (DNPAO) to fund state and local programs aimed specifically at fighting obesity (HHS 2010a). These programs approach the problem of obesity from multiple standpoints and encompass a variety of strategies to combat obesity. For example, some of these initiatives focus on increasing physical activity by creating safe routes to schools (through sidewalk, street safety, and design improvements), encouraging children to engage in active transportation (such as walking or biking), and improving traffic safety near schools (CDC 2012h).

Along with these structural changes, which attempt to address both sides of the Energy Balance Equation, various government agencies devote significant attention and resources to researching obesity. For instance, the National Institutes of Health reports that it spent 830 million research dollars on obesity in 2011 and has plans to spend similar amounts in 2012 and 2013 (NIH 2012).

These newer initiatives suggest a broader approach to what the CDC defines as a pressing health epidemic. Yet only time will reveal their impact and whether they will in fact lead to the CDC's goal of a reduction in obesity prevalence rates. Some observers have already commented that while the Let's Move! campaign has not decreased childhood obesity rates, it has nevertheless increased public awareness of the issue and increased public support for federal initiatives aimed at combating obesity (Emanuel 2012).

In light of their failure to stymie obesity rates, advocates of the health frame might learn a few lessons from others framers, such as proponents of the social justice frame. Perhaps the CDC's inability to garner successful results for the public health agenda stems from its narrow understanding of health. For example, the CDC's attention to physical health tends to overlook psychological and emotional well-being, including the weight stigma at the core of the social justice frame. By neglecting to address fat bias, stigma, and discrimination, public health officials may actually be foiling their policy goals. As researchers have well established and NAAFA advocates repeatedly spell out, weight stigma can lead to individual health consequences such as unhealthy eating and lower physical activity; psychological disorders; stress-induced pathophysiology; and substandard health care and decreased utilization of healthcare services (Puhl and Heuer 2010).

The health frame's failure to combat weight bias also relates to health and social disparities. Here Rebecca Puhl and Chelsea Heuer discuss the interconnection between, on the one hand, weight bias and, on the other, health and social disparities:

> By limiting the national response for obesity to education about individual choices regarding nutrition and physical activity, important societal and environmental causes of obesity are overlooked, the economic and social disparities that contribute to obesity are ignored, and weight stigma and discrimination are equally disregarded. Indeed, public health policy can either protect those afflicted with a disease from discrimination, or can promote unfair treatment and disparities. Unfortunately, the US government has not addressed weight stigma and discrimination in formal legislation, leaving millions of obese people to suffer unfair

treatment because of their weight. These social consequences may intensify the health disparities already faced by obese Americans. Because obesity is especially prevalent among poor or minority groups who live in disadvantaged areas, obese individuals often already belong to marginalized groups and experience multiple stigmatized statuses. (2010, 1025, citation removed)

If Puhl and Heuer are correct, combating weight stigma and discrimination (key policy concerns of the social justice frame) does not necessarily compromise the policy concerns of the health frame. In fact, combating weight stigma and discrimination may actually help advocates of the health frame reach their policy goals of creating a healthy populace. Such approaches might also help prevent further social injustices because, as we have already seen, obesity disproportionately affects underprivileged groups.

Additionally, a broader approach to the health frame's policy initiatives might involve a shift away from what have been labeled aesthetic measures of health. As Annemarie Jutel (2001) maintains, the BMI and other weight/height measures that supposedly project health risks reveal more about morality and sentiments about body aesthetics than they do about physical health. The numbers they produce, such as those in the display of a bathroom scale, tend to reflect and reinforce cultural expectations about how the body *ought* to appear. Or, as NAAFA and HAES allies might put it, they are not real measures of physical and metabolic health. This so-called aesthetics of health or normality (see also Spitzack 1990) may result in prioritization of weight loss and inattention to viable alternatives to dieting, including options that promote overall fitness and well-being (see Aphramor 2005). Adopting a HAES approach to health would mean abandoning the view that health is an objective end state and instead viewing health as a subjective and dynamic process (Burgard 2009). The health frame's potential adaptation of this broader multidimensional operational definition of health might facilitate its policy agenda; moreover, it would align with the World Health Organization's oft-cited definition of health as a "state of complete physical, mental, and social well-being" (WHO 2011).

Finally, while the CCF's free-market policy objectives are necessarily incompatible with some policies of health governance, particularly those health initiatives aimed at certain structural changes such as new taxes on foodstuffs or regulations on food marketing, a few things are worth noting. First, if trends in receiving flu shots, attending college, smoking, or drinking heavily are solid indicators, American adults already exhibit stable or improving levels of personal responsibility (Brownell et al. 2010). Second, the promotion of individual choice and personal responsibility is not necessarily incompatible with corporate responsibility. As Kelly D. Brownell and his colleagues write: "The challenge is to combine personal and collective responsibility approaches in ways that best serve the public good. This begins with viewing these approaches as complementary, if not synergistic, and recognizing that conditions can be changed to create more optimal defaults that support informed and responsible decisions and hence enhance personal freedoms" (2010, 384). According to Brownell and his colleagues (2010), when those advocating the choice and responsibility frame go on "personal responsibility crusades" (Hacker 2006), they can actually undermine personal responsibility. They do so by mislabeling actions that enhance personal choice as "government intrusion," which then stalls much-needed policy changes that can actually help people become more responsible and make more informed choices. In this line of thinking, neither the consumer's right to factual information nor the regulation of food marketing or the imposition of food taxes necessarily clash with the choice and responsibility frame's goal of protecting consumer freedom and encouraging personal responsibility.

FRAMING THE FAT BODY

Framing Fat explores how competing claims makers attempt to define fat and the fat body. In our presentation of four competing frames, or discourses, about the fat body, we discussed their key messages and how each message was conveyed. We saw that the aesthetic and health frames are homogenizing and lead to body conformity, while the choice and responsibility and social justice frames promote body diversity, albeit for different reasons. We also saw how core tenets of the aesthetic, health, and choice and responsibility frames generally accord with public sentiments—a resonance that is, we argue, attributable in part to the salience of the individualistic logic about obesity causation upon which these three frames rest.

This individualistic logic stigmatizes body nonconformists as morally weak and disreputable. Yet, as we have laid out in preceding pages, the burden of body conformity falls unevenly on different groups. For example, aesthetic body norms are gendered, carrying much more weight for women than they do for men. The ability to transform the body is also contingent upon factors directly related to socioeconomic status, including financial resources, leisure time, and nutritional knowledge. Racial segregation correlates positively with obesity risk, and obesity rates are significantly higher in poor communities and among racial/ethnic minorities such as African Americans and Hispanics. Concern for weight loss and identification with medical categories such as "obese" also vary by racial/ethnic groups and socioeconomic status.

Framing Fat then is really about unveiling the cultural discourse that "frames" fat individuals for committing the crime of body nonconformity. The three powerful frames (namely, the aesthetic, health, and choice and responsibility frames) present incriminating evidence, portraying fat people as failures and blaming them for their failure to meet culturally constructed body norms. The National Association to Advance Fat Acceptance's rebuttal, which attempts to exonerate fat people by awakening others to the injustice of these frames, falls on the ears of a mostly unsympathetic jury. While there are multiple constructions in the court of public opinion, not all constructions are equal. Some fat frames win; some lose. The verdict is in: the strong individualistic neoliberal sentiments that permeate modern society skew understandings of beauty and health such that messages condemning fat bodies resonate in the public imagination. *Framing Fat* is ultimately about framing fat bodies.

Several decades ago, Peggy McIntosh (2000 [1988]) introduced the concept of male privilege—a set of unearned and invisible assets and advantages that men possess and women do not. According to McIntosh, as men go about their daily lives they are able to draw on the resources in what she refers to as an invisible knapsack of tools, strategies, maps, and so on, to make life a little easier. Men are often oblivious to this male privilege. They operate as if their lives are normative and morally neutral, and they may even assume that it is merit alone that accounts for their personal successes. Yet cultural and social structures have provided for, and reinforced, these taken-for-granted privileges.

In the same manner, we see how cultural discourses about fat play out in the public arena and create a cultural and social climate in which some bodies are privileged over others (see also Bacon 2009; Kwan 2010). Despite the fact that there are multiple approaches to body aesthetics and new ways of understanding the relationship between fat and health besides the overweight-equals-unhealthy equation, public attitudes equate fat with social, aesthetic, medical, and moral failure. However, as we saw, frames are not static; they can influence and dialogue with one another. Perhaps the day will come when these frames coalesce in such a way as to create greater acceptance of all bodies and to foster a society in which privilege based on body size is no longer a privilege and, in the words of NAAFA, "people of every size are accepted with dignity and equality in all aspects of life" (2011a).

NOTES

1. A CONTESTED FIELD

1. On fat activism, also see Martin (2002) and Sobal (1999).

2. For an overview of the cultural politics of body size from an anthropological perspective, see Gremillion (2005).

3. On the role of emotions in obesity epidemic discourse, see Fraser, Maher, and Wright (2010).

4. In their typology of "obesity epidemic entrepreneurs," Lee Monaghan, Robert Hollands, and Gary Pritchard (2010) acknowledge the different roles that parties play in shaping public discourse on fat. Their typology includes creators (what we are labeling "producers"), amplifiers/moralizers, legitimators, supporters, enforcers/administrators, and the entrepreneurial self.

5. In our e-mail communication with CREW on December 9, 2010, inquiring about the outcome of this complaint, we were directed to CREW's website for any updates. As of September 1, 2012, no new updates about the complaint appeared on CREW's website, suggesting that the complaint has resulted in no further action and remains unresolved.

6. Membership data is based on our June 16, 2011, communication with NAAFA's Membership and Member Services director, Phyllis Warr.

7. That would also be appropriately labeled a "medical" or "biomedical" frame. We consistently use the term "health" for the sake of simplicity.

8. Kwan discusses all four frames extensively in previous work (see Kwan 2007; 2009b; 2009c), and this book builds off of, and elaborates upon, these previous works.

2. FAT AS FRIGHTFUL

1. Because many advertisements are not archived in a way that lends to their being cited, some of our citations necessarily refer to third-party sources that make mention of the profiled advertisements but do not point directly to their primary sources. As a result, we have provided primary sources whenever possible and the best secondary sources whenever necessary.

2. The *Oxford English Dictionary* (2nd ed.) defines "frightful" as "tending to cause fright; alarming" and "horrible to contemplate, shocking, dreadful, revolting." We have opted to use the term "frightful" because it connotes something that cannot be seen in a positive light and is to be avoided at all costs.

3. On criticisms of the gendered nature of the mind-body dualism, see Bordo (1986).

4. The original Anti-Gym, founded in Denver, Colorado, shut down in January 2009 as a result of problems with the Internal Revenue Service (Husted 2009). It reportedly owed nearly $200,000 in back taxes (Maher 2009). The owner, Michael Karolchyk, relocated to California, where he opened an Anti-Gym in San Diego (Husted 2009); however, this

location also went out of business in 2010. Karolchyk has since made a name for himself by appearing in various media outlets such as *Fox Business* (2011), *America's Morning News* (CBS Houston 2011), and *Dr. Phil* (2010).

5. As seen in, for example, posts on the Yahoo! Fat Studies discussion group.

6. The National Association to Advance Fat Acceptance endorses fat admiration but is quick to critique fat fetishism, noting that it is coercive and dangerous (NAAFA 2011k, "Feederism"). However, some scholars have been less critical of fat fetishism (see LeBesco 2004).

7. Today, the notion that fat is frightful and slender is sexy seems to be a taken-for-granted part of the American cultural landscape. Many of the studies documenting Americans' aesthetic opinions of fat thus date from the 1970s, 1980s, and 1990s.

3. FAT AS FATAL

1. On historical changes in obesity criteria, see Kuczmarski and Flegal (2000).

2. BMI = mass (kg) / height (m)^2.

3. We acknowledge that public health officials express greater concern about the social consequences when it comes to overweight and obese *children*. This may be due to increased social awareness of bullying in recent years. For example, the Let's Move! (2012b) campaign acknowledges that overweight and obese children can be the targets of social discrimination and stigmatization, both of which can cause low self-esteem. Web pages devoted specifically to childhood obesity also acknowledge that "obese children and adolescents have a greater risk of social and psychological problems such as discrimination and poor self-esteem" (CDC 2012b).

4. 347 U.S. 483 (1954).

5. For a recent review on obesity and inequality, see Lee (2011).

6. Whitney Houston, vocal performance of "Greatest Love of All," by Michael Masser and Linda Creed, on *Whitney Houston*, Arista ARCD 8212, 1985, compact disc.

7. Interestingly, while the CCF argues that 35 million were affected, other sources, including the one we reference earlier in chapter 3 (Cohen and McDermott 1998), indicate that the redefinition affected 25 million individuals. Other sources indicate the figure at 29 million (e.g., Squires 1998). The original NIH press release does not specify a figure (NIH 1998). These competing estimates themselves point to the contested nature of the BMI and related issues.

8. In its attempt to debunk (what the group believes is) the myth that obesity has made diabetes an epidemic, the CCF also exposes a similar redefinition that changed the standards for diabetes diagnosis: "In 1997, the American Diabetes Association (ADA) and the federal government lowered the *per se* standard for diagnosing diabetes from a fasting blood glucose level of 140 mg/dL to 126 mg/dL" (CCF 2005a, 115). We focus on the BMI reclassification example as it is a prominent exemplar that received substantial media exposure.

9. It is worth restating here that, as we saw earlier, despite widespread usage of the BMI in its publications and on its website, the CDC acknowledges the BMI's limitations and insists on the use of other measures such as waist circumference.

10. Cartoon by Jim Borgman (*Cincinnati Inquirer*, April 27, 1997).

11. For a scholarly summary of the debate on deaths attributable to obesity, including a timeline of events, see McHugh (2006).

12. We acknowledge that the CCF recognizes that "extreme obesity remains a genuine health risk" (2005a, 1) and in this way aligns itself with the health frame. The CCF's challenge to the health frame is in reference to the overweight or obese body, not the extremely obese condition.

13. Cartoon by Alex Gregory (*New Yorker*, May 22, 2006).
14. Comments posted at the YouTube website hosting the podcast (HHS 2010c).
15. On critical layperson understandings of weight, see Monaghan (2007).

4. FAT AND FOOD POLITICS

1. The CCF published the first edition of *An Epidemic of Obesity Myths* in 2004. That edition focused on debunking seven "myths": that obesity kills 400,000 Americans a year, that you can't be overweight and healthy, that obesity is a disease, that overeating is the primary cause of obesity, that soda causes childhood obesity, that 64 percent of Americans are overweight or obese, and that obesity costs the U.S. economy $117 billion annually (CCF 2004a). These same "myths" are again allegedly debunked, albeit more elaborately, in the second edition (CCF 2005a). One visible difference in the second edition is the addition of a section entitled "Myth Makers: Financially Conflicted Obesity Research" (CCF 2005a, 127–174). The CCF does not mention specific organizational actors in the first edition, and, while it mentions individual researchers in the first edition, the attacks on these individuals are not as explicit as they are in the second edition. In the second edition, the CCF takes on several professional organizations and individuals that it accuses of directly profiting from, and therefore having a stake in, perpetuating these so-called myths. The CCF's criticisms of these specific professional organizations and individuals in the later edition suggest that its tactics are becoming more focused and more aggressive.

2. This chapter presents quite a few quotes that the CCF uses to back its claims. The CCF's main strategy is to pit research (or, in many cases, research quotes) favorable to its position against research that appears to advocate the health frame. In this battle of research studies, we do not take a normative stance. Instead, in this chapter (and throughout the book), we present the data, quotes, etc., that a cultural producer employs to illuminate the strategies and rhetoric it uses to convey its message and shape public opinions about the fat body.

3. While the CCF criticizes the CDC for citing allegedly methodologically problematic research, the CDC's health frame has ample research evidence upon which to draw to support its position central claims. These research studies not only acknowledge a diverse range of causal factors, from endocrine disruptors to mating patterns (see Keith et al. 2006), but employ longitudinal methods that are more likely (than cross-sectional studies) to establish a causal relationship between food consumption and health risk (Mozaffarian et al. 2011). In 2006, the agency also released a publication that summarizes longitudinal research on the relationship between sugar-sweetened beverages and weight gain (CDC 2006).

4. Cartoon by Larry Wright (*Detroit News*, February 9, 2006), reproduced at CCF (2009).
5. Cartoon by Gary Brookins (*Richmond Times Dispatch*, 1997), reproduced at CCF (2001).
6. The CCF also devotes extensive energy to criticizing the animal activist group People for the Ethical Treatment of Animals (PETA). Many of its cartoons and print advertisements accuse the group of hypocrisy (one CCF advertisement reads "Two on PETA staff charged with cruelty to animals"), not caring for human beings (one CCF advertisement reads "'Even if animal research results in a cure for AIDS we'd be against it.'—Ingrid Newkirk, President People for the Ethical Treatment of Animals"), and being extremist (one CCF advertisement reads, "'It would be great if all the fast-food outlets, slaughterhouses, these laboratories, and the banks who fund them exploded tomorrow.'—Bruce Friedrich, Campaign Director for People for the Ethical Treatment of Animals"; CCF 2011a). The CCF even has a website called www. petakillsanimals.com.

7. For example, New York City enacted a law in 2008 that bans the use of trans fats in New York City restaurants and requires restaurants to include nutrition facts (such as caloric content) on their menus (MSNBC 2006).

8. *Pelman v. McDonald's Corp.*, 237 F. Supp. 2d 512 (S.D.N.Y. 2003).

9. The 2004 Personal Responsibility in Food Consumption Act (aka the Cheeseburger Bill) would have placed limitations on litigation against food producers and retailers for making their customer's obese; however, after passing the House, it failed to receive approval from the Senate.

10. Cartoon by Henry Payne (*Detroit News*, November 15, 2003).

11. On how food and agriculture lobbies influenced the former United States Department of Agriculture (USDA) Food Pyramid, along with other examples, see Nestle (1993, 2002).

12. Some of the individual "myth makers" the CCF shames are tied to these three professional organizations.

13. The Food and Drug Administration recently approved a gel patch that freezes and destroys unwanted fat cells (Chang and Netter 2010).

14. For a recent review of beauty bias including the social disadvantages incurred by body nonconformists, see Rhode (2010).

5. FAT AND FAIR TREATMENT

1. On legal outcomes of appearance discrimination cases including size discrimination, see Rhode (2010), Solovay (2000), and Trautner and Kwan (2010).

2. The policy's thresholds—33.5 inches for men and 35.4 inches for women—were based on recommendations by the International Diabetes Federation as guidelines for identifying health risks (Onishi 2008).

3. This is NAAFA's primary source on discrimination.

4. Debra Gimlin (2002) observes that, despite NAAFA's civil rights orientation, many of the group's activities are social.

5. Because the solutions offered by NAAFA's social justice frame are in reaction to the two dominant frames, and because NAAFA's human-rights focus makes it action oriented, this chapter emphasizes solutions more than previous chapters do.

6. In an even larger venue, NAAFA board member Paul Campos (2010), writing in the *New Republic*, forwards similar challenges to Mrs. Obama, exposing her alarmist claims about childhood obesity and her role in promoting fat stigma.

7. We do not focus here on the resonance of NAAFA's call for diet industry regulation; however, we note that consumer advocates have questioned the safety and effectiveness of diet products. Over a decade ago, the Bureau of Consumer Protection of the Federal Trade Commission and other federal agencies, along with representatives from academia, the weight-loss industry, and consumer advocacy groups, convened a conference to evaluate commercial weight-loss products and programs (Cleland et al. 1997). The presiding panel acknowledged that many weight-loss marketers fail to conduct research on, or only make partial disclosures about, their products. Like NAAFA, consumer advocate groups have maintained that this lack of information may jeopardize the health of consumers. This was particularly evident in the 1990s with Federal Drug Administration (FDA)–approved appetite suppressants such as fenfluramine and phentermine (used in combination as "Fen-Phen"), which were eventually linked to serious cardiac-valvular disease. In recent years, legal scholars have also chimed in on debates about diet industry regulation, arguing that "misleading and scientifically implausible" claims are no longer just harmless "puffery"; therefore, weight-loss marketers who make

unsubstantiated scientific claims should not be afforded First Amendment protection (Gross 2006). In other words, weight-loss products have major health ramifications for consumers, and their manufacturers should be rightly held accountable for claims they make.

8. At least one study has found that study subjects do not associate overweight workers with stereotypical beliefs (see Roehling, Roehling, and Odland 2008).

9. See One Thousand Fat Cranes (2008).

6. FRAMING FAT BODIES

1. On obesity and attribution theory, also see Rodin et al. (1989) and Weiner, Perry, and Magnusson (1988).

2. As the other framers make abundantly clear, because the American public seems to respond well to research, and citing research increases the credibility of the message, marketers do sometimes turn to research findings in their advertisements. For example, the makers of the Medifast diet claims that it is "recommended by over 20,000 doctors" (Medifast, Inc. 2012).

3. Our discussion of policy does not assess the specific policies of the CDC, the CCF, and NAAFA. We deemed them too numerous and too extensive to review in this work. Others have laid out these policies critically in reports such as *F as in Fat: How Obesity Policies Are Failing in America* (Trust for America's Health 2006) and *Weight Bias: The Need for Public Policy* (Rudd 2008). Instead, our discussion focuses on select ways in which the policies of these three groups are unexpectedly compatible. Moreover, because our goal is to illuminate the social construction of fat, including various public policy approaches, our discussion of policy should not be taken to mean that we advocate a particular framer's policy agenda.

REFERENCES

ABA (American Beverage Association). 2012. "Active Members." www.ameribev.org/members/active-members (accessed May 13).

Abel, Emily K. 1986. "Adult Daughters and Care for the Elderly." *Feminist Studies* 12 (3): 479–497.

ACSM (American College of Sports Medicine). 2011. *ACSM American Fitness Index: Health and Community Fitness Status of the 50 Largest Metropolitan Areas.* Indianapolis, IN: ACSM.

Aguiar, Mark, and Erik Hurst. March 2007. "Measuring Trends in Leisure: The Allocation of Time over Five Decades." *Quarterly Journal of Economics* 122 (3): 969–1006.

Allison, David B., Kevin R. Fontaine, JoAnn E. Manson, June Stevens, and Theodore B. VanItallie. 1999. "Annual Deaths Attributable to Obesity in the United States." *Journal of the American Medical Association* 282 (16): 1530–1538.

Allison, David B., Raffaella Zannolli, and K. M. Venkat Narayan. 1999. "The Direct Health Care Costs of Obesity in the United States." *American Journal of Public Health* 89 (8): 1194–1199.

Altabe, Madeline, and Keisha-Gaye N. O'Garo. 2002. "Hispanic Body Images." In *Body Image: A Handbook of Theory, Research, and Clinical Practice,* edited by Thomas F. Cash and Thomas Pruzinsky, 250–256. New York: Guilford.

American Medical Association. 2011. "AMA Adopts New Policies at Annual Meeting." News release, June 21. www.ama-assn.org/ama/pub/news/news/a11-new-policies.page (accessed August 21, 2012).

Americans Against Food Taxes. 2011. "'Give Me a Break' Americans Against Food Taxes TV Ad." YouTube video, posted January 13. www.youtube.com/watch?v=hWi7JI55G-c (accessed May 8, 2012).

American Society for Aesthetic Plastic Surgery. 2009. "Despite Recession, Overall Plastic Surgery Demand Drops only 2 Percent from Last Year." March 9. www.surgery.org/media/news-releases/despite-recession-overall-plastic-surgery-demand-drops-only-2-percent-from-last-year (accessed August 21, 2012).

American Society for Metabolic and Bariatric Surgery. 2011. "Fact Sheet: Metabolic and Bariatric Surgery." http://s3.amazonaws.com/publicASMBS/MediaPressKit/MetabolicBariatricSurgeryOverviewJuly2011.pdf (accessed August 21, 2012).

Andersen, Arnold E., Paul J. Woodward, Adela Spalder, and Marlene Koss. 1993. "Body Size and Shape Characteristics of Personal ('In Search Of') Ads." *International Journal of Eating Disorders* 14 (4): 111–115.

Andreyeva, Tatiana, Michael W. Long, Kathryn E. Henderson, and Gabrielle M. Grode. 2010. "Trying to Lose Weight: Diet Strategies among Americans with Overweight or Obesity in 1996 and 2003." *Journal of the American Dietetic Association* 110 (4): 535–542.

Andreyeva, Tatiana, Rebecca M. Puhl, and Kelly D. Brownell. 2008. "Changes in Perceived Weight Discrimination among Americans: 1995–1996 through 2004–2006." *Obesity* 16 (5): 1129–1134.

Anti-Gym. 2011a. "Are You a Bearded Lady?" www.theantigym.com/beardedlady.html (accessed May 16, 2011; site discontinued).

———. 2011b. "Commercials." www.theantigym.com/caughtintheact.html (accessed May 16, 2011; site discontinued).

———. 2011c. "Intensity. Motivation. Accountability. Results." www.theantigym.com/exposed.html (accessed May 16, 2011; site discontinued).

———. 2011d. "No Chubbies Allowed." www.theantigym.com/blowyourmind.html (accessed May 16, 2011; site discontinued).

Aphramor, Lucy. 2005. "Is a Weight-Centred Health Framework Salutogenic? Some Thoughts on Unhinging Certain Dietary Ideologies." *Social Theory and Health* 3:315–340.

———. 2010. "Validity of Claims Made in Weight Management Research: A Narrative Review of Dietetic Articles." *Nutrition Journal* 9:30.

Apidexin. 2011. "Apidexin." www.apidexin.com/?gclid=COTsopT1hakCFSF17AodoGXusQ (accessed May 2, 2012).

Arterburn, David E., Matthew L. Maciejewski, and Joel Tsevat. 2005. "Impact of Morbid Obesity on Medical Expenditures on Adults." *International Journal of Obesity* 29 (3): 334–339.

Associated Press. 2011. "Ohio Woman Upset with Army over Son's Diet Death." *Sandusky Register*, March 26.

Atkinson, Michael. 2008. "Exploring Male Femininity in the 'Crisis': Men and Cosmetic Surgery." *Body and Society* 14 (1): 67–87.

Bacon, Linda. 2008. *Health at Every Size: The Surprising Truth about Your Weight.* Dallas: Benbella.

———. 2009. "Reflections on Fat Acceptance: Lessons Learned from Privilege." Essay based on keynote speech presented at the conference of the National Association to Advance Fat Acceptance, August 1, 2009. www.lindabacon.org/Bacon_ThinPrivilege080109.pdf (accessed August 21, 2012).

Bacon, Linda, Judith S. Stern, Marta D. Van Loan, and Nancy L. Keim. 2005. "Size Acceptance and Intuitive Eating Improve Health for Obese, Female Chronic Dieters." *Journal of the American Dietetic Association* 105 (6): 929–936.

Bariatric Care Centers. 2009. "Lose Weight, Enjoy Life!" www.drbrianmirza.com (accessed August 21, 2012).

Barry, Colleen L., Victoria L. Brescoll, Kelly D. Brownell, and Mark Schlesinger. 2009. "Obesity Metaphors: How Beliefs about the Causes of Obesity Affect Support for Public Policy." *Milbank Quarterly* 87 (1): 7–47.

Bartky, Sandra Lee. 1990. *Femininity and Domination: Studies in the Phenomenology of Oppression.* New York: Routledge.

———. 2010 [1988]. "Foucault, Femininity, and the Modernization of Patriarchal Power." In *The Politics of Women's Bodies: Sexuality, Appearance, and Behavior*, 3rd ed., edited by Rose Weitz, 76–97. New York: Oxford University Press.

Becker, Howard S. 1963. *Outsiders: Studies in the Sociology of Deviance.* New York: Free Press.

Belcher, Britni R., David Berrigan, Kevin W. Dodd, B. Adar Emken, Chih-ping Chou, and Donna Spruijt-Metz. 2010. "Physical Activity in US Youth: Effect of Race/Ethnicity, Age, Gender and Weight Status." *Medicine and Science in Sports and Exercise* 42 (12): 2211–2221.

Benford, Robert D., and David A. Snow. 2000. "Framing Processes and Social Movements: An Overview and Assessment." *Annual Review of Sociology* 26:611–639.

Berger, Joseph, M. Hamit Fisek, Robert Z. Norman, and Morris Zelditch Jr. 1977. *Status Characteristics and Social Interaction.* New York: Elsevier.

Best, Joel. 1989. *Images of Issues: Typifying Contemporary Social Problems.* New York: Aldine de Gruyter.

Block, Jason P., Richard A. Scribner, and Karen B. DeSalvo. 2004. "Fast Food, Race/Ethnicity, and Income: A Geographic Analysis." *American Journal of Preventive Medicine* 27 (3): 211–217.

Blommaert, Jan. 2005. *Discourse: A Critical Introduction*. Cambridge: Cambridge University Press.

Blumer, Herbert. 1971. "Social Problems as Collective Behavior." *Social Problems* 18 (3): 298–306.

Boas, Taylor C., and Jordan Gans-Morse. 2009. "Neoliberalism: From New Liberal Philosophy to Anti-liberal Slogan." *Studies in Comparative International Development* 44 (2): 137–161.

Bobel, Chris, and Samantha Kwan. 2011. *Embodied Resistance: Challenging the Norms, Breaking the Rules*. Nashville, TN: Vanderbilt University Press.

Boero, Natalie. 2007. "All the News That's Fat to Print: The American 'Obesity Epidemic' and the Media." *Qualitative Sociology* 30 (1): 41–60.

———. 2009. "Fat Kids, Working Moms, and the Obesity Epidemic." In Rothblum and Solovay 2009, 113–119.

———. 2010. "Bypassing Blame: Bariatric Surgery and the Case of Biomedical Failure." In *Biomedicalization: Technoscience, Health, and Illness in the U.S.*, edited by Adele E. Clarke, Laura Mamo, Jennifer Ruth Fosket, Jennifer R. Fishman, and Janet K. Shim, 307–330. Durham, NC: Duke University Press.

Bond, John. 2002. "The Medicalization of Dementia." *Journal of Aging Studies* 6 (4): 397–403.

Bookwala, Jamila, and Jenny Boyar. 2008. "Gender, Excessive Body Weight, and Psychological Well-Being in Adulthood." *Psychology of Women Quarterly* 32 (2): 188–195.

Bordo, Susan. 1986. "The Cartesian Masculinization of Thought." *Signs* 11 (3): 439–456.

———. 2003. *Unbearable Weight: Feminism, Western Culture, and the Body*. 2nd ed. Berkeley: University of California Press.

Bourdieu, Pierre. 1978. "Sport and Social Class." *Social Science Information* 17 (6): 819–840.

———. 1986. "The Forms of Capital." In *Handbook of Theory and Research for the Sociology of Education*, edited by John G. Richardson, 241–258. New York: Greenwood.

Brewis, Alexandra A., Amber Wutich, Ashlan Faletta-Cowden, and Isa Rodriguez-Soto. 2011. "Body Norms and Fat Stigma in Global Perspective." *Current Anthropology* 52 (2): 269–276.

Brink, Pamela J., and Kristi Ferguson. 1998. "The Decision to Lose Weight." *Western Journal of Nursing Research* 20 (1): 84–102.

Brochu, Paula M., and Melanie A. Morrison. 2007. "Implicit and Explicit Prejudice toward Overweight and Average-Weight Men and Women: Testing Their Correspondence and Relation to Behavioral Intentions." *Journal of Social Psychology* 147 (6): 681–706.

Brown, Alexander. 2009. *Personal Responsibility: Why It Matters*. New York: Continuum.

Brownell, Kelly D., Rogan Kersh, Davis S. Ludwig, Robert C. Post, Rebecca M. Puhl, Marlene B. Schwartz, and Walter C. Willett. 2010. "Personal Responsibility and Obesity: A Constructive Approach to a Controversial Issue." *Health Affairs* 29 (3): 379–387.

Brownell, Kelly D., Rebecca M. Puhl, Marlene B. Schwartz, and Leslie Rudd, eds. 2005. *Weight Bias: Nature, Consequences and Remedies*. New York: Guilford.

Browner, C. H., and Nancy Press. 1996. "The Production of Authoritative Knowledge in American Prenatal Care." *Medical Anthropology Quarterly* 10 (2): 141–156.

Bruno, Barbara Altman, and Debora Burgard. 2009. *Guidelines for Therapists Who Treat Fat Clients*. National Association to Advance Fat Acceptance. www.naafaonline.com/dev2/assets/documents/NAAFA_Therapists_2010_v03.pdf (accessed August 21, 2012).

Burgard, Deb. 2009. "What Is 'Health at Every Size'?" In Rothblum and Solovay 2009, 42–53.

Bury, M. R. 1986. "Social Constructionism and the Development of Medical Sociology." *Sociology of Health and Illness* 8 (2): 137–169.

Campos, Paul. 2004. *The Obesity Myth: Why America's Obsession with Weight Is Hazardous to Your Health*. New York: Gotham Books.

————. 2010. "Childhood Shmobesity." *New Republic*, February 11.

Campos, Paul, Abigail Saguy, Paul Ernsberger, Eric Oliver, and Glenn Gaesser. 2006. "The Epidemiology of Overweight and Obesity: Public Health Crisis or Moral Panic?" *International Journal of Epidemiology* 35 (1): 55–60.

Canner, Liz, director. 2009. *Orgasm Inc.* DVD. West Groton, MA: Astrea Media.

Carmon, Irin. 2010. "Charming Facebook Fat-Bashers Maybe Practicing Hate Speech." Jezebel, July 9. http://jezebel.com/5583086/are-facebook-fat+bashers-practicing-hate-speech (accessed August 21, 2012).

Carollo, Kim, and Lara Salahi. 2011. "Pound for Pound, Worst Foods for Weight Gain." *ABC News*, June 22.

Carr, Deborah, and Michael A. Friedman. 2006. "Body Weight and the Quality of Interpersonal Relationships." *Social Psychology Quarterly* 69 (2): 127–149.

Case, Anne, and Christina Paxson. 2001. "Mothers and Others: Who Invests in Children's Health?" *Journal of Health Economics* 20 (3): 301–328.

Cawley, John. 2004. "The Impact of Obesity on Wages." *Journal of Human Resources* 39 (2): 451–474.

CBS Houston. 2011. "Regulating the Fast Food Industry." *America's Morning News*, August 15. http://houston.cbslocal.com/2011/08/15/regulating-the-fast-food-industry/ (accessed September 21, 2012).

CCF (Center for Consumer Freedom). 1997–2012a. Main website. www.consumerfreedom. com (accessed August 21, 2012).

————. 1997–2012b. "CSPIscam: Our Advertisements." www.cspiscam.com/ads.cfm (accessed May 7, 2012).

————. 2001. "Uncle Sam." Center for Consumer Freedom. July 1. www.consumerfreedom .com/2001/07/uncle-sam (accessed August 21, 2012).

————. 2004a. *An Epidemic of Obesity Myths*. Washington, DC: Center for Consumer Freedom.

————. 2004b. "Today Let's Blame Obesity On . . ." June 30. www.consumerfreedom .com/2004/06/today-lets-blame-obesity-on (accessed August 21, 2012).

————. 2005a. *An Epidemic of Obesity Myths*. Washington, DC: Center for Consumer Freedom.

————. 2005b. "He Plays Football for Four Hours a Day!" March 29. www.consumerfreedom .com/2005/03/he-plays-football-for-four-hours-a-day/ (accessed August 2, 2012).

————. 2005c. "If Obesity = Disease, the Diet Drugs = Insurance $." December 28. www .consumerfreedom.com/2005/12/if-obesity-disease-the-diet-drugs-insurance/ (accessed August 21, 2012).

————. 2005d. "I'm Suing Bathing Suit Makers for Causing Skin Cancer." August 2. www .consumerfreedom.com/2005/08/im-suing-bathing-suit-makers-for-causing-skin-cancer (accessed August 21, 2012).

————. 2007a. "Changes in Work." July 25. www.consumerfreedom.com/2007/07/ changes-in-work/.

————. 2007b. *Small Choices, Big Bodies: How Countless Daily Decisions Contribute to America's Burgeoning Waistline*. Washington, DC: Center for Consumer Freedom.

————. 2007c. "Something's Just Not Right . . ." June 22. www.consumerfreedom .com/2007/06/somethings-just-not-right (accessed August 21, 2012).

————. 2007d. "Today's Medical News." April 12. www.consumerfreedom.com/2007/04/ todays-medical-news (accessed August 21, 2012).

————. 2009. "Exercise TV." November 10. www.consumerfreedom.com/tag/cartoon/ page/2 (accessed August 21, 2012).

———. 2011a. "Archives: Print Ads." Last modified December 22. www.consumerfreedom.com/tag/print (accessed August 21, 2012).

———. 2011b. "Biography: Dr. Marion Nestle." ActivistCash.com. http://activistcash.com/biography.cfm/b/3381-marion-nestle-dr (accessed November 22, 2011).

———. 2012. "About Us." Center for Consumer Freedom. Accessed April 30. www.consumerfreedom.com/about (accessed April 30, 2012).

CDC (Centers for Disease Control and Prevention). 1996. "Historical Perspectives History of CDC." *Morbidity and Mortality Weekly Report* 45 (25): 526–530.

———. 2006. "Does Drinking Beverages with Added Sugars Increase the Risk of Overweight?" Research to Practices Series no. 3, September. www.cdc.gov/nccdphp/dnpa/nutrition/pdf/r2p_sweetend_beverages.pdf (accessed September 6, 2012).

———. 2010a. "About CDC." www.cdc.gov/about/history/ourstory.htm (accessed September 6, 2012).

———. 2010b. "Adult Obesity." *CDC Vitalsigns*. www.cdc.gov/VitalSigns/pdf/2010-08-vitalsigns.pdf (accessed September 6, 2012).

———. 2010c. "More US Adults Report Being Obese." News release, August 3. www.cdc.gov/media/pressrel/2010/r100803.htm (accessed September 6, 2012).

———. 2010d. "Presentation: The Childhood Obesity Epidemic: Threats and Opportunities." www.cdc.gov/about/grand-rounds/archives/2010/06-June.htm (accessed September 6, 2012).

———. 2011a. "Balancing Calories." www.cdc.gov/healthyweight/calories/index.html (accessed September 6, 2012).

———. 2011b. "CDC's LEAN Works!—A Workplace Obesity Prevention Program." www.cdc.gov/leanworks (accessed September 6, 2012).

———. 2011c. *FY 2011 Justification of Estimates for Appropriation Committees*. www.cdc.gov/fmo/topic/Budget%20Information/appropriations_budget_form_pdf/FY2011_CDC_CJ_Final.pdf (accessed September 6, 2012).

———. 2011d. "Healthy Weight—It's Not a Diet, It's a Lifestyle." www.cdc.gov/healthyweight/success/index.html (accessed September 6, 2012).

———. 2011e. "Obesity Cost Calculator." www.cdc.gov/leanworks/costcalculator/index.html (accessed September 6, 2012).

———. 2011f. "Obesity: Halting the Epidemic by Making Health Easier: At a Glance 2011." www.cdc.gov/chronicdisease/resources/publications/aag/pdf/2011/Obesity_AAG_WEB_508.pdf (accessed September 6, 2012).

———. 2011g. "The Obesity Epidemic." Podcast video, July 22. www.cdc.gov/cdctv/Obesity Epidemic (accessed September 6, 2012).

———. 2012a. "Adult Obesity Facts." www.cdc.gov/obesity/data/adult.html (accessed May 9, 2012).

———. 2012b. "Basics about Childhood Obesity." www.cdc.gov/obesity/childhood/basics.html (accessed September 6, 2012).

———. 2012c. "Causes and Consequences." www.cdc.gov/obesity/adult/causes/index.html (accessed September 6, 2012).

———. 2012d. "Data and Statistics." www.cdc.gov/obesity/data/childhood.html (accessed September 6, 2012).

———. 2012e. "Defining Overweight and Obesity." www.cdc.gov/obesity/adult/defining.html (accessed September 6, 2012).

———. 2012f. "Facts." www.cdc.gov/obesity/data/facts.html (accessed September 6, 2012).

———. 2012g. "Overweight and Obesity." www.cdc.gov/obesity/index.html (accessed September 6, 2012).

——. 2012h. "Program Highlights." www.cdc.gov/obesity/stateprograms/highlights.html (accessed September 6, 2012).

——. 2012i. "Resources and Publications." www.cdc.gov/obesity/resources/index.html (accessed September 6, 2012).

Cellulite MD. 2011. Main website. www.cellulitemd.com (accessed August 21, 2012).

Chang, Juju, and Sarah Netter. 2010. "Freezing Fat: Weight Loss Treatment Zeltiq Approved by FDA." *ABC News*, September 15.

Chang, Robert Y., director. 2006. *Nothing to Lose*. DVD. Watertown, MA: Documentary Educational Resources.

Chang, Virginia W. 2006. "Racial Residential Segregation and Weight Status among US Adults." *Social Science and Medicine* 63 (5): 1289–1303.

Chang, Virginia W., Amy E. Hillier, and Neil K. Mehta. 2009. "Neighborhood Racial Isolation, Disorder and Obesity." *Social Forces* 87 (4): 2053–2092.

Chauncey, George. 1994. *Gay New York: Gender, Urban Culture, and the Making of the Gay Male World, 1890–1940*. New York: Basic Books.

Chen, Eunice Y., and Molly Brown. 2005. "Obesity Stigma in Sexual Relationships." *Obesity Research* 13 (8): 1393–1397.

Chernin, Kim. 1994. *The Obsession: Reflections on the Tyranny of Slenderness*. New York: Harper Perennial.

Choate, Laura Hensley. 2005. "Toward a Theoretical Model of Women's Body Image Resilience." *Journal of Counseling and Development* 83 (3): 320–330.

Christou, Nicolas V., Didier Look, and Lloyd D. MacLean. 2006. "Weight Gain after Short- and Long-Limb Gastric Bypass in Patients Followed for Longer than 10 Years." *Annals of Surgery* 244 (5): 734–740.

Church, Timothy S., Corby K. Martin, Angela M. Thompson, Conrad P. Earnest, Catherine R. Mikus, and Steven N. Blair. 2009. "Changes in Weight, Waist Circumference, and Compensatory Responses with Different Doses of Exercise among Sedentary, Overweight Postmenopausal Women." *PLoS One* 4 (2): e4515.

Clarke, Adele, E., Janet K. Shim, Laura Mamo, Jennifer Ruth Fosket, and Jennifer R. Fishman. 2003. "Biomedicalization: Technoscientific Transformations of Health, Illness, and U.S. Biomedicine." *American Sociological Review* 68 (2): 161–194.

——. 2010. "Biomedicalization: A Theoretical and Substantive Introduction." In *Biomedicalization: Technoscience, Health, and Illness in the U.S.*, edited by Adele E. Clarke, Laura Mamo, Jennifer Ruth Fosket, Jennifer R. Fishman, and Janet K. Shim, 1–44. Durham, NC: Duke University Press.

Cleland, Richard, Dean C. Graybill, Van Hubbard, Laura Kettel Khan, Judith S. Stern, Thomas A. Wadden, Roland Weinsier, and Susan Yanovski. 1997. *Commercial Weight Loss Products and Programs: What Consumers Stand to Gain and Lose*. Conference proceedings, October 16–17, Washington, DC. www.ftc.gov/os/1998/03/weightlo.rpt.htm (accessed August 21, 2012).

Cloud, John. 2009. "Why Exercise Won't Make You Thin." *Time*, August 9.

Cohen, Elizabeth, and Anne McDermott. 1998. "Who's Fat? New Definition Adopted." CNN, June 17. www.cnn.com/HEALTH/9806/17/weight.guidelines (accessed August 21, 2012).

Colditz, Graham A. 1999. "Economic Costs of Obesity and Inactivity." *Medicine and Science in Sports and Exercise* 31 (11): S663–S667.

Cole, Cheryl L., and Amy Hribar. 1995. "Celebrity Feminism: Nike Style Post-Fordism, Transcendence, and Consumer Power." *Sociology of Sport* 12 (4): 347–369.

Collins, Patricia Hill. 2000. *Black Feminist Thought: Knowledge, Consciousness, and the Politics of Empowerment*. 2nd ed. New York: Routledge.

————. 2004. *Black Sexual Politics: African Americans, Gender, and the New Racism*. New York: Routledge.

Conley, Dalton, and Rebecca Glauber. 2007. "Gender, Body Mass, and Socioeconomic Status: New Evidence from the PSID." *Advances in Health Economics and Health Services Research* 17:253–275.

Connell, R. W. 1995. *Masculinities*. Berkeley: University of California Press.

Connell, R. W., and James W. Messerschmidt. 2005. "Hegemonic Masculinity: Rethinking the Concept." *Gender and Society* 19 (6): 832–859.

Conrad, Peter. 1992. "Medicalization and Social Control." *Annual Review of Sociology* 18:209–232.

Conrad, Peter, and Deborah Potter. 2000. "From Hyperactive Children to Adult ADHD: Observations on the Expansion of Medical Categories." *Social Problems* 47 (4): 559–582.

Conrad, Peter, and Joseph W. Schneider. 1980. *Deviance and Medicalization: From Badness to Sickness*. St. Louis: C. V. Mosby.

Correll, Shelley J., and Cecilia J. Ridgeway. 2003. "Expectation States Theory." In *Handbook of Social Psychology*, edited by John Delamater, 29–51. New York: Kluwer.

CRA (Corn Refiners Association). 2011a. "SweetSurprise.com: The Facts about High Fructose Corn Syrup." www.sweetsurprise.com (accessed September 11, 2012).

————. 2011b. "Myth vs. Facts." http://sweetsurprise.com/hfcs-myths-and-facts (accessed September 3, 2012).

Crandall, Christian S. 1994. "Prejudice against Fat People: Ideology and Self-Interest." *Journal of Personality and Social Psychology* 66 (5): 882–894.

Crandall, Christian S., and Monica Biernat. 1990. "The Ideology of Anti-fat Attitudes." *Journal of Applied Social Psychology* 20 (3): 227–243.

Crandall, Christian S., Silvana D'Anello, Nuray Sakalli, Eleana Lazarus, Grazyna Wieczorkowska Nejtardt, and N. T. Feather. 2001. "An Attribution-Value Model of Prejudice: Anti-fat Attitudes in Six Nations." *Personality and Social Psychology Bulletin* 27 (1): 30–37.

Crandall, Christian S., and Rebecca Martinez. 1996. "Culture, Ideology, and Antifat Attitudes." *Personality and Social Psychology Bulletin* 22 (11): 1165–1176.

Crandall, Christian S., Angela Nierman, and Michelle Hebl. 2009. "Anti-fat Prejudice." In *Handbook of Prejudice, Stereotyping, and Discrimination*, edited by Todd D. Nelson, 469–487. New York: Taylor & Francis.

Crawford, David, Neville Owen, Dorothy Broom, Marian Worcester, and Graeme Oliver. 1998. "Weight-Control Practices of Adults in a Rural Community." *Australian and New Zealand Journal of Public Health* 22 (1): 73–79.

Crawford, Robert. 1980. "Healthism and the Medicalization of Everyday Life." *International Journal of Health Services* 10 (3): 365–388.

————. 1994. "The Boundaries of the Self and the Unhealthy Other: Reflections on Health, Culture and AIDS." *Social Science and Medicine* 38 (10): 1347–1365.

————. 2006. "Health as a Meaningful Social Practice." *Health* 10 (4): 401–420.

Crespo, Carlos J., Ellen Smit, Ross E. Andersen, Olivia Carter-Pokras, and Barbara E. Ainsworth. 2000. "Race/Ethnicity, Social Class and Their Relation to Physical Inactivity during Leisure Time: Results from the Third National Health and Nutrition Examination Survey, 1988–1994." *American Journal of Preventive Medicine* 18 (1): 46–53.

CREW (Citizens for Responsibility and Ethics in Washington). 2004. "CREW Files Complaint against Center for Consumer Freedom Alleging Violations of Tax Exempt Status." News release, November 16. www.citizensforethics.org/press/entry/831 (accessed August 21, 2012).

Crosnoe, Robert. 2007. "Gender, Obesity, and Education." *Sociology of Education* 80 (3): 241–260.

Crosnoe, Robert, Anna Strassmann Mueller, and Kenneth Frank. 2008. "Gender, Body Size and Social Relations in American High Schools." *Social Forces* 86 (3): 1189–1216.

CSPI (Center for Science in the Public Interest). 2010. "Class Action Lawsuit Targets McDonald's Use of Toys to Market to Children." December 15. www.cspinet.org/new/201012151 .html (accessed August 21, 2012).

———. 2011. "Mission Statement." February 15. www.cspinet.org/about/mission.html (accessed August 21, 2012).

Darlin, Damon. 2006. "Extra Weight, Higher Costs." *New York Times*, December 2.

Davis, Kathy. 1991. "Remaking the She-Devil: A Critical Look at Feminist Approaches to Beauty." *Hypatia* 6 (2): 21–43.

Davis, Simon. 1990. "Men as Success Objects and Women as Sex Objects: A Study of Personal Advertisements." *Sex Roles* 23 (1/2): 43–50.

DeJong, William. 1980. "The Stigma of Obesity: The Consequences of Naïve Assumptions concerning the Causes of Physical Deviance." *Journal of Health and Social Behavior* 21 (1): 75–87.

Dellinger, Kirsten, and Christine L. Williams. 1997. "Makeup at Work: Negotiating Appearance Rules in the Workplace." *Gender and Society* 11 (2): 151–177.

Dermology. 2011. "Dermology Stretch Mark Prevention." http://coupon.dermology.com/ 6C6A0ED5?aid=228979&mhcp=417033&serialized[http_ref_over]=http%253A%252F %252Fwww.topstretchmarkcreams.com%252F&serialized[custom_site_id]=0 &serialized[cpa_flag]=0&cp_code=&cid=&api_opt1=&api_opt2=&api_opt3 =&frame=1&serialized[store_name]=&reload= (accessed May 2, 2012).

Deutsch, Francine M., Carla M. Zalenski, and Mary E. Clark. 1986. "Is There a Double Standard of Aging?" *Journal of Applied Social Psychology* 16 (9): 771–785.

Dion, Karen, Ellen Berscheid, and Elaine Walster. 1972. "What Is Beautiful Is Good." *Journal of Personality and Social Psychology* 24 (3): 285–290.

Dixon, Jane, and Christine Winter. 2007. "The Environment of Competing Authorities: Saturated with Choice." In *Seven Deadly Sins of Obesity: How the Modern Diet Is Making Us Fat*, edited by Jane Dixon and Dorothy H. Broom, 126–147. Sydney: University of New South Wales Press.

Donaldson James, Susan. 2009. "Critics Slam Overweight Surgeon General Pick, Regina Benjamin." *ABC News*, July 21.

Dor, Avi, Christine Ferguson, Casey Langwith, and Ellen Tan. 2010. *A Heavy Burden: The Individual Costs of Being Overweight and Obese in the United States*. Washington, DC: George Washington University School of Public Health and Health Services, Department of Health Policy.

Dr. Phil. 2010. "The Fat Debate." Television program, April 6. www.drphil.com/shows/ show/1438 (accessed May 2, 2012).

Dworkin, Shari L., and Faye Linda Wachs. 2004. "'Getting Your Body Back': Postindustrial Fit Motherhood in *Shape Fit Pregnancy* Magazine." *Gender and Society* 18 (5): 610–624.

———. 2009. *Body Panic: Gender, Health, and the Selling of Fitness*. New York: New York University Press.

Dykman, April. 2011. "The Financial Cost of Obesity." *Forbes*, July 26.

Edgley, Charles, and Dennis Brissett. 1990. "Health Nazis and the Cult of the Perfect Body: Some Polemical Observations." *Symbolic Interaction* 13 (2): 257–279.

Elizabeth Arden, Inc. 2012. "Prevage." www.prevageskin.com/prevage-body-treatment (accessed May 3, 2012).

Elliott, Stuart. 1997. "The Body Shop's Campaign Offers Reality, Not Miracles." *New York Times*, August 26.

Emanuel, Ezekiel. 2012. "Let's Move, She Said—and We Have." *Opinionator* (blog). *New York Times*, February 13. http://opinionator.blogs.nytimes.com/2012/02/13/lets-move-she -said-and-we-have (accessed August 21, 2012).

Emslie, Carol, Kate Hunt, and Sally Macintyre. 2001. "Perceptions of Body Image among Working Men and Women." *Journal of Epidemiology and Community Health* 55 (6): 406–407.

Entman, Robert M. 1993. "Framing: Toward a Clarification of a Fractured Paradigm." *Journal of Communication* 43 (4): 51–58.

Epstein, Laura, and Jane Ogden. 2005. "A Qualitative Study of GPs' Views of Treating Obesity." *British Journal of General Practice* 55 (519): 750–754.

Ernsberger, Paul, and Richard J. Koletsky. 1993. "Weight Cycling and Mortality: Support from Animal Studies." *Journal of the American Medical Association* 269 (9): 1116.

Esacove, Anne W. 2004. "Dialogic Framing: The Framing/Counterframing of 'Partial-Birth' Abortion." *Sociological Inquiry* 74 (1): 70–101.

Etcoff, Nancy. 1999. *Survival of the Prettiest: The Science of Beauty*. New York: Doubleday.

Evans, Tom. 2010. "Unattainable Beauty." *Amanpour* (blog). CNN, February 12. http:// amanpour.blogs.cnn.com/tag/beauty (accessed August 21, 2012).

Evans, W. Douglas, Eric A. Finkelstein, Douglas B. Kamerow, and Jeanette M. Renaud. 2005. "Public Perceptions of Childhood Obesity." *American Journal of Preventive Medicine* 28 (1): 26–32.

Fabrey, William J. 2001. "Thirty-Three Years of Size Acceptance in Perspective—How Has It Affected the Lives of Real People?" Keynote address presented at the Big as TEXAS Spring Event, Houston, Texas, March 16–17. http://bigastexas.tripod.com/2001event/ keynote2001.html (accessed September 10, 2012).

Featherstone, Mike. 1982. "The Body in Consumer Culture." *Theory, Culture and Society* 1 (2): 18–33.

———. 2010. "Body, Image and Affect in Consumer Culture." *Body and Society* 16 (1): 193–221.

Fernandez, Elizabeth. 2002. "Teacher Says Fat, Fitness Can Mix: S.F. Mediates Complaint Jazzercise Showed Bias." *San Francisco Chronicle*, February 24.

Finkelstein, Eric A., Olga A. Khavjou, Hope Thompson, Justin G. Trogdon, Liping Pan, Bettylou Sherry, and William Dietz. 2012. "Obesity and Severe Obesity Forecasts through 2030." *American Journal of Preventive Medicine* 42 (6): 563–570.

Finkelstein, Eric A., Justin G. Trogdon, Joel W. Cohen, and William Dietz. 2009. "Annual Medical Spending Attributable to Obesity: Payer- and Service-Specific Estimates." Web exclusive. *Health Affairs* 28 (5): w822–w831.

Fiske, John. 1986. "Television, Polysemy and Popularity." *Critical Studies in Mass Communication* 3 (4): 391–408.

———. 1989. *Understanding Popular Culture*. London: Unwin Hyman.

———. 1994. *Media Matters: Everyday Culture and Political Change*. Minneapolis: University of Minnesota Press.

Flegal, Katherine M., Margaret D. Carroll, Cynthia L. Ogden, and Lester R. Curtin. 2010. "Prevalence and Trends in Obesity among US Adults, 1999–2008." *Journal of the American Medical Association* 303 (3): 235–241.

Flegal, Katherine M., Barry I. Graubard, David F. Williamson, and Mitchell H. Gail. 2005. "Excess Deaths Associated with Underweight, Overweight, and Obesity." *Journal of the American Medical Association* 293 (15): 1861–1867.

Fletcher, Dan. 2009. "Brief History: The Fat-Acceptance Movement." *Time*, July 31.

Florida, Richard. 2011. "America's Fittest Cities." *Atlantic*, May 27.

Foster, Gary D., Thomas A. Wadden, Angela P. Makris, Duncan Davidson, Rebecca Swain Sanderson, David B. Allison, and Amy Kessler. 2003. "Primary Care Physicians' Attitudes about Obesity and Its Treatment." *Obesity Research* 11 (10): 1168–1177.

Foucault, Michel. 1973. *The Birth of the Clinic: An Archaeology of Medical Perception,* translated by A. M. Sheridan Smith. New York: Pantheon.

———. 1979. *Discipline and Punish: The Birth of the Prison.* New York: Vintage.

———. 1980. *Power/Knowledge: Selected Interviews and Other Writings, 1972–1977.* New York: Pantheon.

———. 1984. "Bio-Power." In *The Foucault Reader,* edited by Paul Rabinow, 258–289. New York: Pantheon.

Fox Business. 2011. "America's Becoming Soft." May 6. http://video.foxbusiness.com/v/3890830/americas-becoming-soft/ (accessed September 18, 2012).

Fraser, Laura. 2009. "The Inner Corset: A Brief History of Fat in the United States." In Rothblum and Solovay 2009, 11–14.

Fraser, Suzanne, JaneMaree Maher, and Jan Wright. 2010. "Between Bodies and Collectives: Articulating the Action of Emotion in Obesity Epidemic Discourse." *Social Theory and Health* 8 (2): 192–209.

Frederickson, Barbara L., and Tomi-Ann Roberts. 1997. "Objectification Theory: Towards Understanding Women's Lived Experiences and Mental Health Risks." *Psychology of Women Quarterly* 21 (2): 173–206.

Friedan, Betty. 1963. *Feminine Mystique.* New York: W. W. Norton.

Friedman, Kelli E., Simona K. Reichmann, Philip R. Costanzo, Arnaldo Zelli, Jamile A. Ashmore, and Gerard J. Musante. 2005. "Weight Stigmatization and Ideological Beliefs: Relation to Psychological Functioning in Obese Adults." *Obesity Research* 13 (5): 907–916.

Frisco, Michelle L., Jason N. Houle, and Molly A. Martin. 2009. "Adolescent Weight and Depressive Symptoms: For Whom Is Weight a Burden?" *Social Science Quarterly* 90 (4): 1019–1038.

Gaesser, Glenn A. 1999. "Thinness and Weight Loss: Beneficial or Detrimental to Longevity?" *Medicine and Science in Sports and Exercise* 31 (8): 1118–1128.

———. 2002. *Big Fat Lies: The Truth about Your Weight and Your Health.* Updated ed. Carlsbad, CA: Gürze Books.

———. 2003. "Is It Necessary to Be Thin to Be Healthy?" *Harvard Health Policy Review* 4 (2): 40–47.

Gagné, Patricia, and Deanna McGaughey. 2002. "Designing Women: Cultural Hegemony and the Exercise of Power among Women Who Have Undergone Elective Mammoplasty." *Gender and Society* 16 (6): 814–838.

Gamson, William A. 1992. *Talking Politics.* New York: Cambridge University Press.

Gamson, William A., and Kathryn E. Lasch. 1983. "The Political Culture of Social Welfare Policy." In *Evaluating the Welfare State: Social and Political Perspectives,* edited by Shimon E. Spiro and Ephraim Yuchtman-Yaar, 397–415. New York: Academic Press.

Gamson, William A., and Andre Modigliani. 1987. "The Changing Culture of Affirmative Action." *Research in Political Sociology* 3:137–177.

Gard, Michael. 2009. "Friends, Enemies and the Cultural Politics of Critical Obesity Research." In *Biopolitics and the "Obesity Epidemic": Governing Bodies,* edited by Jan Wright and Valerie Harwood, 31–44. Abingdon: Routledge.

Gard, Michael, and Jan Wright. 2005. *The Obesity Epidemic: Science, Morality and Ideology.* New York: Routledge.

Garro, Linda C. 1995. "Individual or Societal Responsibility? Explanations of Diabetes in an Anishinaabe (Ojibway) Community." *Social Science and Medicine* 40 (1): 37–46.

George, Robert. 2010. "Research Shows Sugary Drinks Do Not Cause Weight Gain." *Medical News Today,* August 10. www.medicalnewstoday.com/articles/197265.php (accessed May 2, 2012).

Giddens, Anthony. 1991. *Modernity and Self Identity: Self and Society in the Late Modern Age.* Cambridge: Polity Press.

Gillespie, Charmaine. 2010. "Health and Beauty News." *Inside the Institute* (blog). *Good Housekeeping,* October 5. www.goodhousekeeping.com/product-testing/from-the-lab -blog/2011-health-and-beauty-news (accessed August 21, 2012).

Gimlin, Debra L. 2000. "Cosmetic Surgery: Beauty as Commodity." *Qualitative Sociology* 23 (1): 77–98.

———. 2002. *Body Work: Beauty and Self-Image in American Culture.* Berkeley: University of California Press.

———. 2007. "What Is 'Body Work'? A Review of the Literature." *Sociology Compass* 1 (1): 353–370.

Giovanelli, Dina, and Stephen Ostertag. 2009. "Controlling the Body: Media Representations, Body Size, and Self-Discipline." In Rothblum and Solovay 2009, 289–296.

Glass, Christy M., Steven A. Haas, and Eric N. Reither. 2010. "The Skinny on Success: Body Mass, Gender and Occupational Standing across the Life Course." *Social Forces* 88 (4): 1777–1806.

Goffman, Erving. 1959. *The Presentation of Self in Everyday Life.* New York: Doubleday.

———.1974. *Frame Analysis: An Essay on the Organization of Experience.* Cambridge, MA: Harvard University Press.

———. 1979. *Gender Advertisements.* New York: Harper & Row.

Gorman, James. 2004. "Plastic Surgery Gets a New Look." *New York Times,* April 27.

Granberg, Ellen M. 2011. "'Now My "Old Self" Is Thin': Stigma Exits after Weight Loss." *Social Psychology Quarterly* 74 (1): 29–52.

Greener, Joe, Flora Douglas, and Edwin van Teijlingen. 2010. "More of the Same? Conflicting Perspectives of Obesity Causation and Intervention amongst Overweight People, Health Professionals and Policy Makers." *Social Science and Medicine* 70 (7): 1042–1049.

Greenlees, I. A., and William C. McGrew. 1994. "Sex and Age Differences in Preferences and Tactics of Mate Attraction: Analysis of Published Advertisements." *Ethology and Sociobiology* 15 (2): 59–72.

Gremillion, Helen. 2005. "The Cultural Politics of Body Size." *Annual Review of Anthropology* 34:13–32.

Gross, Jennifer E. 2006. "The First Amendment and Diet Industry Advertising: How 'Puffery' in Weight-Loss Advertisements Has Gone Too Far." *Journal of Law and Health* 20:325–355.

Guthman, Julie. 2009. "Neoliberalism and the Constitution of Contemporary Bodies." In Rothblum and Solovay 2009, 187–196.

Guthman, Julie, and Melanie DuPuis. 2006. "Embodying Neoliberalism: Economy, Culture, and the Politics of Fat." *Environment and Planning D: Society and Space* 24 (3): 427–448.

Guyll, Max, Karen A. Matthews, and Joyce T. Bromberger. 2001. "Discrimination and Unfair Treatment: Relationship to Cardiovascular Reactivity among African American and European American Women." *Health Psychology* 20 (5): 315–325.

Haas, Jennifer S., Lisa B. Lee, Celia P. Kaplan, Dean Sonneborn, Kathryn A. Phillips, and Su-Ying Liang. 2003. "The Association of Race, Socioeconomic Status, and Health Insurance Status with the Prevalence of Overweight among Children and Adolescents." *American Journal of Public Health* 93 (12): 2105–2110.

Hacker, Jacob S. 2006. *The Great Risk Shift: The Assault on American Jobs, Families, Health Care and Retirement and How You Can Fight Back.* New York: Oxford University Press.

HAES (Health at Every Size). 2012. "The Pledge." http://haescommunity.org/pledge.php (accessed May 5, 2012).

Hagan, Caitlin. 2009. "Extreme Diets: Life on 800 Calories a Day." CNN, December 15.

Hakim, Catherine. 2010. "Erotic Capital." *European Sociological Review* 26 (5): 499–518.

Hall, Stuart. 1980. "Encoding/Decoding." In *Culture, Media, Language: Working Papers in Cultural Studies, 1972–1979*, edited by Stuart Hall, Andrew Lowe, Dorothy Hobson, and Paul Willis, 128–138. Birmingham: Centre for Contemporary Cultural Studies, University of Birmingham.

Hamburg, David A. 1994. *Today's Children: Creating a Future for a Generation in Crisis*. New York: Time Books.

Harriger, Jennifer A., Rachel M. Calogero, David C. Witherington, and Jane Ellen Smith. 2010. "Body Size Stereotyping and Internalization of the Thin Ideal in Preschool Girls." *Sex Roles* 63 (9/10): 609–620.

Harris, Mary B., Richard J. Harris, and Stephen Bochner. 1982. "Fat, Four-Eyed, and Female: Stereotypes of Obesity, Glasses, and Gender." *Journal of Applied Social Psychology* 12 (6): 503–516.

Harris Interactive. 2010. "Overweight? Obese? Or Normal Weight? Americans Have Hard Time Gauging Their Weight." Harris Polls, September 2.

Harvey, David. 2005. *A Brief History of Neoliberalism*. New York: Oxford University Press.

Harvey, Emma L., and Andrew J. Hill. 2001. "Health Professionals' Views of Overweight People and Smokers." *International Journal of Obesity* 25 (8): 1253–1261.

Hebl, Michelle R., and Todd F. Heatherton. 1998. "The Stigma of Obesity in Women: The Difference Is Black and White." *Personality and Social Psychology Bulletin* 24 (4): 417–426.

Hebl, Michelle R., and Julie M. Turchin. 2005. "The Stigma of Obesity: What about Men?" *Basic and Applied Social Psychology* 27 (3): 267–275.

Henderson, Nia-Malika. 2010. "After Delays, Final Vote Set for Child Nutrition Bill." *Washington Post*, December 2.

Hendrie, Gillian Anne, John Coveney, and David Cox. 2008. "Exploring Nutrition Knowledge and the Demographic Variation in Knowledge Levels in an Australian Community Sample." *Public Health Nutrition* 11 (12): 1365–1371.

Hensley, Scott. 2010. "In Obesity Fight, a Third of Americans Support Soda Tax." *Shots* (blog). National Public Radio, April 21. www.npr.org/blogs/health/2010/04/in_obesity_fight_a_third_of_am.html (accessed August 21, 2012).

Herndon, April Michelle. 2005. "Collateral Damage from Friendly Fire? Race, Nation, Class and the 'War against Obesity.'" *Social Semiotics* 15 (2): 127–141.

———. 2010. "Mommy Made Me Do It: Mothering Fat Children in the Midst of the Obesity Epidemic." *Food, Culture and Society* 13 (3): 331–349.

Herrick, Clare. 2009. "Shifting Blame/Selling Health: Corporate Social Responsibility in the Age of Obesity." *Sociology of Health and Illness* 31 (1): 51–65.

Hesse-Biber, Sharlene. 1996. *Am I Thin Enough Yet? The Cult of Thinness and the Commercialization of Identity*. New York: Oxford University Press.

Heussner, Ki Mae. 2009. "11 Photo-Editing Flubs: Ralph Lauren Ad Sparks Controversy." *ABC News*, October 8.

HHS (U.S. Department of Health and Human Services). 2001. *The Surgeon General's Call to Action to Prevent and Decrease Overweight and Obesity*. Rockville, MD: U.S. Department of Health and Human Services, Public Health Service, Office of the Surgeon General. www.surgeongeneral.gov/library/calls/obesity/CalltoAction.pdf (accessed September 6, 2012).

———. 2008. *2008 Physical Activity Guidelines for Americans*. www.health.gov/paguidelines/pdf/paguide.pdf (accessed September 6, 2012).

———. 2010a. *American Recovery and Reinvestment Act Prevention and Wellness Initiative: Communities Putting Prevention to Work*. www.cdc.gov/chronicdisease/recovery/PDF/HHS_CPPW_CommunityFactSheet.pdf (accessed September 6, 2012).

—————. 2010b. *State Indicator Report on Physical Activity, 2010 National Action Guide.* www .cdc.gov/physicalactivity/downloads/PA_State_Indicator_Report_2010_Action _Guide.pdf (accessed September 6, 2012).

—————. 2010c. "Surgeon General: Healthy and Fit." SurgeonGeneral.gov. Podcast video, January 28. www.surgeongeneral.gov/videos/2010/01/healthy-fit.html (accessed September 6, 2012); posted with viewer comments at www.youtube.com/watch?v=fvUYWms8P3w (accessed September 20, 2012.)

—————. 2010d. *The Surgeon General's Vision for a Healthy and Fit Nation 2010.* www.surgeon general.gov/initiatives/healthy-fit-nation/obesityvision2010.pdf (accessed September 6, 2012).

Hilgartner, Stephen, and Charles L. Bosk. 1988. "The Rise and Fall of Social Problems: A Public Arenas Model." *American Journal of Sociology* 94 (1): 53–78.

Holland, Kate E., R. Warwick Blood, Samantha I. Thomas, Sophie Lewis, Paul A. Komesaroff, and David J. Castle. 2011. "'Our Girth Is Plain to See': An Analysis of Newspaper Coverage of Australia's Future 'Fat Bomb.'" *Health, Risk and Society* 13 (1): 31–46.

Horowitz, Jason, and Nia-Malika Henderson. 2010. "Some GOP Stalwarts Defend First Lady's Anti-obesity Campaign from Palin's Shots." *Washington Post*, December 29.

Hudson, James I., Eva Hiripi, Harrison G. Pope Jr., and Ronald C. Kessler. 2007. "The Prevalence and Correlates of Eating Disorders in the National Comorbidity Survey Replication." *Biological Psychiatry* 61 (3): 348–358.

Hughes, Christina. 2002. *Key Concepts in Feminist Theory and Research.* London: Sage.

Hughes, Jane. 2011. "Breastfed Babies 'Develop Fewer Behaviour Problems.'" *BBC News*, May 9.

Hunter, Aina. 2010. "Christina Hendrick's 15-Pound Weight Gain Made Her Feel Sexy." *CBS News*, July 2.

Husted, Bill. 2009. "Denver's Anti-Gym Shuttered by IRS, Karolchyk Vows to Move On." *The Peek* (blog). *Denver Post*, January 30. http://blogs.denverpost.com/husted/2009/01/30/ denvers-anti-gym-shuttered-by-irs-karolchyk-vows-to-move-on/787 (accessed August 21, 2012).

IFICF (International Food Information Council Foundation). 2011. *2011 Food and Health Survey: Consumer Attitudes towards Food Safety, Nutrition, and Health.* Washington, DC: IFICF. www.foodinsight.org/Content/3840/2011%20IFIC%20FDTN%20Food%20and %20Health%20Survey.pdf (accessed August 21, 2012).

Iyengar, Shanto. 1991. *Is Anyone Responsible? How Television Frames Political Issues.* Chicago: University of Chicago Press.

Jain, Anjali. 2005. "Treating Obesity in Individuals and Populations." *British Medical Journal* 331 (7529): 1387–1390.

Jeffery, Robert W., and Simone A. French. 1996. "Socioeconomic Status and Weight Control Practices among 20- to 45-Year-Old Women." *American Journal of Public Health* 86 (7): 1005–1010.

Jhally, Sut. 1987. *The Codes of Advertising: Fetishism and the Political Economy of Meaning in the Consumer Society.* New York: St. Martin's Press.

Joelving, Frederik. 2010. "If You're 70 and Overweight, You May Live Longer." Reuters, February 2.

Johnston, Josée, and Judith Taylor. 2008. "Feminist Consumerism and Fat Activists: A Comparative Study of Grassroots Activism and the Dove Real Beauty Campaign." *Signs* 33 (4): 941–966.

Jones, Jeffrey M. 2009. "In U.S., More Would Like to Lose Weight Than Are Trying To." Gallup, November 20. www.gallup.com/poll/124448/in-u.s.-more-lose-weight-than-trying -to.aspx (accessed August 22, 2012).

Jones, Meredith. 2008. *Skin Tight: An Anatomy of Cosmetic Surgery.* Oxford: Berg.

Jordan, Brigitte. 1997. "Authoritative Knowledge and Its Construction." In *Childbirth and Authoritative Knowledge: Cross-Cultural Perspectives,* edited by Robbie E. Davis-Floyd and Carolyn F. Sargent, 55–79. Berkeley: University of California Press.

JourneyLite. 2007. "Healthy Is the New Beautiful." Lap-Band advertisement. *St. Petersburg Times,* October 25. http://news.google.com/newspapers?nid=888&dat=20071025&id =wPlRAAAAIBAJ&sjid=sXQDAAAAIBAJ&pg=4076,4272611 (accessed August 22, 2012).

Jutel, Annemarie. 2001. "Does Size Really Matter? Weight and Values in Public Health." *Perspectives in Biology and Medicine* 44 (2): 283–296.

Kantor, Jodi. 2007. "As Obesity Fight Hits Cafeteria, Many Fear a Note from School." *New York Times,* January 8.

Karra, Cindy. 1994. "Dr. C. Everett Koop Launches A New 'Crusade' to Combat Obesity in America." Shape Up, America. News release, December 6. www.shapeup.org/about/ arch_pr/120694.php (accessed August 22, 2012).

Katz, Sidney. 2007. "The Importance of Being Beautiful." In *Down to Earth Sociology: Introductory Readings,* 14th ed., edited by James M. Henslin, 341–348. New York: Free Press.

Kawamura, Kathleen Y. 2002. "Asian American Body Images." In *Body Image: A Handbook of Theory, Research, and Clinical Practice,* edited by Thomas F. Cash and Thomas Pruzinsky, 243–249. New York: Guilford.

Keith, Scott W., David T. Redden, Peter T. Katzmarzyk, Mary M. Boggiano, Erin C. Hanlon, Ruth M. Benca, Douglas M. Ruden, Angelo Pietrobelli, Jamie L. Barger, Kevin R. Fontaine, Chenxi Wang, Louis J. Aronne, Suzanne M. Wright, Monica Baskin, Nikhil V. Dhurandhar, Maria C. Lijoi, Carlos M. Grilo, Maria DeLuca, Andrew O. Westfall, and David B. Allison. 2006. "Putative Contributors to the Secular Increase in Obesity: Exploring the Roads Less Traveled." *International Journal of Obesity* 30: 1585–1594.

Kennedy, Randall. 2002. *Nigger: The Strange Career of a Troublesome Word.* New York: Pantheon.

Kersh, Rogan, and James Morone. 2002. "How the Personal Becomes Political: Prohibitions, Public Health, and Obesity." *Studies in American Political Development* 16 (2): 162–195.

Kilbourne, Jean. 1999. *Can't Buy My Love: How Advertising Changes the Way We Think and Feel.* New York: Touchstone.

———. 2012. "Video." Jean Kilbourne. www.jeankilbourne.com/videos (accessed August 22, 2012).

Kilpatrick, Marcus, Christine Ohannessian, and John B. Bartholomew. 1999. "Adolescent Weight Management and Perceptions: An Analysis of the National Longitudinal Study of Adolescent Health." Abstract. *Journal of School Health* 69 (4): 148–152.

Kim, Sei-Hill, and L. Anne Willis. 2007. "Talking about Obesity: News Framing of Who Is Responsible for Causing and Fixing the Problem." *Journal of Health Communication* 12 (4): 359–376.

Kitsuse, John I., and Malcolm Spector. 1973. "Toward a Sociology of Social Problems: Social Conditions, Value-Judgments, and Social Problems." *Social Problems* 20 (4): 407–419.

Kleinman, Sherryl. 2002. "Why Sexist Language Matters." *Qualitative Sociology* 25 (2): 299–304.

Koplan, Jeffrey P., and Kelly D. Brownell. 2010. "Response of the Food and Beverage Industry to the Obesity Threat." *Journal of the American Medical Association* 304 (13): 1487–1488.

Kramer, Paul M. 2011. *Maggie Goes on a Diet.* Maui, HI: Aloha Publishers.

Kuczmarski, Robert J., and Katherine M. Flegal. 2000. "Criteria for Definition of Overweight in Transition: Background and Recommendations for the United States." *American Journal of Clinical Nutrition* 72 (5): 1074–1081.

Kulick, Don, and Anne Meneley, eds. 2005. *Fat: The Anthropology of an Obsession.* New York: Jeremy P. Tarcher/Penguin.

Kwan, Samantha. 2007. "Contested Meanings about Body, Health, and Weight: Frame Resonance, Strategies of Action, and the Uses of Culture." Ph.D. dissertation, University of Arizona.

————. 2009a. "Competing Motivational Discourses for Weight Loss: Means to Ends and the Nexus of Beauty and Health." *Qualitative Health Research* 19 (9): 1223–1233.

————. 2009b. "Framing the Fat Body: Contested Meanings between Government, Activists, and Industry." *Sociological Inquiry* 79 (1): 25–50.

————. 2009c. "Individual versus Corporate Responsibility: Market Choice, the Food Industry, and the Pervasiveness of Moral Models of Fatness." *Food, Culture and Society* 12 (4): 477–495.

————. 2010. "Navigating Public Spaces in Everyday Life: Gender, Race, and Body Privilege." *Feminist Formations* 22 (2): 144–166.

Kwan, Samantha, and Mary Nell Trautner. 2009. "Beauty Work: Individual and Institutional Rewards, the Reproduction of Gender, and Questions of Agency." *Sociology Compass* 3 (1): 49–71.

Lake Snell Perry and Associates. 2003. "Obesity as a Public Health Issue: A Look at Solutions." www.phsi.harvard.edu/health_reform/poll_results.pdf (accessed September 3, 2012).

Landau, Elizabeth. 2009. "Thinner Is Better to Curb Global Warming, Study Says." CNN, April 20.

Landy, David, and Harold Sigall. 1974. "Beauty Is Talent: Task Evaluation as a Function of the Performer's Physical Attractiveness." *Journal of Personality and Social Psychology* 29 (3): 299–304.

Lawrence, Regina G. 2004. "Framing Obesity: The Evolution of News Discourse on a Public Health Issue." *Press/Politics* 9 (3): 56–75.

Leading Edge Marketing Inc. 2012. "Leading Edge Herbals: Products to Enhance Your Lifestyle: How It Works." www.leadingedgeherbals.com/products/stretchmark.html (accessed September 3, 2012).

LeBesco, Kathleen. 2004. *Revolting Bodies? The Struggle to Redefine Fat Identity.* Amherst: University of Massachusetts Press.

————. 2009. "Quest for a Cause: The Fat Gene, the Gay Gene, and the New Eugenics." In Rothblum and Solovay 2009, 65–74.

Lee, Chris. 2010. "Kevin Smith's Southwest Airlines Incident Sets Web All A-Twitter," *Los Angeles Times,* February 16.

Lee, Hedwig. 2011. "Inequality as an Explanation for Obesity in the United States." *Sociology Compass* 5 (3): 215–232.

Let's Move! 2010. "Child Nutrition Reauthorization: Healthy, Hunger-Free Kids Act of 2010." U.S. White House news release, December 13. www.whitehouse.gov/sites/default/files/Child_Nutrition_Fact_Sheet_12_10_10.pdf (accessed May 6, 2012).

————. 2012a. "About Let's Move!" www.letsmove.gov/about (accessed April 30, 2012).

————. 2012b. "Health Problems and Childhood Obesity." www.letsmove.gov/health -problems-and-childhood-obesity (accessed May 2, 2012).

Lewis, Megan. 2009. "Women's Health and Beauty Day Slated for Saturday." *University of Toledo News,* April 30.

Lissner, Lauren, Patricia M. Odell, Ralph B. D'Agostino, Joseph Stokes III, Bernard E. Kreger, Albert J. Belanger, and Kelly D. Brownell. 1991. "Variability of Body Weight and Health Outcomes in the Framingham Population." *New England Journal of Medicine* 324 (26): 1839–1844.

Lovejoy, Meg. 2001. "Disturbances in the Social Body: Differences in Body Image and Eating Problems among African American and White Women." *Gender and Society* 15 (2): 239–261.

Luker, Kristin. 1984. *Abortion and the Politics of Motherhood.* Berkeley: University of California Press.

Lupton, Deborah. 1995. *The Imperative of Health: Public Health and the Regulated Body.* London: Sage.

Lyons, Linda. 2004. "Teaching Kids to Be Fit: Who's Responsible?" Gallup, August 10. www .gallup.com/poll/12652/teaching-kids-fit-whos-responsible.aspx (accessed August 22, 2012).

Maher, JaneMaree, Suzanne Fraser, and Jo M. Lindsay. 2010. "Between Provisioning and Consuming? Children, Mothers and 'Childhood Obesity.'" *Health Sociology Review* 19 (3): 304–316.

Maher, JaneMaree, Suzanne Fraser, and Jan Wright. 2010. "Framing the Mother: Childhood Obesity, Maternal Responsibility and Care." *Journal of Gender Studies* 19 (3): 233–247.

Maher, Jared Jacang. 2009. "How Much Does Anti-Gym's Michael Karolchyk Owe to the IRS?" *Latest Word* (blog). *Denver Westword.* February 25. http://blogs.westword.com/latestword/2009/02/how_much_does_anti-gyms_michae.php (accessed August 22, 2012).

Mallyon, Anna, Mary Holmes, John Coveney, and Maria Zadoroznyj. 2010. "I'm Not Dieting, 'I'm Doing It for Science': Masculinities and the Experience of Dieting." *Health Sociology Review* 19 (3): 330–342.

Mann, Traci, A. Janet Tomiyama, Erika Westling, Ann-Marie Lew, Barbra Samuels, and Jason Chatman. 2007. "Medicare's Search for Effective Obesity Treatments: Diets Are Not the Answer. *American Psychologist* 62 (3): 220–233.

Marikar, Sheila. 2010. "Britney Spears, Kelly Clarson and More Go under the (Digital) Knife." *ABC News*, April 14.

Marketdata Enterprises. 2008. *The U.S. Market for Self-Improvement Products and Services.* Tampa, FL: Marketdata Enterprises.

———. 2011. *The U.S. Weight Loss and Diet Control Market.* 11th ed. Tampa, FL: Marketdata Enterprises.

Markula, Pirkko. 1995. "Firm but Shapely, Fit but Sexy, Strong but Thin: The Postmodern Aerobicizing Female Bodies." *Sociology of Sport Journal* 12 (4): 424–453.

Marshall, Simon J., Deborah A. Jones, Barbara E. Ainsworth, Jared P. Reis, Susan S. Levy, and Caroline A. Macera. 2007. "Race/Ethnicity, Social Class, and Leisure-Time Physical Inactivity." *Medicine and Science in Sports and Exercise* 39 (1): 44–51.

Martin, Courtney E. 2007. *Perfect Girls, Starving Daughters: The Frightening New Normalcy of Hating Your Body.* New York: Simon & Schuster.

Martin, Daniel D. 2002. "From Appearance Tales to Oppression Tales: Frame Alignment and Organizational Identity." *Journal of Contemporary Ethnography* 31 (2): 158–206.

Martin, Michel. 2009. "Nation's Obesity Problem Puts Strain on Health Care Costs." National Public Radio, July 29.

Mayer, Caroline E., and Amy Joyce. 2005. "The Escalating Obesity Wars." *Washington Post*, April 27.

McAuley, Paul A., Peter F. Kokkinos, Ricardo B. Oliveira, Brian T. Emerson, and Jonathan N. Myers. 2010. "Obesity Paradox and Cardiorespiratory Fitness in 12,417 Male Veterans Aged 40 to 70 Years." *Mayo Clinic Proceedings* 85 (2): 115–121.

McHugh, Matthew D. 2006. "Fit or Fat? A Review of the Debate on Deaths Attributable to Obesity." *Public Health Nursing* 23 (3): 264–270.

McIntosh, Peggy. 2000 [1988]. "White Privilege and Male Privilege: A Personal Account of Coming to See Correspondences through Work in Women's Studies." In *Gender Basics,* 2nd ed., edited by Anne Minas, 30–38. Belmont, CA: Wadsworth.

McKinley, Nita M. 1999. "Ideal Weight/Ideal Women: Society Constructs the Female." In *Weight Issues: Fatness and Thinness as Social Problems,* edited by Jeffrey Sobal and Donna Maurer, 97–115. New York: Aldine de Gruyter.

McLaren, Lindsay, and Diana Kuh. 2004. "Women's Body Dissatisfaction, Social Class, and Social Mobility." *Social Science and Medicine* 58 (9): 1575–1584.

McMurray, Coleen. 2004. "Public: Lifestyle, Not Disease, Causes Obesity." Gallup, August 10. www.gallup.com/poll/12661/public-lifestyle-disease-causes-obesity.aspx (accessed August 22, 2012).

Mead, George Herbert. 1934. *Mind, Self, and Society from the Standpoint of a Social Behaviorist.* Chicago: University of Chicago Press.

Medifast, Inc. 2012. Medifast Program. www.medifast1.com/how_it_works/why_it_works/the_medifast_difference.jsp?campaign=g000869&gclid=CPX-6MLewK0CFUZjTAod wFlRPw (accessed September 11, 2012).

Menashe, Claudia L., and Michael Siegel. 1998. "The Power of a Frame: An Analysis of Newspaper Coverage of Tobacco Issues—United States, 1985–1996." *Journal of Health Communication* 3 (4): 307–325.

Mendes, Elizabeth. 2010. "Obesity Linked to Lower Emotional Wellbeing." Gallup, September 17. www.gallup.com/poll/143045/obesity-linked-lower-emotional-wellbeing.aspx (accessed August 22, 2012).

Merten, Michael J., K. A. S. Wickrama, and Amanda L. Williams. 2008. "Adolescent Obesity and Young Adult Psychosocial Outcomes: Gender and Racial Differences." *Journal of Youth and Adolescence* 37 (9): 1111–1122.

Meyer, Jonathan M. 2002. "Awareness of Obesity and Weight Issues among Chronically Mentally Ill Inpatients: A Pilot Study." *Annals of Clinical Psychiatry* 14 (1): 39–45.

Milkie, Melissa A. 1999. "Social Comparisons, Reflected Appraisals, and Mass Media: The Impact of Pervasive Beauty Images on Black and White Girls' Self-Concepts." *Social Psychology Quarterly* 62 (2): 190–210.

Miller, Carol T., and Kathryn T, Downey. 1999. "A Meta-analysis of Heavyweight and Self-Esteem." *Personality and Social Psychology Review* 3 (1): 68–84.

Mintel International Group Ltd. 2011. "Parents Concerned, but Confused about How to Fix Childhood Obesity." News release, May 14. www.mintel.com/press-centre/press-releases/354/parents-concerned-but-confused-about-how-to-fix-childhood-obesity (accessed August 22, 2012).

Mizell, Jill. 2011. "Economic Opportunity, Human Rights, and the Role of Government." *Public Opinion Monthly,* July 27. http://opportunityagenda.org/public_opinion_monthly_july_2011 (accessed September 11, 2012).

Moffat, Tina. 2010. "The 'Childhood Obesity Epidemic': Health Crisis or Social Construction?" *Medical Anthropology Quarterly* 24 (1): 1–21.

Mokdad, Ali H., James S. Marks, Donna F. Stroup, and Julie L Gerberding. 2004. "Actual Causes of Death in the United States, 2000." *Journal of the American Medical Association* 291 (10): 1238–1245.

Monaghan, Lee F. 2007. "Body Mass Index, Masculinities and Moral Worth: Men's Critical Understandings of 'Appropriate' Weight-for-Height." *Sociology of Health and Illness* 29 (4): 584–609.

———. 2008. "Men, Physical Activity, and the Obesity Discourse: Critical Understandings from a Qualitative Study." *Sociology of Sport Journal* 25 (1): 97–129.

Monaghan, Lee F., Robert Hollands, and Gary Pritchard. 2010. "Obesity Epidemic Entrepreneurs: Types, Practices and Interests." *Body and Society* 16 (2): 37–71.

Moss, Michael. 2010. "While Warning about Fat, U.S. Pushes Cheese Sales." *New York Times*, November 6.

Mozaffarian, Dariush, Tao Hao, Eric B. Rimm, Walter C. Willett, and Frank B. Hu. 2011. "Changes in Diet and Lifestyle and Long-Term Weight Gain in Women and Men." *New England Journal of Medicine* 364 (25): 2392–2404.

MSNBC. 2006. "New York City Passes Trans Fat Ban." December 5.

Mulvey, Laura. 1975. "Visual Pleasure and Narrative Cinema." *Screen* 16 (3): 6–18.

Murray, Samantha. 2008. *The "Fat" Female Body*. New York: Palgrave Macmillan.

NAAFA (National Association to Advance Fat Acceptance). 2010. "NAAFA Challenges the First Lady." *NAAFA Newsletter*, February. www.naafaonline.com/newsletterstuff/old newsletterstuff/February%202010%20NAAFA%20Newsletter.html (accessed August 22, 2012).

———. 2011a. "About Us." http://naafaonline.com/dev2/about (accessed August 22, 2012).

———. 2011b. "Boards Members." www.naafaonline.com/dev2/about/Board.html (accessed August 22, 2012).

———. 2011c. "Education." www.naafaonline.com/dev2/education/index.html (accessed August 22, 2012).

———. 2011d. "The Issues: Education." www.naafaonline.com/dev2/the_issues/education .html (accessed August 22, 2012).

———. 2011e. "Frequently Asked Questions." www.naafaonline.com/dev2/education/faq .html (accessed August 22, 2012).

———. 2011f. "Health at Every Size (HAES)." www.naafaonline.com/dev2/education/haes .html (accessed August 22, 2012).

———. 2011g. "Healthcare." www.naafaonline.com/dev2/the_issues/health.html (accessed August 22, 2012).

———. 2011h. "The Issues." www.naafaonline.com/dev2/the_issues/index.html (accessed August 22, 2012).

———. 2011i. "Media Outreach." www.naafaonline.com/dev2/about/media.html (accessed August 22, 2012).

———. 2011j. NAAFA home page. www.naafaonline.com/dev2/index.html (accessed August 22, 2012).

———. 2011k. "Official Policies." www.naafaonline.com/dev2/about/docs.html (accessed August 22, 2012).

———. 2011l. "Recommended Reading." www.naafaonline.com/dev2/education/booklist .html (accessed August 22, 2012).

———. 2011m. "Work." www.naafaonline.com/dev2/the_issues/worklife.html (accessed August 22, 2012).

NAAFA-LA (National Association to Advance Fat Acceptance, Los Angeles Chapter). 2012. National Association to Advance Fat Acceptance–Los Angeles Chapter, Myspace website. www.myspace.com/naafala (accessed September 3, 2012).

Nano, Stephanie. 2010. "Study Says Even Being a Bit Overweight Is Risky." *Washington Times*, December 1.

National Eating Disorders Association. 2011. "Facts and Statistics." New York: National Eating Disorders Association. www.nationaleatingdisorders.org/information-resources/general -information.php#facts-statistics (accessed August 22, 2012).

Nestle, Marion. 1993. "Food Lobbies, the Food Pyramid, and U.S. Nutritional Policy." *International Journal of Health Services* 23 (3): 483–496.

————. 2002. *Food Politics: How the Food Industry Influences Nutrition and Health.* Berkeley: University of California Press.

Neumark-Sztainer, Dianne, Mary Story, Peter J. Hannan, and Jillian Croll. 2002. "Overweight Status and Eating Patterns among Adolescents: Where Do Youths Stand in Comparison with the Healthy People 2010 Objectives?" *American Journal of Public Health* 92 (5): 844–851.

Newport, Frank. 2008. "Impact of Smoking, Being Overweight on a Person's Image." Gallup, July 21. www.gallup.com/poll/108925/impact-smoking-being-overweight-persons-image.aspx (accessed August 22, 2012).

————. 2009a. "Americans on Healthcare Reform: Top 10 Takeaways." Gallup, July 31. www.gallup.com/poll/121997/americans-healthcare-reform-top-takeaways.aspx (accessed August 22, 2012).

————. 2009b. "Republican Base Heavily White, Conservative, Religious." Gallup, June 1. www.gallup.com/poll/118937/republican-base-heavily-white-conservative-religious.aspx (accessed August 22, 2012).

New York Daily News. 2010. "With Perfect Grinch Timing, a Consumer Group Has Sued McDonald's Demanding That It Take the Toys Out of Its Happy Meals." Discussions. www.nydailynews.com/forums/thread.jspa?threadID=118765&start=0&tstart=0 (site discontinued).

Nichter, Mimi. 2000. *Fat Talk: What Girls and Their Parents Say about Dieting.* Cambridge, MA: Harvard University Press.

Nichter, Mimi, and Nancy Vukovic. 1994. "Fat Talk: Body Image among Adolescent Girls." In *Many Mirrors: Body Image and Social Relations,* edited by Nicole Landry Sault, 109–131. New Brunswick, NJ: Rutgers University Press.

Nielsen. 2011. "Super Bowl XLV Most Viewed Telecast in U.S. Broadcast History." Nielsen Wire, February 7. http://blog.nielsen.com/nielsenwire/media_entertainment/super-bowl-xlv-most-viewed-telecast-in-broadcast-history (accessed August 22, 2012).

NIH (National Institutes of Health). 1998. "First Federal Obesity Clinical Guidelines Released." News release, July 17. www.nih.gov/news/pr/jun98/nhlbi-17.htm (accessed August 22, 2012).

————. 2012. "Estimates of Funding for Various Research, Condition, and Disease Categories (RCDC)." Research Portfolio Online Reporting Tools (RePORT). http://report.nih.gov/categorical_spending.aspx (accessed May 6, 2012).

Norton, Amy. 2011. "Are C-Sections Fueling the Obesity Epidemic?" Reuters, May 12.

Norton, Kevin I., Timothy S. Olds, Scott Olive, and Stephen Dank. 1996. "Ken and Barbie at Life Size." *Sex Roles* 34 (3/4): 287–294.

OECD (Organization for Economic Co-Operation and Development). 2009. "Special Focus: Measuring Leisure in OECD Countries." In *Society at a Glance: OECD Social Indicators,* edited by OECD, 19–49. Paris, France: OECD.

Ogden, Jane, and Zakk Flanagan. 2008. "Beliefs about the Causes and Solutions to Obesity: A Comparison of GPs and Lay People." *Patient Education and Counseling* 71 (1): 72–78.

Oliver, J. Eric. 2006. *Fat Politics: The Real Story behind America's Obesity Epidemic.* New York: Oxford University Press.

Oliver, J. Eric, and Taeku Lee. 2005. "Public Opinion and the Politics of Obesity in America." *Journal of Health Politics, Policy and Law* 30 (5): 923–954.

Olson, Walter. 2010. "McDonald's Suit over Happy Meal Toys by California Mom Monet Parham New Low in Responsible Parenting." *New York Daily News,* December 15.

One Thousand Fat Cranes. 2008. 1,000 Fat Cranes. Home page. www.myspace.com/1000fatcranes (accessed August 22, 2012).

Onishi, Norimitsu. 2008. "Japan, Seeking Trim Waists, Measures Millions." *New York Times,* June 13.

Pampel, Fred C., Patrick M. Krueger, and Justin T. Denney. 2010. "Socioeconomic Disparities in Health Behaviors." *Annual Review of Sociology* 36:349–370.

Park, Madison. 2010. "Ex-Military Leaders: Young Adults 'Too Fat to Fight.'" CNN, April 20.

Parker, Sheila, Mimi Nichter, Mark Nichter, Nancy Vuckovic, Colette Sims, and Cheryl Rittenbaugh. 1995. "Body Image and Weight Concerns among African American and White Adolescent Females: Differences That Make a Difference." *Human Organization* 54 (2): 103–114.

Parmenter, Kate, Jo Waller, and Jane Wardle. 1999. "Demographic Variation in Nutrition Knowledge in England." *Health Education Research* 15 (2): 163–174.

Parsons, Talcott. 1951. *The Social System.* London: Routledge & Kegan Paul.

Patt, Madhavi Reddy, Anthereca E. Lane, Cheryl P. Finney, Lisa R. Yanek, and Diane M. Becker. 2002. "Body Image Assessment: Comparison of Figure Rating Scales among Urban Black Women." *Ethnicity and Disease* 12 (1): 54–62.

Pew Research Center. 2006. *In the Battle of the Bulge, More Soldiers than Successes.* Pew Social and Demographic Trends. www.pewsocialtrends.org/files/2010/11/Exercise.pdf (accessed August 22, 2012).

———. 2011. *Less Optimism about America's Long-Term Prospects: Economy Dominates Public's Agenda, Dims Hopes for the Future.* Washington, DC: Pew Research Center.

Plunkett Research, Ltd. 2011. "U.S. Food Industry Overview." www.plunkettresearch.com/Food%20beverage%20grocery%20market%20research/industry%20statistics (accessed August 22, 2012).

Pollan, Michael. 2009. *Food Rules.* New York: Penguin.

Pope, Harrison G., Jr., Katharine A. Phillips, and Roberto Olivardia. 2000. *The Adonis Complex: The Secret Crisis of Male Body Obsession.* New York: Free Press.

Popenoe, Rebecca. 2005. "Ideals." In *Fat: The Anthropology of an Obsession,* edited by Don Kulick and Anne Meneley, 9–28. New York: Jeremy P. Tarcher/Penguin.

PRNewswire. 2011. "Diet Pepsi Debuts Its Sleek, New Look at Mercedes-Benz Fashion Week." Pepsico news release, February 8. www.pepsico.com/PressRelease/Diet-Pepsi-Debuts-its-Sleek-New-Look-at-Mercedes-Benz-Fashion-Week02082011.html (accessed August 22, 2012).

Procellix Cellulite Cream. 2012. "Procellix." www.procellix-cellulite-cream.com (accessed May 2, 2012).

Proctor & Gamble. 2012. "Metamucil." http://beautifyyourinside.com (accessed May 2, 2012).

Puhl, Rebecca M., Tatiana Andreyeva, and Kelly D. Brownell. 2008. "Perceptions of Weight Discrimination: Prevalence and Comparison to Race and Gender Discrimination in America." *International Journal of Obesity* 32 (6): 992–1000.

Puhl, Rebecca M., and Chelsea A. Heuer. 2009. "The Stigma of Obesity: A Review and Update." *Obesity* 17 (5): 941–964.

———. 2010. "Obesity Stigma: Important Considerations for Public Health." *American Journal of Public Health* 100 (6): 1019–1028.

Rabin, Roni Caryn. 2008. "In the Fatosphere, Big is In, or at Least Accepted." *New York Times,* January 22.

Reinarman, Craig. 1988. "The Social Construction of an Alcohol Problem: The Case of Mothers Against Drunk Drivers and Social Control in the 1980s." *Theory and Society* 17 (1): 91–120.

Rettner, Rachael. 2011. "Obesity's Big Fat Costs to States: 15 Billion per Year." MSNBC, August 23.

Revitol. 2012. "Revitol." www.revitol.com/site/Revitol_Cellulite_Solution (accessed May 2, 2012).

Rhode, Deborah. L. 2010. *The Beauty Bias: The Injustice of Appearance in Life and Law.* New York: Oxford University Press.

Rich, Emma, and John Evans. 2005. "'Fat Ethics'—the Obesity Discourse and Body Politics." *Social Theory and Health* 3 (4): 341–358.

Richardson, Laurel. 2004 [1987]. "Gender Stereotyping in the English Language." In *Feminist Frontiers,* 6th ed., edited by Laurel Richardson, Verta Taylor, and Nancy Whittier, 89–93. Boston: McGraw-Hill.

Rivers, Christopher. 1994. *Face Value: Physiognomical Thought and the Legible Body in Marivaux, Lavater, Balzac, Gautier, and Zola.* Madison: University of Wisconsin Press.

Robinson, Beatrice E., Jane G. Bacon, and Julia O'Reilly. 1993. "Fat Phobia: Measuring, Understanding, and Changing Anti-fat Attitudes." *International Journal of Eating Disorders* 14 (4): 467–480.

Robison, Jennifer. 2002. "Teens' Views Offer Insight into 'Obesity Epidemic.'" Gallup, June 11. www.gallup.com/poll/6169/teens-views-offer-insight-into-obesity-epidemic.aspx (accessed August 22, 2012).

Rodin, Miriam, Judy Price, Francisco Sanchez, and Sharel McElligot. 1989. "Derogation, Exclusion, and Unfair Treatment of Persons with Social Flaws: Controllability of Stigma and the Attribution of Prejudice." *Personality and Social Psychology Bulletin* 15 (3): 439–451.

Roehling, Mark V. 1999. "Weight-Based Discrimination in Employment: Psychological and Legal Aspects." *Personnel Psychology* 52 (4): 969–1016.

Roehling, Mark V., Patricia V. Roehling, and L. Maureen Odland. 2008. "Investigating the Validity of Stereotypes about Overweight Employees: The Relationship between Body Weight and Normal Personality Traits." *Group and Organization Management* 33 (4): 392–424.

Rose, Nikolas. 1996. "Governing 'Advanced' Liberal Democracies." In *Foucault and Political Reason: Liberalism, Neo-liberalism, and Rationalities of Government,* edited by Andrew Barry, Thomas Osborne, and Nikolas Rose, 37–64. Chicago: University of Chicago Press.

Rothblum, Esther D. 1990. "Women and Weight: Fad and Fiction." *Journal of Psychology* 124 (1): 5–24.

———. 1992. "The Stigma of Women's Weight: Social and Economic Realities." *Feminism and Psychology* 2 (1): 61–73.

Rothblum, Esther, and Sondra Solovay, eds. 2009. *The Fat Studies Reader.* New York: New York University Press.

Rudd (Rudd Center for Food Policy and Obesity). 2008. *Weight Bias: The Need for Public Policy.* New Haven, CT: Rudd Center for Food Policy and Obesity.

———. 2010. *Focus Groups with Parents: What Do They Think of Food Marketing to Their Kids.* New Haven, CN: Rudd Center for Food Policy and Obesity.

———. 2011. "Legislation Database." www.yaleruddcenter.org/legislation (accessed August 22, 2012).

Rudolph, Cort W., Charles L. Wells, Marcus D. Weller, and Boris B. Baltes. 2009. "A Meta-Analysis of Empirical Studies of Weight-Bias in the Worplace." *Journal of Vocational Behavior* 74 (1): 1–10.

Ryan, Charlotte. 1991. *Prime Time Activism: Media Strategies for Grass Roots Organizing.* Boston: South End Press.

Ryan, Matthew. 2011. "Many Don't Believe Their Obesity Poses Health Risks." *USA Today,* October 21.

Ryan, William. 1976. *Blaming the Victim.* New York: Vintage Books.

Saad, Lydia. 2003. "Public Balks at Obesity Lawsuits." Gallup, July 21. www.gallup.com/poll/8869/public-balks-obesity-lawsuits.aspx (accessed August 22, 2012).

————. 2009. "CDC Tops Agency Ratings; Federal Reserve Board Lowest." Gallup, July 27. www.gallup.com/poll/121886/cdc-tops-agency-ratings-federal-reserve-board-lowest.aspx (accessed August 22, 2012).

————. 2010. "Access Still Top Health Concern in US; Gov't Role Gains Ground." Gallup, November 17. www.gallup.com/poll/144776/access-still-top-health-concern-u.s.-govt -role-gains-ground.aspx (accessed August 22, 2012).

Saguy, Abigail C., and Rene Almeling. 2008. "Fat in the Fire? Science, the News Media and the 'Obesity Epidemic.'" *Sociological Forum* 23 (1): 53–83.

Saguy, Abigail C., and Kjerstin Gruys. 2010. "Morality and Health: News Media Constructions of Overweight and Eating Disorders." *Social Problems* 57 (2): 231–250.

Saguy, Abigail C., Kjerstin Gruys, and Shanna Gong. 2010. "Social Problem Construction and National Context: News Reporting on 'Overweight' and 'Obesity' in the United States and France." *Social Problems* 57 (4): 586–610.

Saguy, Abigail C., and Kevin W. Riley. 2005. "Weighing Both Sides: Morality, Mortality, and Framing Contests over Obesity." *Journal of Health Politics, Policy, and Law* 30 (5): 869–921.

Salk, Rachel H., and Renee Engeln-Maddox. 2011. "'If You're Fat, Then I'm Humongous!' Frequency, Content, and Impact of Fat Talk among College Women." *Psychology of Women Quarterly* 35 (1): 18–28.

Santry, Heena P., Daniel L. Gillen, and Diane S. Lauderdale. 2005. "Trends in Bariatric Surgical Procedures." *Journal of the American Medical Association* 294 (15): 1909–1917.

Schafer, Markus H., and Kenneth F. Ferraro. 2011. "The Stigma of Obesity: Does Perceived Weight Discrimination Affect Identity and Physical Health?" *Social Psychology Quarterly* 74 (1): 76–97.

Schieman, Scott, Tetyana Pudrovska, and Rachel Eccles. 2007. "Perceptions of Body Weight among Older Adults: Analyses of the Intersection of Gender, Race, and Socioeconomic Status." *Journals of Gerontology Series B: Psychological Sciences and Social Sciences* 62 (6): S415–S423.

Schlosser, Eric, 2001. *Fast Food Nation: The Dark Side of the All-American Meal.* Boston: Houghton Mifflin.

Schneider, Joseph W. 1985. "Social Problems Theory: The Constructionist View." *Annual Review of Sociology* 11:209–229.

Schroeder, Charles Roy. 1992. *Fat Is Not a Four-Letter Word.* Minneapolis: Chronimed.

Schuler, Petra B., Debra Vinci, Robert M. Isosaari, Steven F. Philipp, John Todorovich, Jane L. P. Roy, and Retta R. Evans. 2008. "Body-Shape Perceptions and Body Mass Index of Older African American and European American Women." *Journal of Cross-Cultural Gerontology* 23 (2): 255–264.

Schultz, E. J. 2011. "Weight Watchers Picks a New Target: Men." *Advertising Age*, April 22.

Schulz, Leslie O., Peter H. Bennett, Eric Ravussin, Judith R. Kidd, Kenneth K. Kidd, Julian Esparza, and Mauro E. Valencia. 2006. "Effects of Traditional and Western Environments on Prevalence of Type 2 Diabetes in Pima Indians in Mexico and the U.S." *Diabetes Care* 29 (8): 1866–1871.

Schulz, Muriel R. 1975. "The Semantic Derogation of Woman." In *Language and Sex: Difference and Dominance*, edited by Barrie Thorne and Nancy Henley, 64–75. Rowley, MA: Newbury House.

Schwartz, Hillel. 1986. *Never Satisfied: A Cultural History of Diets, Fantasies, and Fat.* New York: Free Press.

Schwartz, Marlene, Lenny R. Vartanian, Brian A. Nosek, and Kelly D. Brownell. 2006. "The Influence of One's Own Body Weight on Implicit and Explicit Anti-fat Bias." *Obesity* 14 (3): 440–447.

Scott, Linda M. 1993. "Fresh Lipstick—Rethinking Images of Women in Advertising." *Media Studies* 7 (1/2): 141–155.

Seid, Roberta Pollack. 1989. *Never Too Thin: Why Women Are at War with Their Bodies.* New York: Prentice Hall.

Sensa Products, LLC. 2012. "Sensa Weight-Loss System." http://start.trysensa.com/dms2229 (accessed May 10, 2012).

Serrano, Solange Queiroga, Maria Gorete Lucena de Vasconcelos, Gisélia Alves Pontes da Silva, Mônica Maria Osório de Cerqueria, and Cleide Maria Pontes. 2010. "Obese Adolescents' Perceptions about the Repercussions of Obesity on Their Health." *Revista da Escola de Enfermagem da USP* 44 (1): 25–31.

Shearn, Ian T. 2010. *Investigative Report: CCF's Richard Berman.* Washington, DC: Humane Society of the United States.

Shilling, Chris. 2003. *The Body and Social Theory.* 2nd ed. London: Sage.

———. 2004. "Physical Capital and Situated Action: A New Direction for Corporeal Sociology." *British Journal of Sociology of Education* 25 (4): 473–487.

Shilling, Chris, and Philip A. Mellor. 1996. "Embodiment, Structuration Theory and Modernity: Mind/Body Dualism and the Repression of Sensuality." *Body and Society* 2 (4): 1–15.

Singleton, Royce A., and Bruce C. Straits. 2010. *Approaches to Social Research.* 5th ed. New York: Oxford University Press.

Sixel, L. M. 2011. "Man Fired at 680 Pounds Says Weight Didn't Hurt His Work." *Houston Chronicle*, September 29.

Smith, Jane E., V. Ann Waldorf, and David L. Trembath. 1990. "Single White Male Looking for Thin, Very Attractive . . ." *Sex Roles* 23 (11/12): 675–685.

Smith, Morgan C. 2009. "Obesity as a Social Problem in the United States: Application of the Public Arenas Model." *Policy, Politics, and Nursing Practice* 10 (2): 134–142.

Snow, David A., and Robert D. Benford. 1988. "Ideology, Frame Resonance, and Participant Mobilization." *International Social Movement Research* 1:197–217.

———. 1992. "Master Frames and Cycles of Protest." In *Frontiers in Social Movement Theory,* edited by Aldon D. Morris and Carol McClurg Mueller, 133–155. New Haven, CT: Yale University Press.

Sobal, Jeffery. 1995. "The Medicalization and Demedicalization of Obesity." In *Eating Agendas: Food and Nutrition as Social Problems,* edited by Donna Maurer and Jeffery Sobal, 67–90. New York: Aldine de Gruyter.

———. 1999. "The Size Acceptance Movement and the Social Construction of Body Weight." In *Interpreting Weight: The Social Management of Fatness and Thinness,* edited by Jeffery Sobal and Donna Maurer, 231–249. New York: Aldine de Gruyter.

Solovay, Sondra. 2000. *Tipping the Scales of Justice: Fighting Weight-Based Discrimination.* Amherst, NY: Prometheus Books.

Solovay, Sondra, and Esther Rothblum. 2009. Introduction to Rothblum and Solovay 2009, 1–7.

Sørensen, Thorkild I. A., Aila Rissanen, Maarit Korkeila, and Jaakko Kaprio. 2005. "Intention to Lose Weight, Weight Changes, and 18-y Mortality in Overweight Individuals without Co-Morbidities." *PLoS Medicine* 2 (6): e171.

Spector, Malcolm, and John I. Kitsuse. 1973. "Social Problems: A Re-formulation." *Social Problems* 21 (2): 145–159.

Speers, Sarah, Jennifer Harris, Amir Goren, Marlene B. Schwartz, and Kelly D. Brownell. 2009. *Public Perceptions of Food Marketing to Youth: Results of the Rudd Center Public Opinion Poll, May 2008*. New Haven, CT: Rudd Center for Food Policy and Obesity.

Spitzack, Carole. 1990. *Confessing Excess: Women and the Politics of Body Reduction*. Albany: State University of New York Press.

Spurlock, Morgan, director. 2004. *Super Size Me*. DVD. Culver City, CA: Columbia TriStar Home Entertainment.

Squires, Sally. 1998. "About Your BMI (Body Mass Index): Optimal Weight Threshold Lowered." *Washington Post*, June 4.

Starr, Paul. 1982. *The Social Transformation of American Medicine: The Rise of a Sovereign Profession and the Making of a Vast Industry*. New York: Basic Books.

Stearns, Peter. 2002. *Fat History: Bodies and Beauty in the Modern West*. 2nd ed. New York: New York University Press.

Steger, Manfred B., and Ravi K. Roy. 2010. *Neoliberalism: A Very Short Introduction*. New York: Oxford University Press.

Stokes, Paul. 2008. "Schoolgirl Hanged Herself Because She Felt Fat and Ugly, Inquest Told." *Telegraph*, November 26.

Story, Mary, Karen M. Kaphingst, Ramona Robinson-O'Brien, and Karen Glanz. 2008. "Creating Healthy Food and Eating Environments: Policy and Environmental Approaches." *Annual Review of Public Health* 29: 253–272.

Strawbridge, William J., Margaret I. Wallhagen, and Sarah J. Shema. 2000. "New NHLBI Clinical Guidelines for Obesity and Overweight: Will They Promote Health?" *American Journal of Public Health* 90 (3): 340–343.

Swahn, Monica H, Megan Reynolds, Melissa Tice, Cecilia M. Miranda-Pierangeli, Courtney Jones, and India Jones. 2009. "Perceived Overweight, BMI, and Risk for Suicide Attempts: Findings from the 2007 Youth Risk Behavior Survey." *Journal of Adolescent Health* 45 (3): 292–295.

Swami, Viren, and Martin J. Tovee. 2009. "Big Beautiful Women: The Body Size Preferences of Male Fat Admirers." *Journal of Sex Research* 46 (1): 89–96.

Sweeting, Helen, and Patrick West. 2002. "Gender Differences in Weight Related Concerns in Early to Late Adolescence." *Journal of Epidemiology and Community Health* 56 (9): 700–701.

Swidler, Ann. 1986. "Culture in Action: Symbols and Strategies." *American Sociological Review* 51 (2): 273–286.

———. 2001. *Talk of Love: How Culture Matters*. Chicago: University of Chicago Press.

Teachman, Bethany A., Katherine D. Gapinski, Kelly D. Brownell, Melissa Rawlins, and Subathra Jeyaram. 2003. "Demonstrations of Implicit Anti-fat Bias: The Impact of Providing Causal Information and Evoking Empathy." *Health Psychology* 22 (1): 68–78.

Thomas, Andria M., Ginger Moseley, Rayvelle Stallings, Gloria Nichols-English, and Peggy J. Wagner. 2008. "Perceptions of Obesity: Black and White Differences." *Journal of Cultural Diversity* 15 (4): 174–180.

Thompson, Becky Wangsgaard. 1992. "'A Way Outa No Way': Eating Problems among African-American, Latina, and White Women." *Gender and Society* 6 (4): 546–561.

Throsby, Karen. 2008. "Happy Re-birthday: Weight Loss Surgery and the 'New Me.'" *Body and Society* 14 (1): 117–133.

Thulitha Wickrama, K. A., Kandauda A. S. Wickrama, and Chalandra M. Bryant. 2006. "Community Influence on Adolescent Obesity: Race/Ethnic Differences." *Journal of Youth and Adolescence* 35 (4): 641–651.

Tiefer, Leonore. 2006. "Female Sexual Dysfunction: A Case Study of Disease Mongering and Activist Resistance." *PLoS Medicine* 3 (4): e178.

Tilly, Charles. 2004. *Social Movements, 1768–2004.* Boulder, CO: Paradigm.

TMZ. 2010. "Gabourey Sidibe: Beauty Comes in All Sizes." March 26. www.tmz.com/2010/03/16/gabourey-sidibe-weight-loss-product-healthy (accessed August 22, 2012).

Trautner, Mary Nell, and Samantha Kwan. 2010. "Gendered Appearance Norms: An Analysis of Employment Discrimination Lawsuits, 1973–2006." *Research in the Sociology of Work* 20:127–150.

Trust for America's Health. 2006. *F as in Fat: How Obesity Policies Are Failing in America.* Washington, DC: Trust for America's Health.

Umberson, Debra, and Michael Hughes. 1987. "The Impact of Physical Attractiveness on Achievement and Psychological Well-Being." *Social Psychology Quarterly* 50 (3): 227–236.

Unilever. 2012. "The Dove Campaign for Real Beauty." www.dove.us/Social-Mission/campaign-for-real-beauty.aspx (accessed May 5, 2012).

USDA (United States Department of Agriculture). 2001. *Results from the USDA's 1994–96 Diet and Health Knowledge Survey.* Washington, DC: USDA.

———. 2010. "Part B. Section 2: The Total Diet: Combining Nutrients, Consuming Food." In *Report of the Dietary Guidelines Advisory Committee on the Dietary Guidelines for Americans, 2010*, B1-1–B3-10. www.cnpp.usda.gov/Publications/DietaryGuidelines/2010/DGAC/Report/B-2-TotalDiet.pdf (accessed August 22, 2012).

———. 2012. "USDA Unveils Historic Improvements to Meals Served in America's Schools." News release, January 25. www.fns.usda.gov/cga/PressReleases/2012/0023.htm (accessed May 6, 2012).

Vaughan, Christine A., and Carolyn T. Halpern. 2010. "Gender Differences in Depressive Symptoms during Adolescence: The Contributions of Weight-Related Concerns and Behaviors." *Journal of Research on Adolescence* 20 (2): 389–419.

Venturini, Beatrice, Luigi Castelli, and Silvia Tomelleri. 2006. "Not All Jobs Are Suitable for Fat People: Experimental Evidence of a Link between Being Fat and 'Out-of-Sight' Jobs." *Social Behavior and Personality* 34 (4): 389–398.

Vermeire, E., H. Hearnshaw, P. Van Royen, and J. Denekens. 2001. "Patient Adherence to Treatment: Three Decades of Research. A Comprehensive Review." *Journal of Clinical Pharmacy and Therapeutics* 26 (5): 331–342.

Wade, Lisa. 2010. "De-curving Christina." *Sociological Images* (blog), September 29. http://thesocietypages.org/socimages/2010/09/29/de-curving-christina (accessed May 2, 2012).

Wang, Catharine, and Elliot J. Coups. 2010. "Causal Beliefs about Obesity and Associated Health Behaviors: Results from a Population-Based Survey." *International Journal of Behavioral Nutrition and Physical Activity* 7 (1): 19–25.

Wang, Youfa, May A. Beydoun, Lan Liang, Benjamin Caballero, and Shiriki K. Kumanyika. 2008. "Will All Americans Become Overweight or Obese? Estimating the Progression and Cost of the U.S. Obesity Epidemic." *Obesity* 16 (10): 2323–2330.

Wann, Marilyn. 1998. *Fat!So? Because You Don't Have to Apologize for Your Size!* Berkeley, CA: Ten Speed Press.

———. 2009. Foreword to Rothblum and Solovay 2009, ix–xxv.

Wardle, Jane, and J. Griffith. 2001. "Socioeconomic Status and Weight Control Practices in British Adults." *Journal of Epidemiology and Community Health* 55 (3): 185–190.

Webster, Murray, Jr., and James E. Driskell Jr. 1983. "Beauty as Status." *American Journal of Sociology* 89 (1): 140–165.

WeConnectFashion. 2011. *USA Apparel Market Research Report.* New York: WeConnectFashion.

Wee, Christina C., Daniel B. Jones, Roger B. Davis, Ashley C. Bourland, and Mary Beth Hamel. 2006. "Understanding Patients' Value of Weight Loss and Expectations for Bariatric Surgery." *Obesity Surgery* 16 (4): 496–500.

Weiner, Bernard, Raymond P. Perry, and Jamie Magnusson. 1988. "An Attributional Analysis of Reactions to Stigmas." *Journal of Personality and Social Psychology* 55 (5): 738–748.

Weinstock, Jacqueline, and Michelle Krehbiel. 2009. "Fat Youth as Common Targets for Bullying." In Rothblum and Solovay 2009, 120–126.

WHO (World Health Organization). 2011. "Definition of Health." www.who.int/about/definition/en/print.html (accessed September 21, 2012).

Wiederman, Michael W. 1993. "Evolved Gender Differences in Mate Preferences: Evidence from Personal Advertisements." *Ethology and Sociobiology* 14 (5): 331–351.

Wienke, Chris. 2005. "Male Sexuality, Medicalization, and the Marketing of Cialis and Levitra." *Sexuality and Culture* 9 (4): 29–57.

Williams, Rhys H. 2004. "The Cultural Contexts of Collective Action: Constraints, Opportunities, and the Symbolic Life of Social Movements." In *The Blackwell Companion to Social Movements*, edited by David A. Snow, Sarah A. Soule, and Hanspeter Kriesi, 91–115. Malden, MA: Blackwell.

Wolf, Anne M., and Graham A. Colditz. 1996. "Social and Economic Effects of Body Weight in the United States." *American Journal of Clinical Nutrition* 63 (3): 466S–469S.

———. 1998. "Current Estimates of the Economic Cost of Obesity in the United States." *Obesity Research* 6 (2): 97–106.

Wolf, Naomi. 1991. *The Beauty Myth: How Images of Beauty Are Used against Women*. New York: William Morrow.

Wooley, Susan C., and Orland W. Wooley. 1979. "Obesity and Women—I. A Closer Look at the Facts." *Women's Studies International Quarterly* 2 (1): 69–79.

Zola, Irving Kenneth. 1972. "Medicine as an Institution of Social Control." *Sociological Review* 20 (4): 487–504.

Zones, Jane Sprague. 1997. "Beauty Myths and Realities and Their Impact on Women's Health." In *Women's Health: Complexities and Differences*, edited Sheryl Burt Ruzek, Virginia L. Oleson, and Adele E. Clarke, 249–275. Columbus: Ohio State University Press.

INDEX

The letters *f* and *t* appended to page numbers refer to figures and tables. Note locators are indicated by the page number, the letter *n*, and the note number.

ABOUT THE AUTHORS

SAMANTHA KWAN is an assistant professor of sociology at the University of Houston. She is co-editor of *Embodied Resistance: Challenging the Norms, Breaking the Rules* (Vanderbilt University Press, 2011).

JENNIFER GRAVES is a professor of sociology at Houston Community College and a sociology instructor at the University of Houston. Her research focuses on fat studies, social problems, and gender.

CPSIA information can be obtained at www.ICGtesting.com
Printed in the USA
BVOW020300280313

316653BV00002B/4/P